Passing on the Right

Passing on the Right

Conservative Professors in the Progressive University

JON A. SHIELDS
JOSHUA M. DUNN SR.

OXFORD
UNIVERSITY PRESS

OXFORD
UNIVERSITY PRESS

Oxford University Press is a department of the University of Oxford. It furthers the University's objective of excellence in research, scholarship, and education by publishing worldwide. Oxford is a registered trade mark of Oxford University Press in the UK and certain other countries.

Published in the United States of America by Oxford University Press
198 Madison Avenue, New York, NY 10016, United States of America.

© Oxford University Press 2016

Library of Congress Cataloging-in-Publication Data
Names: Shields, Jon A., author. | Dunn Sr., Joshua M., author.
Title: Passing on the right : conservative professors in the progressive university / Jon A. Shields and Joshua M. Dunn Sr.
Description: New York, NY : Oxford University Press, [2016]
Identifiers: LCCN 2015027217 | ISBN 9780199863051 (hardback : alk. paper)
Subjects: LCSH: College teachers—Political activity—United States. | College teaching—Political aspects—United States. | Conservatism—United States. | Right and left (Political science)
Classification: LCC LB2331.72 .S55 2016 | DDC 378.1/25—dc23 LC record available at http://lccn.loc.gov/2015027217

1 3 5 7 9 8 6 4 2
Printed by Sheridan, USA

To my mother, Bonnie, for her love and life itself—JAS

*To my children, Joshua, Benjamin, Elizabeth, and Evangeline
(aka, Banjo)—JMD*

Contents

List of Tables

Acknowledgments

WRITING A BOOK about professors for a largely academic readership is a daunting task. Nearly everyone believes that they are experts on the subject, and not without some justification. Others wonder why anyone would write a book about professors, especially given all the important and less familiar subjects outside our domain. Studying professors, however, is a far less lonely and obscure endeavor than it would have been just a decade ago, thanks to the work of a handful of scholars. They revived interest in a subject that had been nearly dormant ever since Everett Carl Ladd and Seymour Martin Lipset penned their classic, *The Divided Academy*, in 1975. We therefore owe a special debt to Ethan Fosse, Neil Gross, Daniel Klein, Robert Lichter, Stanley Rothman, Solon Simmons, Christian Smith, April-Kelly Woessner, Matthew Woessner, and George Yancey, among others. These scholars also deepened our understanding of the modern academy in ways that enriched our book immeasurably.

Others read our manuscript in full and offered thoughtful suggestions. They include Gerard Alexander, Brian Balogh, Mark Blitz, Jonathan Imber, Joshua Muravchik, Stephanie Muravchik, Bonnie Shields, Steve Teles, Paul Quirk, and Jonathan Zimmerman. We are also grateful for the insightful comments of three anonymous reviewers at Oxford University Press, as well as the intelligence, cheer, and patience of our editor, Cynthia Read. Thanks as well to our outstanding copy editor, Victoria Danahy, and others who assisted with the production of the book, especially Gina Chung and Sunoj Sankaran.

Fieldwork is a costly enterprise. For this reason we are especially grateful for the generous financial support of the Randolph Foundation, the Earhart Foundation, and the Salvatori Center for the Study of Individual Freedom in the Modern World. Grants from these institutions paid for our travel, transcription services, and sabbatical support. We owe a special debt to Mark Blitz, the director of the Salvatori Center, for supporting our work in myriad ways.

Fieldwork is also taxing on our subjects, of course. And so we thank the scores of professors who gave so generously of their time and patiently waited for our arrival as we navigated unfamiliar cities and universities. Thanks as well to our outstanding research assistants, Kirstyn Jacobs and Clay Spence.

We also thank our friends for providing needed distractions from the book itself. Shields especially thanks Martha Bayles, Zach Courser, Lenny Fukshansky, Mahindan Kanaratnam, Maxwell Porter, and Peter Skerry. Dunn thanks James Null, Daniel DiSalvo, Joseph Postell, Shep Melnick, and Inhan Kim for their helpful conversations on this project and many others. He owes a special thanks to his late mentor, Martha Derthick, for her invaluable support and advice.

And, finally, we thank our families, especially Stephanie and Kelly, for their love and support. They make everything possible.

Passing on the Right

Introduction

PROGRESSIVES RULE HIGHER education. Their rule is not absolute. But conservatives are scarcer in academia than in just about any other major profession, including the entertainment industry. Progressives' dominance is especially impressive in those humanistic fields where politics falls close to the subjects of inquiry. Conservatives are so scarce, in fact, that Marxists outnumber them. While less than 10% of social scientists and humanities professors identify themselves as Republicans, nearly 18% of social scientists regard themselves as Marxists, and 25% of sociologists do, too.[1]

The marginality of conservatives cannot be blamed on the 1960s. Although the academy drifted leftward after the 1960s, progressive dominance is long-standing. When Republican candidate Dwight D. Eisenhower easily won the presidency in 1952, a substantial majority of American professors cast their votes for the Democratic candidate, Adlai Stevenson. And prior to national surveys, scattered evidence suggests that academics stood well to the left of most other Americans. In 1939, for example, hundreds of professors signed a manifesto that expressed faith in Soviet communism. During these years the Communist Party was so successful recruiting academics that it became a source of frustration. One report on American communism noted that there was "more rejoicing in [the party's] headquarters over the recruiting of one common laborer than over ten Ph.D.s."[2]

Today scholars argue over the scope and power of leftist radicalism in the professoriate, but none deny the marginality of conservatism. Five major studies with quite different methodological approaches all placed the percentage of Republican professors between 7% and 9% in the social sciences, and somewhere between 6% and 11% in the humanities. And they all found that the percentage of self-identified conservatives ranges between 5% and 17% in the social sciences and between 4% and 8% in the humanities (see Table I.1). Such consistent results across multiple studies constitute what social scientists call a very robust finding.

The scarcity of conservatives in academia is not simply an interesting curiosity. It is also a source of concern to a growing number of thinkers from across the political spectrum and from varied disciplinary backgrounds. They argue that the presence of a full spectrum of vantage points, including conservative ones, is essential to the health of the social sciences and humanities.[3] Some politicians outside the Republican fold agree. At Harvard's commencement in 2014, Michael Bloomberg told its graduates that while gender and ethnic diversity matters, "a university cannot be great so long as its faculty is politically homogenous."[4]

Table I.1 Five Surveys of Professors' Ideology and Partisanship

	Klein, Stern, & Western*	NAASS**	Cardiff & Klein***	PAP****	Carnegie
Social Sciences					
Republicans	9	7	8	7	NA
Conservatives	NA	8	NA	5	17
Humanities					
Republicans	7	6	9	11	NA
Conservatives	NA	8	NA	4	7

* Measures voting behavior to assess partisanship rather than self-identification and includes only six disciplines.

** North American Academic Study Survey.

*** Uses voter registration to assess partisanship.

**** Politics of the American Professoriate Survey.

Sources: Daniel B. Klein, Charlotta Stern, and Andrew Western, "Documenting the One-Party Campus," *Academic Questions* 18(1) 2004–2005: 40–52; Stanley Rothman and S. Robert Lichter, "The Vanishing Conservative—Is There a Glass Ceiling?" in Robert Maranto, Richard E. Redding, and Frederick M. Hess, eds., *The Politically Correct University: Problems, Scope, and Reform* (Washington, DC: AEI Press, 2009), 60–76; Christopher F. Cardiff and Daniel B. Klein, "Faculty Partisan Affiliation in All Disciplines: A Voter Registration Study," *Critical Review* 17(3–4) 2005: 237–255; Neil Gross and Solon Simmons, "The Social and Political Views of American Professors," Working Paper, 24 September 2007, 1–76; and Daniel B. Klein and Charlotta Stern, "Liberal vs. Conservative Stinks," *Society* 45(6) 2008: 488–495.

And yet this call for more diversity remains a minority view. Most partisans on both sides of the political divide continue to regard academia as an inappropriate career choice for conservatives. The right, in fact, has long steered young conservatives away from academic careers by highlighting the excesses of far-left professors and the trials of their conservative students.[5] Pillorying the university for its liberalism, of course, has been part of the modern right's rhetorical arsenal ever since the 1950s when William Buckley penned *God and Man at Yale*.[6] While such polemics do not generally offer explicit career advice, the implicit message has always been that universities are "unsafe spaces" for conservatives. Those who do not discourage academia altogether urge intellectually inclined conservatives to find refuge in right-wing colleges and think tanks, rather than seek careers in mainstream academia. "Conservatives will unfortunately have to develop their own schools of thought at conservative institutions like Hillsdale College," lamented Ron Radosh, at least "until liberal academia holds out a welcome mat for conservatives."[7]

Progressive professors, meanwhile, seem inclined to offer similar career advice to conservatives, albeit for different reasons. While liberal professors almost certainly think that conservatives are good at some vocations (such as banking or military command), many nonetheless insist that they lack the needed psychological and cognitive traits for high-level academic work, such as creativity and open-mindedness.[8] Conservatives, in this view, are not graced with what the sociologist Paul Lazarsfeld influentially called an *academic mind*.[9] And because conservatives do not possess academic minds, many liberals presume their enduring scarcity in academia is a benign consequence of a well-functioning meritocracy. Indeed, liberals increasingly suggest that there are already *too many* conservatives in higher education. Progressives, for example, say that right-wing groups, such as the Koch Foundation, are compromising the university's integrity by paying conservative professors to do their bidding.[10] In this context, liberals wonder why anyone would suggest that the university needs *more* conservative professors.

While many on the right and left conclude that academia is not an appropriate career choice for conservatives, they do so without knowing very much about the right-wing thinkers who are already quietly making a living as professors. Our book corrects that shortcoming by illuminating the hidden world of right-wing professors.[11] We interviewed and surveyed 153 conservative professors in six disciplines in the social sciences and humanities—economics, political science, sociology, history, philosophy, and literature—at eighty-four universities. We asked them to provide an intellectual biography, one that would give us a rich sense of their politics, intellect, and work life. What we found should prompt conservatives and liberals alike to rethink their views on higher education and the place of conservatives in it.

Conservative academics, for example, generally told us that the academy is far more tolerant than right-wing critics of the progressive university seem to imagine. Many right-wing academics, in fact, actually first began drifting toward conservatism in the academy itself—through their coursework, friendships with right-wing students, and even their research. That so many conservative professors abandoned their liberalism when confronted with new perspectives suggests that their minds are not especially closed ones. And partly because the university is often the cradle of their intellectual and political identities, conservative professors are not a movement of outsiders looking to storm progressives' academic citadel. Most conservatives feel indebted and connected to the university, which is why they have at times been the staunchest and ablest defenders of its traditions.[12] They are thus unlikely to become the academic minions of the Koch brothers.

In fact, many conservative academics feel more at home in the progressive academy than in the Republican Party. This alienation is not because most conservative academics we interviewed are Rockefeller Republicans. In some respects, they are *more conservative* than self-identified Republicans in the general population. Instead, the Republican Party tends to trouble even the most conservative professors because they share with the American founders a small-c conservatism that is sensitized to the dangers of democratic movements. This political orientation inclines conservative professors to look askance at the populism that has shaken up the Republican Party in recent years, especially the Tea Party and its fiery candidates. In contrast to progressive academics, who often celebrate mass movements as necessary antidotes to the inegalitarian tendencies of our economic and political order, and who lament the ways our political regime frustrates progressive revolutions,[13] right-wing professors are usually comforted by the domestication of conservative movements. Their antipopulism also makes them unlikely crusaders for any right-wing organization that lobbies the academy from the outside.

Even if they were more enthusiastic partisans, many conservatives would still feel at home in academia. This is because they are often immersed in research topics, methods, and theoretical perspectives that they share with their liberal colleagues. Such professors tend to regard themselves as political scientists or economists who happen to be conservatives, rather than conservative political scientists or economists. And this means that conservatives are often tolerated by their progressive peers not because they are repressing their politics in a sharply ideological work environment or even because of the broad-mindedness of liberal academics—they are tolerated because large swaths of the academy itself are not very politicized to begin with.

We do not mean to suggest, however, that conservatives always feel accepted in academia. As a stigmatized minority, many conservatives must manage what sociologist Erving Goffman called a "spoiled" professional identity.[14] That is, they must manage the widespread presupposition that conservatives are unsuited for the life of the mind. They do so by practicing many of the same coping strategies that gays and lesbians have used in the military and other inhospitable work environments.[15] Approximately a third of the conservatives we interviewed, for example, concealed their politics prior to tenure by "passing" as liberals. Such closeted conservatives generally wait until they are tenured before venturing out of the ivory tower's shadows, a fact that should give pause to those right-wing thinkers who recommend getting rid of tenure.[16] Uncloseted professors, meanwhile, select from a broad range of strategies to navigate the liberal academy. Most decide to challenge their colleagues' prejudices by practicing conspicuous civility, temperance, and broad-mindedness, but a few opt to be defiant and combative. Others minimize open conflicts by either avoiding liberal peers or by steering clear of politicized disciplines and subfields. As one of our subjects put it, "If you are conservative, there [are] such huge no-go zones." Some of these zones are large enough to encompass nearly entire disciplines, such as sociology or literature. Thus, unlike those of progressive scholars, conservatives' decisions to specialize in one field rather than another take place within a relatively constrained set of professional choices.[17]

Academia's unwelcoming "no-go zones" have been deeply influenced by something like what Christian Smith has called a progressive "spiritual project"—a project that Smith analyzes in the context of his home discipline of sociology, but is embedded in other areas of academia as well. Academics laboring in such spiritualized academic fields, Smith says, are driven by impulses and purposes that are sacred in the Durkheimian sense that they are "hallowed, revered, and honored as beyond questioning or disrespect." At their deepest levels, therefore, sociology and its related fields seek more than a disinterested understanding of the social world. The substance of this spiritual project, Smith explains, is committed to "realizing the emancipation, equality, and moral affirmation of all human beings as autonomous, self-directing, individual agents." It is a radical project, one that seeks systemic, even revolutionary, social change.[18] When conservative professors venture into such spiritualized academic terrain, they often report mistreatment in small and large ways for their intellectual profanity.

The nature of professors' conservatism matters too, not just their field of study. Devotees of economic conservatism, for example, tend to report much more welcoming work environments than do cultural conservatives. The former were more often exposed to arguments on behalf of their ideals in college, less likely to enter the academic closet, and far less likely to report persecution by their progressive colleagues. Many on the libertarian right found an especially welcoming intellectual home inside economics. Economics, in fact, is the only social science discipline with anything approaching a rough partisan balance between Democrats and Republicans. This anomalous development is partly because economics is also the sole academic discipline with deep roots in the work of a conservative Enlightenment thinker—Adam Smith.

The conservative economists we spoke with even insisted that their discipline has become *more tolerant* of scholars who harbor free-market ideals in recent decades. There are good reasons to trust this assessment. As the progressive social movements of the 1960s and 1970s brought scores of activist-scholars into fields like sociology, literature, and history, the regulatory experiments of that era helped to revive economists' traditional appreciation of markets.[19] In the wake of the Great Society, prominent free-market economists were even honored with the Nobel Prize in economics, including Friedrich Hayek in 1974 and Milton Friedman in 1976. And so, as conservative intellectuals were grieving over the radicalization of the humanities, economists were actually drifting rightward toward a neoclassical consensus.

Thus we can tell something like a tale of two conservatives: As the academy became more receptive to the interests and concerns of libertarians, it grew less friendly to traditionalists. These political currents in academia roughly mirrored—and perhaps contributed to—shifts in American public opinion, which liberalized on many social issues, but on few economic ones.[20]

While free-market enthusiasts often find a congenial intellectual home in the discipline of economics, cultural conservatives can find no comparable quarters. Sociology might be cultural conservatives' most natural home, since it is a discipline that takes culture and social institutions such as the family and religion seriously. Yet, as this book will show, outspoken cultural conservatives in sociology confront a life of isolation and persecution. In light of this finding, we must regretfully conclude that cultural conservatives—the defenders of an intellectual tradition with roots in important thinkers from the ancient world (Aristotle) to the Enlightenment (Hume and Burke)—may be wise to stay out of the one discipline that is most singularly devoted to the study of culture. This observation underscores a more general and troubling truth: Conservatives are least welcome in fields where they are most needed.

Despite such problems, our conversations with conservative professors suggest that the right-wing critique of the university is overdrawn. We certainly do not want to minimize the real challenges many conservatives confront in academia. Some of the accounts in this book, after all, are quite troubling, even shocking. But while conservatives contemplating a career in academia—especially those on the cultural right—are certainly well served by knowing the challenges of being a political minority, the many successful conservatives in academia show that they do not have to become debilitating challenges. There is also a long history of out-groups—from Marxists to libertarians—that successfully created their own sizable niches inside the university. The problems that do exist, moreover, will probably not get better until more conservatives enter academia—a development that is inadvertently slowed by right-wing attacks on the university.

While the right's distorted views of the academy are rooted in its isolation from the university, the scarcity of conservatives in academia compels liberal professors to associate conservatism almost entirely with its populist expressions. This is partly why so many liberal professors continue to believe that the *academic mind* is a progressive one and why they especially fear the right-wing populists who attempt to shape the university from outside its walls. Our findings should quiet those anxieties. While a few right-wing professors are combative and many others accept monies from the coffers of right-wing foundations, there is also little reason to suppose that a surge in conservative academics would undermine the mission and integrity of the university, at least not if they resemble the ones already laboring in it.

Why Conservatives Matter

Our book invites partisans on both sides to consider the possibility that conservatives fit better in the university than they suppose. That reconsideration is long overdue, especially since the scarcity of conservatives in academia really does matter, though not for the reasons right-wing critics tend to emphasize. Little evidence, for example, supports the conservative trope that universities are places where impressionable students are routinely indoctrinated by leftist professors.

It is better to think of the teaching problem as a missed opportunity, rather than one of indoctrination. The university is one of the few institutions that could better prepare students for lives as citizens by exposing them to civil and respectful debates. But that sort of example is hard to provide with so few conservatives about. Their absence also limits the exposure of all students to importance perspectives. And it deprives conservative student activists of mentors who might deepen their politics and direct them away from the populist tactics that are increasingly popular in large universities.[21]

Some might suppose that a university dominated by progressives could still achieve these same general ends by introducing their students to a wide spectrum of thinkers. It seems doubtful, however, that liberal professors generally prepare their students for a life as citizens by exposing them to broad range of conservative thinkers, not when so many continue to dismiss conservatism as a symptom of closed minds. Even if there were no such prejudices, many bodies of knowledge are so imbued with progressive politics that it would be easy to overlook the occasional dissonant voice.

Beyond the classroom, the near absence of conservative thinkers in many areas of inquiry undermines knowledge-seeking by making it more difficult for scholars to converge on the best approximation of the truth. This is an inevitable outcome of homogeneity, at least in those research areas where political and moral considerations fall close to the subjects of inquiry. Politically diverse epistemic communities are better at converging on the truth partly because they generate a broader range of research interests and interpretations. Diverse communities are also better because of the tenacious power of "confirmation bias." This is the tendency of human beings to accept findings and theories that are consistent with their preexisting beliefs. Norms of objectivity in academia cannot adequately check confirmation bias because, as psychologists Philip Tetlock and Gregory

Mitchell explain, "biased information processing is deeply wired into human nature."[22]

Without the reality check afforded by a more diverse professoriate, well-meaning progressive professors in the social sciences and humanities are also tempted to abuse their intellectual authority outside the ivory tower. When academics are broadly united around some pressing moral issue—as they have been in a number of conflagrations in the culture wars—they sometimes overstate their knowledge. This is especially the case in legal battles in which scholarly expertise is granted special weight. Enlisting in moral crusades may fulfill professors' political convictions, but at the risk of compromising the integrity of the academy and undermining its authority.

Predictably, such campaigns leave the academy vulnerable to retaliation from Republican governors—a development that should concern progressive *and* conservative professors. Republican governors, for example, have recently sought to redistribute state resources away from the social sciences and humanities in favor of the natural sciences. Democratic opponents respond by insisting that the purpose of the humanities and social sciences is to broaden young minds. Yet conservative politicians reasonably wonder how well the social sciences and humanities actually broaden minds, especially when these fields are shaped so deeply by a progressive spiritual project. In any case, progressive academics cannot have it both ways: They cannot lend their credentials to political crusades *and* expect to be treated like a nonpartisan institution floating above a factionalized political world.

Though the scarcity of conservatives in the professoriate is a problem, it is not clear that much can be done to improve their numbers. Affirmative action has been the most common means of increasing pluralism in higher education. And recently a number of thinkers from across the political spectrum have recommended some version of it for conservative professors and graduate students.[23] If affirmative action for right-wing professors ever gets any political traction, it must overcome the near absence of support for it in the professoriate. Far from preferring to hire right-wing thinkers, in fact, many progressive professors say that, if given the choice, they would hire a liberal over a conservative, everything else being equal. In some disciplines, professors even report a preference for hiring Marxists rather than Republicans.[24] These preferences may not always be driven by animus. As conservatives have pointed out in disputes over residential segregation, such preferences may be rooted in a natural fondness for like-minded communities, rather than in small-minded prejudices.[25] Prejudice, how-ever, is probably at work too, especially since so many liberal professors believe that conservatism is incompatible with the life of the mind.[26]

The conservative professors we spoke with are ambivalent about right-wing affirmative action. On the one hand, they generally think that the academy needs more political pluralism, and some even support hiring conservative applicants over equally qualified liberals. In a few important instances, conservatives have also built right-wing academic centers that resemble programs designed to help women and minorities. On the other hand, most of the conservative professors we spoke with—and nearly all their Republican allies outside the academy—are opposed to any sort of preferences for right-wing academics in hiring and promotion.

In any case, if progressive rule over higher education ever wanes, it will not be because of affirmative action. It will happen when larger numbers of young conservatives decide that they want to be professors.

In Search of the Conservative Professoriate

Finding conservative professors to interview presented both methodologi-cal and practical challenges. At the outset we decided to limit our study to professors in the social sciences and humanities. We did so because in these humanistic fields politics falls close to the subjects of inquiry, rendering objectivity an elusive ideal and ideological pluralism impor-tant.[27] This is partly why Everett Carl Ladd and Seymour Martin Lipset referred to the social sciences as "the political sciences" in their classic *The Divided Academy*.[28] To be sure, some areas of study in the natural sci-ences become politicized on occasion, such as climatology. However, in humanistic disciplines, the nature of the subject matter itself renders poli-tics a permanent problem and source of controversy.[29] If all the engineers and physicists in the country were a Marxist, while the social sciences were balanced ideologically, observers would certainly regard these facts as odd-ities, but few would express much interest or concern. There would be no David Horowitz warning us about radical professors who teach and write on engineering from a Marxist or feminist slant.

We further restricted our study to six disciplines within the social sci-ences and humanities—economics, political science, sociology, history, philosophy, and literature. These fields were selected because they rep-resent a broad spectrum of humanistic knowledge and because they each have distinct political valences. Even so, these fields probably represent a conservative slice of the social sciences and humanities. While this study included relatively conservative fields, such as economics and political science, it also excluded many progressive disciplines, such as psychology, anthropology, linguistics, and education. And, of course, we excluded by necessity the various area studies. These are fields where even moderate professors do not tread, much less conservative ones. They include gender studies, cultural studies, American studies, Chicano studies, Middle Eastern studies, and black studies.[30] On the other hand, we also excluded professional schools, such as those in law, public policy, and business, which are comparatively moderate and technocratic in their orientation.[31]

Having pared our study down to a manageable number of disciplines, we then had to decide who should count as a conservative. Because American conservatism is best understood as a diverse coalition against modern liberalism—one that includes social conservatives, libertarians, and foreign policy hawks—it made little sense to define conservatism in a way that required our subjects to share a common set of philosophical or policy views.[32] Thus we simply decided to classify professors as conservative if they identified as such. Given our coalitional understanding of modern conservatism, we also included professors in our sample if they self-identified as libertarians. Self-identified libertarians were included because they are sometimes anxious to distinguish themselves from their right-wing allies, despite the fact that they remain an important coalitional partner against post–New Deal liberalism.[33]

These initial choices, hard as they were, still left us with the difficult task of identifying conservative professors. After all, conservative professors are scarce. When hearing how many professors we hoped to interview, one conservative political scientist incredulously asked us if we were "going to raise the dead." As well, one cannot always spot a conservative professor by reading his or her scholarship. We therefore created an initial list of conservative professors by culling names from right-wing journals and academic membership lists with distinct ideational profiles. They included an online directory of libertarian professors, writers for the traditionalist *Intercollegiate Review*, and members of the University Faculty for Life. Writers for the *Claremont Review of Books*, a big-tented conservative magazine, and the former fellows at Princeton University's James Madison Program supplemented these more sectarian conservative sources.[34] We then asked the professors culled from these sources to help us grow our snowball sample by identifying other scholars that are likely to self-identify as political conservatives or libertarians. Many cooperated, though some did not, out of either indifference or evident suspicion. The scholars to whom we were led by the first batch of professors were then asked to confirm their political identities and name other conservative scholars. This process was repeated many times, generating 249 confirmed conservative professors.[35] We stopped asking professors to name names only when it was clear that our pestering was unearthing few new identities.

Because subjects tend to give more of their time and attention in face-to-face meetings, all the interviews were conducted in person. The interviews themselves confirmed this expectation. The modal interview lasted about one hour, and many were twice as long. To reach our scattered population of conservative professors, we embarked on ten research trips to five different regions of the country: three out West; three in the South; one in the Midwest; two in the Mid-Atlantic states; and one in the Northeast. During these regional trips, we interviewed as many professors as possible, completing 153 interviews at eighty-four colleges and universities (see Table I.2).[36] With one exception, the identities of the professors have been concealed.[37] Typically we identify only their discipline and the type of institution they work in, such as a "sociologist at a Catholic college." In those few cases in which a particular subject is discussed at significant length, we assigned the subject a code name, such as Professor F, to improve the readability of the book. We protected the identities of our subjects because so many of them insisted on it and because of the sensitive nature of the subject matter. Although the term "right-wing" sometimes implies "far-right," we use it as simply a synonym for conservatism throughout the book.

All subjects were asked to walk us through their political and intellectual development—and to think carefully about the relationship between their politics and intellectual life. Nearly every interview was recorded and transcribed,[38] which left us with thousands of pages of text to analyze. To prevent us from missing the forest for the trees, our subjects were also asked to complete a formal survey that covered roughly the same terrain in a much more general way.

The scholars we interviewed, of course, are not representative of all conservative professors in the social sciences and humanities. Since we culled our initial sample from ideological sources, they are probably somewhat more conservative than the typical professor on the right. This conclusion is further supported by a recent survey, which found that the policy views of Republican professors place them to the left of the average party

Table I.2 Academic Institutions of Conservative Professors

Amherst College	San Jose State
Assumption College	Seattle University
Auburn University	Smith College
Ashland University	Southern Methodist University
Baylor University	Stanford University
Berry College	SUNY–Buffalo
Blinn College	Texas A&M University
Boston University	Texas Christian University
Bridgewater State University	Towson University
Brown University	Tulane University
California Institute of Technology	U.S. Naval Academy
Cal State Los Angeles	University of Alabama
Cal State San Bernardino	UC–Los Angeles
Catholic University	UC–Riverside
Central Connecticut State University	UC–San Diego
Christopher Newport University	UC–Santa Barbara
College of New Jersey	University of Colorado
Emory University	University of Dallas
Florida State University	University of Houston
George Mason University	University of Illinois–Urbana Champagne
Georgia Perimeter College	University of Maryland, Baltimore County
Georgia State University	University of Maryland, College Park
Harvard University	University of Massachusetts–Amherst
Hillsdale College	University of Missouri
Holy Cross University	University of Montana
Kennesaw State University	University of North Carolina, Chapel Hill
Louisiana State University	University of Pennsylvania
Loyola University–Baltimore	University of San Francisco
Miami-Ohio	University of Southern California
New York University	University of St. Thomas
North Lake College	University of Texas–Arlington
Oglethorpe University	University of Texas–Austin
Ohio University	University of Texas–Dallas
Pasadena City College	University of Virginia
Pepperdine University	University of Washington
Providence College	Vanderbilt University
Princeton University	Villanova University
Radford University	Wellesley College
Rice University	Wesleyan University
Rutgers University	Western Connecticut State University
Saint John's College	William Patterson University
Saint Vincent's College	Yale University
Sam Houston State University	

Table I.3 Professional Profile of Conservative Professors

Academic Discipline	
Political Science	25%
Economics	22%
History	19%
Literature	15%
Philosophy	10%
Sociology	9%
N:	153

Academic Rank	
Full Professor	53%
Associate Professor	27%
Assistant Professor	8%
Visitor/Adjunct	9%
Emeritus	4%
N:	142

Academic Institution	
Ph.D. granting	60%
M.A. granting	18%
B.A. granting	19%
Community college	4%
N:	142

member.[39] The attitudes of the professors we sampled, however, were quite conservative on average, as Chapter One will show. What is also obviously distinctive about the conservatives we interviewed is that they are far more engaged in scholarship than the average professor, with some 60% working at a doctorate-granting institution (see Table I.3). Many of these professors work at the best research universities in the nation. Even professors employed by those institutions that do not grant doctorates are unusually active scholars. For example, one of the community college professors we interviewed has authored many books. By participating actively in scholarship, these conservatives are engaged in a wider community of conversation than their less accomplished peers—one that transcends the particular universities they call home. So although the scholars we inter-viewed do not represent all conservative professors, they matter in and of themselves. These right-wing professors matter because they do tend to be members of an elite conservative professoriate.

And, finally, because this book assumes that politics does shape the work of social scientists, we think it is best to be transparent about our own politics rather than pretend they do not exist or matter. As the sociologist Alvin Gardner suggested decades ago, it is best to reveal the "whole" social scientist lest others are encouraged to "ignore the vulnerability of reason to bias."[40] So, let us just say that we could have been this book's subjects rather than its authors. And, indeed, our interest in this project surely has something to do with our own experiences as a political minority in higher education. Nonetheless we have tried diligently to not allow our presuppositions to shape our interpretation or presentation of evidence. As a safeguard against this danger, we have presented our findings in a way that allows our readers to reach conclusions different from our own. We have done so by letting our subjects speak for themselves by quoting them often and at length. This, we also hope, repays, at least in some small measure, the debts we owe to all the conservative professors who gave so generously of their time.

PART I

The Politics of Conservative Professors

I

The Conservative Minority

OBSERVERS DO NOT always agree on how precisely to characterize the core political and intellectual factions that make up modern American conservatism. Intellectual historian George Nash identifies five camps: libertarians, traditionalists, religious conservatives, neoconservatives, and anticommunists. It is a useful typology. But even Nash acknowledges that it simplifies reality, especially since the American right continues to generate fresh categories and identities. The new century, for example, has witnessed the emergence of "crunchy cons," "theocons," and even "Leocons," the disciples of Leo Strauss.[1] Others suggest a more parsimonious way of thinking about factions within conservatism, one that fingers its principal political tensions rather than subtler distinctions between its fine-tuned intellectual camps. Many journalists and politicians, for example, prefer to think of the Republican Party as a "three-legged stool" that is supported by fiscal, social, and foreign policy conservatives.[2]

Regardless of how one thinks about American conservatives, they are not united by a common agreement on first principles or policy priorities. For this reason, Nash stresses that it is best to think of modern conservatism as a coalition against liberalism rather than as an ideology.[3] Making the same observation with his characteristic humor, political scientist James Ceaser observes that the Republican Party is united "by two self-evident truths: Nancy Pelosi and Barbara Boxer." What conservatives share, in other words, is an antipathy toward modern liberalism rather than deep philosophical affinities.[4] Such a coalition will never be "philosophically tidy," as Nash puts it. "But then," Nash adds, "conservatism was not supposed to be an ideology anyway."[5]

With this coalitional understanding of American conservatism in mind, professors were included in our sample if they self-identified as libertarians as well as conservatives.[6] Had it turned out that many of the libertarian professors in our sample were supporters of the Democratic Party, we would have doubted this methodological decision. But, in fact, not a single libertarian professor we interviewed identifies with the Democratic Party. Instead, most libertarian professors divide their loyalties between the Republican and Libertarian Parties. Social conservatives—occasional rivals of libertarians—made up another distinct cluster of right-wing professors. Unlike libertarians, they tended to be churchgoing Christians, more at home in the Republican Party, as well as strongly opposed to abortion and same-sex marriage. Hawkish foreign policy conservatives in the mold of a Paul Wolfowitz or Elliot Cohen were comparatively scarce, even though many professors who initially gravitated toward conservatism did so because of anticommunism. This is partly because interest in spreading democracy cooled in the wake of the George W. Bush administrations. In between the strong cultural conservatives and libertarians lay many fusionist conservatives who felt more or less equally comfortable with the varied bedfellows that make up American conservatism.

And, finally, with the notable exception of immigration, the policy views of the professors we interviewed—taken as a whole—place them comfortably within the mainstream of the Republican Party. That is, their views mirror those of rank-and-file Republicans in the general population. This fact suggests that our sample of conservative professors reflects the broad intellectual and political diversity that constitutes American conservatism.

While this chapter provides a general portrait of the professors we interviewed, it also focuses on why so many important representatives of this conservative minority embraced a right-wing identity in America's most progressive profession. The conservatives we interviewed beat many paths out of liberalism. While a handful of conservative professors began to rethink their progressive politics after encounters with campus liberals, others were simply moved by political events far beyond the ivory tower's walls. But these were roads less traveled. More frequently, professors found their way to conservatism in and through the progressive academy. Many of these converts moved rightward after taking coursework as both undergraduate and graduate students, especially in economics. Others began drifting away from the left after befriending right-wing students in college. Some professors, in fact, encountered conservatives for the first time as undergraduate students. Such experiences are a reminder that although colleges are sometimes characterized by conservatives as progressive information bubbles, the student populations of universities are often more politically diverse than the high schools of elite students. Some professors, meanwhile, gravitated toward right-wing ideas after engaging in academic labor. For these scholars, the professorial vocation itself paved the way out of liberalism. Yet these same testimonies also suggest that exposure to right-wing ideas is uneven, since the university exposed comparatively few of the professors we interviewed to cultural conservatism.

It is perhaps less surprising that the university itself opened scores of our subjects to conservative ideas, given that so many of them needed to overcome the sense that progressivism is uniquely compatible with the academic mind. As Chapter Three shows, academics often attribute the underrepresentation of right-wing thinkers in the professoriate to the alleged cognitive and psychological limitations of conservatives. Our conservative converts were not unusual in this respect. They too once assumed that the conservative mind was deficient. These former liberals both needed to be exposed to conservative ideas and to witness such ideas compete effectively. And given the intellectualism of our subjects, such political awakenings needed to take place at a fairly high academic level—in college classrooms, through academic research, and through discussions with professors and elite students. Otherwise, many of the professors we interviewed might have never taken conservative ideas seriously, much less embraced a right-wing identity.

While this chapter examines closely some of the turning points in the political development of our subjects, it does not—and cannot—offer a full account of the many factors that shaped their political identity. Such factors, which interact with one another in complex ways, are not fully known even by the individuals who are shaped by them. And this means, of course, that our subjects may place far too much emphasis on, say, a course in economics or on a relationship with a conservative mentor. Even so, such accounts tell us something about how these professors have constructed their political and intellectual identities. It matters, for example, if many right-wing professors regard the university as the birthplace of their conservatism, even if the reality is more untidy and complex. Such professors, after all, will always have to balance any negative professional experiences on account of their politics with the belief that the university is also the cradle of their intellectual and political identities.

This finding should also reassure those progressive scholars eyeing the designs of conservative organizations like the Koch Foundation with

alarm. Given that so many conservative professors developed their intellectual and political selves in the university, they are hardly a movement
of outsiders looking to march through a hostile institution, or ever likely
to become one. For all their complaints, most conservative professors feel
too indebted and connected to the university to wage a guerilla war on it.
Conservatives may be the university's wayward and disgruntled children,
but they are its children nonetheless.

The Conservatives: A Group Portrait

When asked in an open-ended way to label themselves, the professors we
interviewed selected a remarkable range of identities, including Catholic
conservative, Christian traditionalist, Christian humanist, communitarian
conservative, constitutional conservative, paleoconservative, neoconserva-
tive, social conservative, natural rights conservative, classical conservative,
conservative libertarian, free-market conservative, and reactionary. Even
this partial list is a reminder of the factional and fragile nature of modern
American conservatism.

When professors were asked to explain these identities further, they
sometimes offered remarkably idiosyncratic descriptions of their politics.
One professor of history, for example, described himself as someone who
embraces "Hobbitan conservatism." "That is to say, I want to live in the
Shire as described by J. R. Tolkien, [because it] has a sense of natural order
and natural deference."

Despite a few such genuinely idiosyncratic scholars, most fit comfortably within the broad categories Nash identified, with the largest
single cleavage dividing social and economic conservatives. Our sample
included a large contingent of social conservatives. Nearly two-thirds
of the professors we interviewed believe that abortion should be illegal in all or most cases. A somewhat smaller majority of conservative
professors oppose same-sex marriage (see Table 1.1). These views are
rooted partly in the religiosity of our subjects. Approximately half of the
professors we interviewed are Christians who attend church regularly.
In this population, Catholics were especially overrepresented, a not
surprising finding given their intellectual importance to the American
conservative movement.[7] A third of our sample, in fact, comprises
observant Catholics. And approximately 23% of our subjects identify as
"born-again Christians," a group that is mostly, though not exclusively,
Protestant.

Table 1.1 Views on Social Issues

Do you think abortion should be . . .	
Legal in all cases	10%
Legal in most cases	28%
Illegal in most cases	42%
Illegal in all cases	21%
N:	137

Do you favor or oppose allowing gays and lesbians to marry legally?	
Strongly Favor	19%
Favor	18%
Oppose	26%
Strongly Oppose	29%
Don't Know	8%
N:	140

The other large and distinct cluster of professors is made up of libertarian or free-market conservatives—terms that we use more or less synonymously throughout the book. About one-third of the professors we interviewed said that they are libertarians. These professors are far more liberal on social questions than even most Americans, with large majorities supporting abortion rights and same-sex marriage. They are also less religious than nonlibertarian professors. While only 30% of libertarians attend religious services regularly, about 60% of all other conservative professors do so.

Overall, the policy views of the professors we interviewed placed them comfortably within the mainstream of the Republican Party. When we constructed our survey, we drew many of our survey questions from the Pew Research Center's Values Survey so that we could compare the attitudes of conservative professors with those of ordinary Republicans in the general population. As Table 1.2 demonstrates, the professors in our sample broadly share the same policy views of rank-and-file Republicans. Compared with Republicans in the general population, the conservative professors we interviewed are slightly more hawkish, somewhat less in favor of welfare and affirmative action, and moderately more supportive of gay marriage. Their views on abortion and gun rights are nearly identical to those of ordinary Republicans. Thus, in many respects the political views of the conservative professors in our sample are indistinguishable from those of Republicans in the general population.

Table 1.2 Policy Views of Conservative Professors and Republicans in General Population

The government should help more needy people even if it means going deeper in debt.

	All Republicans	Conservative Professors
Agree	20%	11%

We should make every possible effort to improve the position of blacks and other minorities, even if it means giving them preferential treatment.

	All Republicans	Conservative Professors
Agree	12%	5%

The best way to ensure peace is through military strength.

	All Republicans	Conservative Professors
Agree	73%	80%

We should restrict and control people coming to live in our country more than we do now.

	All Republicans	Conservative Professors
Agree	84%	55%

What do you think is more important—to protect the right of Americans to own guns OR to control gun ownership?

	All Republicans	Conservative Professors
Protect Owners	72%	75%

Do you favor or oppose allowing gays and lesbians to marry legally?

	All Republicans	Conservative Professors
Favor	23%	37%

Do you think abortion should be . . .

	All Republicans	Conservative Professors
Legal in All/ Most Cases	34%	37%

Source: Pew Research Center 2012 Values Survey.

Table 1.3 Party Identification of
Conservative Professors

Strong Republicans	49%
Republicans (not strong)	14%
Leaning Republicans	13%
Independents	5%
Leaning Democrats	1%
Democrats (not strong)	0%
Strong Democrats	1%
Libertarian	12%
Other	4%
N:	138

Immigration was the only policy area in which conservative professors significantly parted from their fellow partisans outside academia. While some 84% of all Republicans say that immigration should be more restricted, only a bare majority of conservative professors (55%) agree. In fact, our professors' views on immigration place them in the mainstream of the Democratic Party.[8]

Given that the policy views of conservative professors generally mirror those of supporters of the Republican Party, it is not surprising that they generally identify with the GOP. While about half of the professors in our sample consider themselves *strong* Republicans, an additional 27% identify as either weaker Republicans or Independents who lean toward the Republican Party (see Table 1.3). Another 17% identify as pure Independents or with the Libertarian Party. Meanwhile, only two professors say they are Democrats—a finding that partly reflects the decline of moderates and conservatives in the Democratic Party in recent decades. Conservative professors are even somewhat more inclined to vote for Republicans. Of those professors who cast a ballot in 2000 and 2004, more than 80% voted for George W. Bush. In 2008 support for the Republican ticket declined moderately, especially among libertarian-oriented professors.

As we will see in the following chapter, however, this broad support for Republican presidential candidates belies much deeper concerns about today's GOP. And surveying policy views tell us little about why so many professors we interviewed turned rightward or what they find so compelling about conservatism. To address these questions, we now turn to our interviews.

Many Right Turns

To be sure, some professors reported remarkably stable political identities. A few even felt they were born that way. "I came out of the womb, a 100% capitalist," said one professor. Another agreed: "It's like in my blood, so to speak." So did a third professor: "I was pretty much born this way," he told us. New research on the biological roots of politics suggests there may be something to these claims.[9] Most professors, however, did not insist that they were natural-born conservatives. About 60% of the professors we surveyed, in fact, reported that they have become more conservative over time. Such professors moved rightward from identities that ranged from New Deal liberalism to communism.

Many professors we interviewed began to move rightward after taking course work in economics as both undergraduate and graduate students. Some of these professors were first taught economics by influential free-market conservatives. A professor who now teaches at a large public university, for example, recalled his graduate training at the University of Chicago in the 1960s, a place that was then deeply shaped by Milton Friedman's neoclassical approach to the study of economics. As an undergraduate at an elite liberal arts college, he felt that his progressive professors "just took a lot of things for granted." But at Chicago, he found his economics professors "took nothing for granted." "That was so striking to me compared to the hand-waving and posturing and attitudinizing at [the liberal arts college I attended]," this professor remembered. He was also sensitized to the contestability of progressive ideas when liberal academics visited Chicago. "Just watching [progressives] get slaughtered because they were uttering stuff they thought was self-evident, and it was always shown by Friedman and others not to be self-evident made a big, big impression on me," he recalled.

It is hardly surprising that someone with Friedman's gifts managed to influence some of today's conservative professors. More surprising are the many professors we interviewed who moved to the right after taking a rather ordinary course in microeconomics. During the energy crisis of the 1970s, one of our interviewees took an economics course that changed his life. "Supply and demand really spoke to me," he told us. "Now I understand why I waited in the line to buy gasoline. I mean it was just like the scales falling from my eyes." He became even more politicized later after reading Friedrich Hayek and Friedman's work. "I came [to those works] through economics, it was economics that made me a champion of free markets," he remembered. Another professor, meanwhile, was raised in a union household and strongly identified with New Deal liberalism as a young man. But those familial and political loyalties weakened in college. "I have somehow swung to the completely opposite end of the political spectrum, and I think a lot of it has to do with my economics background," he told us. Unlike the youthful progressivism of the subjects we just described, another subject entered college carrying what he described as "a mixed bag of stupid thoughts." Economics helped him cultivate a more serious and grounded politics: "Microeconomic theory had a big impact on my thinking over the years on the importance of markets."

For a few scholars, their exposure to economics was powerful enough to pull them from the far left. A professor at a regional state college reported that he was a communist as a teenager and deeply troubled by the election of Ronald Reagan in 1980. "I just couldn't believe that these fascists elected Reagan," he recollected. "Then as I started getting into economics, I saw how the research lent itself to studying the effects of regulations and the effects of different policies." Gradually he became committed to economic freedom. Another professor, a red-diaper baby, reported a similar conversion process. "I started learning economics and all of a sudden there was this whole body of work that said, 'markets do things well' and pointed out the unintended consequences of letting government do things," he remembered. "So, that gradually led me to be promarket."

Others who entered college with conservative leanings took economics courses that deepened their commitment to economic freedom. "I had these sort of [free-market] leanings, but with no intellectual foundation there," one professor recalled about his thinking at the time. After this subject immersed himself in the study of economics, he found greater intellectual ballast for his political intuitions. "I discovered that there was this whole intellectual foundation that I had never even seen before," he told us. A professor who teaches at a private university reported a similar encounter with economics as an undergraduate. "I think there's a certain methodological [orientation] within economics that I think directs you towards, if not a libertarian point of view, certainly a more open point of view," he suspected.

Though economics classrooms were often mentioned as sites of political conversion, right-wing professors sometimes recalled the formative influence of courses in other social scientific fields. One philosopher at an elite university, for example, took a course with Harvard's Harvey Mansfield, an irreverent conservative and political theorist of a Straussian bent. "Mansfield was an enormously captivating teacher," he remembered affectionately. He was so captivating, in fact, that this professor believes that his political conversion "was largely a result of exposure to Harvey Mansfield." Fresh off a stint as a volunteer in the dovish McGovern campaign, he was especially impressed by Mansfield's claim that the Soviet Union was actually an "evil empire," as well as his insistence that America needed to confront that moral and existential threat by maintaining a strong military.

More often, however, professors said that they moved right after taking courses with *progressive* scholars. "My first taste of political philosophy was actually from a Rawlsian," a philosopher at a state university informed us. In that class he read Robert Nozick's *Anarchy, State, and Utopia*, an influential libertarian work and rebuttal to the Rawlsian case for a social-welfare state. "He was a fantastic professor who was scrupulously fair to non-Rawlsians," our interviewee said. "I learned a tremendous amount of very fairly presented material [about libertarian philosophy] from someone who was in fact a Rawlsian." Similarly, an economist at a prestigious university recalled taking an influential class from Richard Rorty, a famous postmodern progressive. In Rorty's class he read John Stuart Mill's *On Liberty*, a book that provided him with a deeper philosophical foundation and interest in economic freedom. Mill's work also later compelled him to read Milton Friedman's *Capitalism and Freedom*. A professor of history at an elite university, meanwhile, turned right after taking a course with the Marxist historian Arno Mayer. This admiring historian recalled Mayer announcing to his class, "I'm going to assign the book I most disagree with in the twentieth century, and I'm going to ask you not to critique it, but to recreate its arguments with intellectual empathy." The book was Hayek's *The Road to Serfdom*. "*The Road to Serfdom* was in many ways the first book that I read that challenged my fundamental thinking. It changed my intellectual life." And it set this young historian on the road to conservatism.

As the accounts thus far should suggest, most conservatives who turned right under the direction of their professors did not gravitate toward cultural conservatism. Instead, they generally were sensitized to the virtues of economic conservatism, either through introductory courses in economics or through intellectuals in the classical liberal tradition. There were some exceptions to this tendency, however. One political scientist at a public university, for example, studied ancient philosophy, which she believes exposed her to the dangers of revolutionary and liberationist aspirations. "You can't read Thucydides or Aristotle's *Politics* without realizing that political life is full of factions and you need to be careful in not disturbing political forms, [that one should] be respectful of traditional authorities," she reflected. From such ancient sources, she began to appreciate "just how vulnerable and fragile political life is." A sociologist at an elite public university, meanwhile, first considered the logic of cultural conservatism after reading Linda Waite and Maggie Gallagher's *The Case for Marriage* in graduate school. Reading Waite and Gallagher, he recalled, "pushed me towards, I don't want to say full-blown social conservatism, but definitely I could see the point of it. That book doesn't so much make the case for social conservative policy platforms, so much as it just provides an extremely compelling case for why the family matters."

Another sociologist considered the merits of social conservatism only after frequent disagreements with one on his undergraduate professors. "I would have long conservations [with him] about truth, morality, theology," he recalled. "This professor's basic claim was that there was an objective truth—a transcendent, authoritative, moral order to which we were all obligated and this morality was applicable across time and space." Those deeper arguments opened him to other claims from intellectuals who were still well to his right. As he put it, "That was the first kind of experience that got me moving in a more conservative direction."

Just as often, conservative professors told us that they began drifting away from the left after befriending right-wing students in college. In fact, some professors told us that they encountered conservatives for the first time as undergraduate students. Consider the case of one philosopher who grew up in Brooklyn. He recalled,

> I really can't overstate how important it was for my development to actually start socializing with conservatives, because as I said, in high school, I never met any. So, what limited exposure I had to conservative ideas was always with [an] undercurrent of demonization, [as if] there's got to be some sort of crypto-racism or they're just greedy or they've got this obsession with guns, and all these sort of things.

But all that changed once he left high school for an Ivy League university. "I actually started thinking that some of what they were saying made sense," he recalled. A good example is gun control:

> Growing up in New York City, liberal intellectual family, who on Earth would want a gun, right? Only criminals and rednecks have guns. But arguing with my friends in the conservative group, they would present very rational arguments as to what's the meaning of the Second Amendment and the importance of personal self-defense.

Even when this philosopher was not entirely persuaded by his conservative friends, they compelled him to take conservatism seriously. "It was really eye-opening, once these arguments were presented to me in a non-insane way."

Others had similar experiences. A historian stressed the importance of conservatives who lived in his dorm. "I got to be really good friends with [them], and they were the first people [that I became friends with] who were conservatives," he recalled. "I found them very persuasive so I gradually moved to the right in college." By his senior year, in fact, this subject subscribed to *Reason* magazine. Another historian, meanwhile, developed a friendship with a religious conservative in graduate school who left him doubting his prochoice convictions. "His main argument is [that since] you can't really be sure if it's a human being or not, you should err on the side of caution. I still don't have a good response to [it]," he admitted. A literature professor at a public research university also found the arguments of his conservative college friend provocative, even if not entirely persuasive at the time. "Bill ... kept giving me libertarian ideas, most of which I rejected, but they were interesting to think about. So, I kept thinking about those ideas," he told us. Over the following college break, he began reading libertarian authors, including Ayn Rand and Murray Rothbard.

In other cases, conservative friends simply directed these future professors to right-wing authors. One economist, for example, was encouraged to read Rand's classic *Atlas Shrugged*. "I don't think I can say it too strongly, but literally it just changed my life.... [I]t was like this awakening for me," she recalled. A philosopher at a private university, meanwhile, was pressed into reading a very different conservative work—Allan Bloom's *The Closing of the American Mind*. Afterwards, he said, "[I] became very interested in learning more about Bloom and Straussians." These accounts should remind us that the student bodies of universities are generally far more politically diverse than the professoriate.

Others moved right after engaging in academic labor itself. In this sense, the professorial vocation sometimes paves the way out of liberalism. When one of our subjects first arrived at Berkeley for graduate school, Ronald Reagan had just won his first presidential election. "In Berkeley that was a very surprising result because everyone thought that Carter was too right wing, let alone Reagan," he recalled. The near universal surprise of his fellow historians interested him in writing a dissertation on the intellectual origins of the Reagan Revolution. And that research made him more receptive to conservative ideas. As he explained, "I think the sheer fact of studying conservatism tends to make you take it more seriously, because you can see that there's a lovely internal consistency to the ideas. The people who disagree with them, disagree with the first principles. But if you accept the principles, you can accept the logical playing out of them as well."

Some conservative scholars, meanwhile, simply started reading more broadly after they became professors. For example, a political scientist at an elite university began drifting rightward once he started studying public policy. That growing intellectual interest drew him into an economic literature that was often critical of government regulation. Those economic studies, he remembered, "just made sense." Likewise, when we asked a literature professor at a private research university why he moved to the right, he answered simply, "I read more things." He did so after chafing against the one-sidedness of his education. He explained,

> When you go to graduate school in English, you read Foucault, you read Derrida, you read Marx, and you should read those things. But one should also read Edmund Burke, one should also read Friedrich Hayek. So, I started reading those things.

Those classics drew him into more contemporary and less philosophical works. "Whittaker Chambers' *Witness* gave me a different sense of the McCarthy era and the Cold War, [and] David Horowitz's autobiography *Radical Son* . . . gave me a different sense of the sixties," he remembered. When we asked a political scientist at a state university why he drifted rightward, his response was remarkably similar: "[It was] a desire to read widely that started me shifting [to the right]."

One scholar we interviewed even reported that his teaching helped him see the merits of conservatism. As a historian at a public university, he assigned his students important conservative thinkers that he was not deeply familiar with. "That really gave me the opportunity to read a lot of these texts and think about these things [anew]," he recalled.

Despite the variety of these conversion narratives, professors often emphasized the importance of discovering that conservatism could be compatible with the life of the mind. "I thought conservatives were either stupid or maybe evil," one philosopher confessed. Taking Harvey Mansfield's class at Harvard punctured that assumption. "[I]t was just very surprising to me that an intelligent person would be saying these things," he added. A political scientist had a similar revelatory experience after taking a course with her first conservative professor. "He was conservative and a very thoughtful, serious person, [and] so I think that helped to make me start thinking about the wider range of political possibilities," she remembered fondly. Another subject's awakening happened in graduate school, where he became close to a right-of-center sociologist. "[J]ust knowing that a really smart, really accomplished, really sophisticated social scientist who also had a real appreciation for what Reagan was trying to do was quite influential in shaping my [political views]," he told us. "I certainly considered a range of perspectives that I had not considered previously." After a philosopher read *The Closing of the American Mind* at the urging of friends, he revisited his long-standing political prejudices as well. "I kind of [had] grown up taking for granted [the notion that] since I was smarter than the average person, I was a liberal," confessed this chagrined professor. A historian at an elite university was compelled to confront similar biases as an undergraduate at Harvard. "I grew up with the distinct impression that conservatives were mentally lacking in some sense, that they just weren't as smart as we were, that I was enlightened," he said. So did a professor of philosophy, who struggled to overcome what he called the "reigning 1970s all-intelligent-people-were-liberals thing."

Even professors who never harbored such negative impressions of conservatism still sometimes had a sense that intellectualism was a special characteristic of left-wing thinkers. Despite his libertarian leanings, for example, a professor of economics hung out with what he described as "intellectual friends" on the far left in college. "I had the impression that my viewpoint was more pragmatic, and that real intellectuals were socialists," he recalled. That perspective changed, however, once he started reading Hayek and Ludwig Von Mises both as an undergraduate and graduate student: "[I]t was actually an eye-opening [experience]."

One should not infer from any of the evidence presented thus far that the university *generally* exposes students to a broad range of conservative thought. There are good reasons to suppose that is not true, as the final chapter emphasizes. Nonetheless, our evidence suggests that the ideational pluralism that does exist in the academy has cultivated the development of conservative minds and identities—ones that continue to shape academia.

To be sure, some professors drifted away from progressivism because they were first repelled by campus liberals rather than pulled by its conservative minority. Some were offended by what they regarded as an over-emphasis on American sins. After the World Trade towers were destroyed, for instance, a historian at a public research university said that he reacted sharply against what he called "the anti-Americanism of the post–9/11 atmosphere." "I got fed up with the order-of-magnitude moral errors that people were making," he explained. "Well, yes, the United States may not have clean hands, but can you really compare it to the rest of the world?" The "order-of-magnitude moral errors" alienated another historian as well. When this subject learned more about communism's many crimes, he began to notice more of those errors. "I felt really betrayed by all those professors I had in college [who] talked about Joe McCarthy as if he was Joe Stalin. They blew all of that out of proportion," he fumed. Reacting against the New Left's anti-anticommunism, this professor then embraced what he called "anti-anti-anticommunism." As an immigrant from Poland, one literature professor was also troubled by professors' anti-anticommunism. "American professors didn't know or did not care to know that the entire communist world was basically a slave camp," she lamented. American conservatives did notice—and it made an impression: "I noticed that the only people that really paid attention to the real world were conservatives. So, I was drawn to those people little by little."

Conservative professors perceived a troubling and misplaced emphasis on America's moral failings in the case of domestic affairs as well, especially with respect to race. As a college student, one historian found "the violent passion with which [affirmative action] was defended . . . extremely alarming." "[I]t seemed to me that people of my sex and color were being punished for things that not even our ancestors had done because I had never been there. I'm a Canadian," he protested. A political scientist at an elite public university also felt that he suffered unjustly for America's racial sins. The son of a drug-addicted mother who sometimes turned to prosti-tution to support her habit, he does not think he was saddled with much white privilege. "I'm in the generation that got hit hardest with affirmative action," he told us. As a young, ambitious graduate student, this profes-sor remembered being told that as "a privileged white man, [he needed] to be put to the back of every line." When Reagan ran in 1980, he recalled being "swept away" by his brand of conservatism. Angry and increasingly disaffected from the left, he described Reagan as "the God-sworn enemy of the people who were pissing me off." Another political scientist, mean-while, remembered first encountering the black radical Cornel West as an undergraduate at Harvard. "[H]e was sort of [a] rock star on campus, [and] a figure I really intensely disliked," he recalled. This professor was especially troubled by West's support for Louis Farrakhan, the black leader of the Nation of Islam and notorious anti-Semite. "I found it repellent that someone like Cornel West would give him the time of the day and would legitimize him in this way," he told us.

Other conservatives were especially troubled by what they regarded as the excesses of the student left. One historian recalled his alienation from the dogmatic unreasonableness of campus radicals in the late 1960s. "I didn't like the protesters too much," he told us. "There was a kind of moral arrogance about them that really put me off, like they have the true belief and everybody else is not only morally evil, but practices self-interest [too]. You couldn't have just an honest [difference of] opinion about some-thing," he lamented. Another historian also drifted rightward after con-fronting the political intolerance of the campus left in the 1960s. He and his friends attempted to organize a "Counter Teach In" on the Vietnam War where both defenders and critics of the Vietnam War were invited to speak. It did not go well. "People harassed me," he said. "[I]t was a really searing experience." By his senior year he reluctantly came to accept that he no longer had a home on the left. A political scientist's journey right-ward began after he encountered the antiwar student left as well. "I just could never share the anti-Americanism of the [antiwar] left," he remem-bered. "I knew I was against the people who were against the war."

Even some professors who came of age years after the radicalism of the 1960s reported similar experiences. "I remember this one formative expe-rience" one historian told us. As he explained, "[W]e had a graduate student union, [and] I thought it was silly, partly because its members kept acting like we were being treated like migrant farm workers, and it was so obvi-ously untrue. . . . [T]hey love the rhetoric of suffering and disempowerment and all the rest." A political scientist, meanwhile, recalled his student days at one of the more radical campuses in the University of California system. "I got to [college], and the kids there ... were unreflective Marxists, and so ... I reacted against it pretty strongly," he recalled.

Perhaps the most common value that runs through these personal testimonies is patriotism. As we have seen, so many of those we interviewed drifted rightward because they found that the left overemphasized America's moral failings, whether it was our policies in Vietnam, race relations, or economic inequality. And, in fact, a striking number of conservative professors who immigrated to America recall being initially drawn to our nation's ideals and way of life even when they still identified with the left. They hailed from a wide range of nations: Canada, Britain, the Netherlands, Poland, Romania, Hungary, Mexico, and Japan. Thus a surprising number of America's most accomplished conservative professors were imported.

Consider the example of a historian who now teaches at a private research university in the South. When he first traveled across America in the 1970s as a visitor from Britain, he remembered feeling overwhelmed by our nation's vitality and optimism. America had "this incredible energy," he remembered, "It was like being wide awake for the first time." This professor was especially impressed by the industriousness of the American people. As he recalled,

> When I came to America for the first time the thing that was just so astonishing here was how hard people worked ... it was just incredible.... [I]t's no surprise that Britain was in decline because nobody would do a hard day's work. You know, something would break [in Britain] and everyone would gather around and say, 'oh look at that, it's broken, what a pity.' Where in America, people would say, 'it's broken, we can fix that,' and they would.

Others shared strikingly similar memories. For instance, one sociologist, a Dutch immigrant, said that he "always had a great affection for the United States." "[I had] a basic identification with this country, what it stood for, that it represented a creed of certain ideals, and that it was a very dynamic place," he recollected. A political scientist, a Canadian, was also drawn to the values and dynamism of America. "I identified with heroism and struggling against odds, [and] the Americans to me were always in a sense more exciting," he told us. "[T]o me, the real big bad place to go compete was the United States." Just as some American intellectuals are drawn to the example of European-style social democracies, some conservative intellectuals felt the pull of the world's oldest existing democracy.

And, finally, a handful of professors were drawn to conservatism by observing the world beyond the ivory tower's gates—a reminder that the university is hardly concealed in a hermetically sealed progressive information bubble. A few such professors started drifting right after laboring for progressive causes. As an undergraduate at Berkeley, one of our subjects in political science described himself as someone with "strong beliefs about injustice in the world, and a belief that government was necessary to solve many of them." Those commitments inspired him to take a job working for a community development agency after college. "I was very excited," he told us. Those enthusiasms, however, quickly waned when he discovered that the job involved processing "massive quantities of meaningless paperwork," he explained, and managing "people from HUD that were [always] yelling [about trivial matters]." Years earlier a now-elderly sociologist also reckoned with the gap between liberalism's aspirations and the actual outcomes of its programmatic experiments. He joined the Young People's Socialist League in college and cast his first vote for Norman Thomas in 1948. In the 1950s he moderated politically, though he remained an ardent Adlai Stevenson voter. This subject's own efforts at the Ford Foundation to fight high school delinquency, however, sent him drifting toward neoconservatism by the 1960s. "When I worked for the Ford Foundation, I thought we could make a great deal of difference," he told us. His hopes were soon dashed. "Realistically speaking, it was just not possible to do what this particular branch of the Ford Foundation was starting to do. I discovered that it was much harder to do something about delinquency than we thought," he concluded. He even began to wonder whether "dropping out of a school was such a disaster." An economist at a liberal arts college was similarly disillusioned by a stint at the Department of Commerce. "I interned at the Department of Commerce one summer, and I just realized these people—they were well meaning—but there's no reason they should have any control of the economy," he recalled.

More frequently, however, professors drifted rightward after observing progressive politics from distant vistas. A striking number of these scholars named one presidential administration for encouraging them to reassess liberalism: Jimmy Carter's. "The Carter administration was very disillusioning, because over time the depth of his ineptness was profound," recalled a political scientist at a private research university. In 1980 he joined many so-called Reagan Democrats by voting for Ronald Reagan. One historian offered a remarkably similar explanation for his abandonment of the Democratic Party. "I just figured really that Carter is going to run the country into the ground, if he was president for another term, and that Reagan was worth a shot," he told us. The Carter years, meanwhile, undermined another scholar's faith in government spending during economic downturns. "[I]t seemed to be the decisive refutation of Keynesianism," he explained.

Many were especially troubled by Carter's dovishness in the face of Iranian aggression. "What are you fucking cowards doing talking with these people?" one political scientist remembered wondering. A professor of history posed a similar objection: "Like why aren't we just bombing this country?" A more measured philosopher recollected, "I could see that this confrontational attitude was a problem, but it seemed obvious to me that the alternative was far worse.... [I]t seemed to me that the dovish instincts at the heart of [the Carter administration] just produced a weakness and chaos." In 1980 he voted for Reagan, and four years later he worked as a precinct captain to reelect The Gipper. President Carter also inspired a historian at a regional state college to vote Republican for the first time. "I think it was Carter's hostility to Israel and also his weakness towards the Soviet Union and the Iranian hostage crisis that caused me to vote for Reagan," he surmised.

As this enduring support for the old Cold War liberalism of the Democratic Party might suggest, some conservative professors insisted that their politics have not changed as much as their voting behavior. This view was almost exclusively found among those professors who came of age prior to the 1970s. "[I]f one considers that as of the early '60s, John Kennedy stood for tax cuts, a strong defense and non-discrimination on the basis of race, those were liberal positions in the early '60s," one political scientist at a liberal arts college began. "[But] they are now conservative positions. So, I would say that my ideological position changed somewhat less than the identities of the parties changed." A few Catholic scholars shared his disaffection from Great Society liberalism. "I still have the profile of a 1962 liberal Catholic, which means I vote Republican now," observed another political scientist. A literature professor, meanwhile, bolted from the Democratic Party after it embraced abortion rights. "[I]t became clear after *Roe v. Wade* that the American left was not as I had envisioned it, and didn't share my sense of the dignity and sanctity of human life," he noted regretfully. "I couldn't have a home and good con-science in the Democratic Party."

Today's right-wing professors were often first drawn into conserva-tism because of a particular cause, especially anticommunism, affirma-tive action, abortion, or economic liberty. But these initial breaks with progressivism further compelled them to revisit other liberal political views. After a historian at an elite university became a Cold War hawk, he began to rethink other issues. He did so because of fresh doubts about the deeper foundations of progressive politics. "I wouldn't have [revisited other issues]," he explained, "[without] the experience of find-ing that I and virtually all of the people I admired were wrong about certain foundational things." Similarly, one professor's break with the Democratic Party over abortion prompted him to rethink his long-stand-ing support for the social welfare state. "When I began to look at the life issues, I began to question various other assumptions, unquestioned at that point about the organization of society, about economics, and so on," he explained. Another's disaffection from the Democratic Party over abortion also caused him to revisit his support for the welfare state. After reading George Gilbert's *Wealth and Poverty*, he recalled reconsid-ering the virtues of markets. To a degree, such transformations were by design. As the conservative operative Richard Viguerie noted long ago, the "abortion issue is the door through which many people came into conservative politics."[10] These conversion narratives may also parallel the experiences of many conservative college students. In their qualita-tive study of right-wing student activists, sociologists Amy Binder and Kate Wood found that "a single issue often initially galvanized their conservatism."[11]

Despite such cases of successful fusionism, modern conservatism is still characterized by internal tensions. But as the next chapter shows, these tensions were not as salient as we anticipated. This is because conservative professors generally share a common political philosophy on the proper ordering of American democracy that has surprisingly little to do with their particular understanding of conservatism or their policy ambitions.

2

The Republican Party and Its Discontents

THE COALITIONAL NATURE of the Republican Party presents political advantages and challenges. It may be less vulnerable to schism, since its various factions recognize that the party is not erected on a single philosophical or ideological foundation.[1] But "like all coalitions," observed historian George Nash, it harbors "within itself the potential for its own dissolution."[2] Thus, managing such intraparty tensions has been a preoccupation of Republican operatives and intellectuals ever since Frank Meyer's efforts at *National Review* nurtured "fusionism" between cultural and economic conservatives in the 1950s and 1960s. It is a project that has become more institutionalized over time, thanks in no small measure to Grover Norquist, a self-described "market Leninist" and veteran of the Reagan Revolution. Norquist established a weekly meeting in Washington, D.C., that assembles the party's varied factional interests, including libertarians, representatives of big business, gays from the Log Cabin Republicans, and religious conservatives. Journalists Tom Hamburger and Peter Wallsten, who covered these meetings at the height of their influence during the George W. Bush administration, noted that Norquist works diligently to remind the party's interests of what "might happen if the movement flies apart and the liberals take charge once more."[3]

Before we began interviewing conservative professors, we assumed that their views on the Republican Party would be dominated by these long-standing intraparty tensions and concerns. Our interviews confirmed these provisional expectations to a degree. It is hardly unusual for right-wing professors, like conservative operatives in Washington, to complain about their intraparty rivals. But to our surprise, conservative professors generally share a common political philosophy on the proper ordering of American democracy that has little to do with their particular understanding of conservatism or their policy ambitions.

We call this common philosophy "Madisonian" because it is most resonant with the political thought of James Madison, the architect of the American Constitution. Madison feared democracy's darker proclivities, especially the tendency of groups in democratic regimes to oppress one another and undermine the public interest. To address the "mischiefs of faction," as Madison famously called them in Federalist No. 10, the Constitution was designed to weaken citizen groups as well as to elevate into political office men with broad experience and established reputations for public service. Once in power these statesmen would "refine and enlarge" public sentiments by discerning the general interest through a careful process of deliberation. Ordinary citizens might point such elites to pressing public problems, but they should not be responsible for constructing solutions to these problems, much less elevating their own popular leaders into office. It is a political vision that values the discovery of common ground over ideological purity, learned elites over charismatic leaders, and reasoned appeals over passionate exhortations.[4]

Given this general persuasion, conservative professors found much to dislike in the contemporary Republican Party, particularly as the Tea Party and its populist candidates have reshaped it. Conservatives are troubled by the inability of the Republican Party to moderate interests to their satisfaction and to build durable coalitions that seek incremental, not radical, change. And when pressed, many professors even struggled to identify prominent Republicans in high office whom they regarded as good ambassadors for their conservatism. Thus many right-wing professors are small-c conservatives first and foremost.

Not every conservative professor, of course, opposes revolutionary change or movements. While a few right-wing professors express an unreserved enthusiasm for the Tea Party, radical libertarians are especially frustrated by the realities of coalitional politics in the big-tented GOP and the limits of their own power to effect radical change. This frustration is fueled in part by dreams of a dramatically remade America, one that conforms to classical-liberal ideals. Many libertarian professors, especially the more radical ones, are caught between their high ideals and a sobering, even cynical, sense of their own collective power to realize those same ideals. Some even abstain from voting altogether, since they regard the act as irrational. Thus, while libertarians sometimes share the revolutionary dreams that stir the political imagination of their leftist colleagues, they also seem far more pessimistic about the prospects of political change. And although free-market conservatives tend to feel more at home in the liberal academy than either neoconservatives or cultural conservatives (as the following chapters show), they also experience a deeper sense of political homelessness in America.

The Madisonian Persuasion

In 1964 the Republican nominee for president, Barry Goldwater, electrified the convention delegates by thundering, "moderation in the pursuit of justice is no virtue." With those provocative words, Goldwater attempted to remake the Republican Party by anchoring it to conservative principles. Conservative professors tend to disagree with Goldwater's famous formulation. Moderate in temperament, they insist on the importance of the quintessential conservative virtue of prudence. And they dislike inflammatory rhetoric and political radicalism, even when it is in the service of a right-wing agenda.

For these reasons, condemnation of the Tea Party's radicalism was widespread, though hardly universal. For some professors such excessiveness compromises the political fortunes of the Republican Party. "I do think that they should be a little bit more politically savvy," suggested a philosopher at a private university. "I think that the Tea Party has to be careful that they don't treat politics as if it's theology." Similarly, a political scientist at a state university criticized what he called "their amateurish view of politics." "People have to be realistic," he warned, "they're not going to get everything they want out of politics. The country is not a majority conservative country. It's center-right." A historian at a public research university agreed. "I think the biggest mistake [Tea Partiers] make sometimes is . . . [that they] want their candidates to be pure, to absolutely agree with them on every single issue down the line. Sometimes, they want to condemn a candidate just because he doesn't agree with them on *everything*," he concluded.

One danger of such ideological tests, of course, is backing primary candidates who are unlikely to win general elections. As one worried literature professor at a private research university fretted, "I just hope they don't ruin [the GOP's] chances in 2012." An English professor at a private university even called the "excessiveness" of the Tea Party "inexcusable." This danger was not merely a theoretical one for conservatives. They pointed to the lost opportunities in the 2010 Senate races in Nevada and Delaware. In both cases the nomination of radical Tea Party candidates undermined the power of the Republican Party in the Senate. "That was insane," explained an exasperated political scientist. "I think that they've been unrealistic and really stupid."

Many other professors, however, offered a more sweeping critique of the Tea Party's radicalism. What troubles them is not the inability of ideological candidates to attract moderate voters. Instead, these professors fear that such radicals might win office and undermine a more cautious, prudent conservative agenda. "I'm very disgusted with the Tea Party," said a political scientist at a public university. "They're motivated more by anger than good public policy or common sense, and it's frightening." A literature professor at a public university agreed: "I think that the Republican Party is dealing with a number of crackpotty personalities right now. They may have some good ideas about such and such a thing, but [they] are loose cannons." A sociologist at a public research university was also alienated from the radicalism of the Tea Party, calling it "too extreme." He especially faulted the Tea Party for the "fanatical belief that the market solves all our problems, which is sort of the counterpart to the leftist belief that if you nationalize everything, the whole world will be like an Agora." "I think they are way too intransigent in their demands," another subject told us. "When Michele Bachmann says that she will not vote for increasing the debt ceiling under any circumstances, I think that's just plain irresponsible, and there's too much of that . . . in the Tea Party." A frustrated political scientist at a private research university offered the same assessment:

> [Y]ou get the sense that if many people in the Tea Party were offered a five-for-one deal—right, five dollars in spending cuts for every dollar in tax increases—they would still on principle say 'no' because it involves tax increases. I sympathize with some of the things that they are after, but what I don't like about the Tea Party is [its] absolute unwillingness to compromise in terms of finding fiscal solutions.

"Budget politics is all about compromise," he concluded.

Others criticized Ron Paul in similar terms. "I can agree with [Paul] on a few points," allowed a political scientist at a liberal arts college. "But it's just a case of the perfect becoming the enemy of the good. . . . [I]t becomes [too] ideological." An economist at a public research university harbors the same concerns about Paul. "[H]e frightens me a little bit," he confessed. "Even though I'm sympathetic to [Paul's] ideas, I still think he needs to be more practical about them and understand that, yes, in a libertarian utopia, we wouldn't have [the Federal Reserve System], we'd have a free banking system, and markets would be completely free and whatever else, but that's not reality." An economist at a public university echoed this worry— "[Paul's] a little crazy"—while still another economist expressed a similar, albeit more vague, unease: "I have a feeling, perhaps unjustified, that he's a loose cannon."

Professors' concerns about radicalism in the Republican Party were not directed just at the Tea Party. Even established figures like John McCain, who earned a reputation for bipartisanship, were criticized for their stridency, especially on foreign policy issues. A political scientist at a liberal arts college nearly refused to vote for McCain in 2008, finding his views on foreign policy "disturbing" since they were "not sufficiently informed by prudence." A sociologist at a prominent public university disliked McCain enough to vote for Obama in 2008. "I just can't stand John McCain, I just absolutely loathe him," he said, citing the senator's "impulsiveness." Candidate Obama, on the other hand, seemed to embody the sort of cool, deliberative sense this sociologist admires in presidential candidates. "I feel an instinctive sympathy [for Obama]. He seems like my kind of person, although I disagree with him on basically everything." A libertarian economist at a public university also voted for Obama in 2008 for similar reasons. McCain's "idea, you know, of 'I'll consult my gut, my gut will tell me,' this is outrageous," this economist declared. "Obama," he paused to reflect, "well, let's face it, he's a sort of an intellectual. . . . I can relate." In a more humorous vein, a political scientist at a research university blurted: "I gotta say McCain was worse than Dole as a candidate. God, he was potentially nuts, right? That thing where he had that meltdown, he flew back to Washington, he was going to cancel the debate, then not cancel the debate. . . . That looked like a crazy man at work there."

In addition to expressing their disapproval of rash candidates, many conservative professors also defended the public "waffling" or "flip-flopping" of moderate candidates, preferring to see such changes as evidence of their prudence and reasonableness. Despite harboring strong prolife views, one of our interviewees supported Mitt Romney's prochoice policies as governor of Massachusetts:

> I tend to read ... Romney's flip-flops differently. If you listen to him carefully when he ran [for governor], he never actually says what he believes, he just says what he is not going to do. So, if I were running for governor of Massachusetts, I would actually say, 'Look I am prolife. I understand that the people of this state are not for it, so it's not something on my agenda.' I don't think that's disingenuous.

Another agreed. "[A] politician who advocated my views of the world, would never get elected," he admitted frankly. "I mean like Romney, his honest answer is 'well, look, I did the best I could given the circumstances.'" Thus these two professors defended the compromises Romney made for the sake of political power. They even seem to regard such accommodations as an indication that the American political order is functioning well.

Other professors emphasized the legitimate limits of politics in more general terms. "I'm perfectly willing to talk about marginal changes," one told us. "I have a vision about where I'd like to be, but I don't expect everybody to be there." An economist at a prestigious research university concurred: "I think [improvement] at the margin ... where we get a little smaller government, a little more reliance on markets and individual choices, a little less reliance on government and centralized decisions, would be a step in the right direction." Perhaps the most striking endorsement of moderate change came from the literature professor who announced: "Federalist number 10 is my text." Federalist No. 10 famously defended the Constitution because it "breaks" and "controls" factions, preventing them from convulsing society or imposing their will on the national government. In other words, this professor admires our Constitution precisely because it keeps mass movements like the Tea Party weak.

At times, conservatives' deep affection for public tranquility was evident in their admiration for particular candidates. A professor of history at a public university praised Rudy Giuliani because of "his ability to keep order." "New York under David Dinkins was so scary that you just couldn't go there," he remembered. "The real vast accomplishment of someone like Giuliani in really creating a sort of perfectly normal world, where you can actually walk from one end of Manhattan holding your wallet up in the air to the other without it being taken from you is really kind of amazing."

Other conservatives were dismayed by the efforts of Republican politicians to radically transform the world, especially by promoting democracy in the Middle East. "I think there's a good deal of bungling in American foreign policy," said one literature professor. "I mean I do think we've got a kind of sense of self-righteousness . . . that can get us into a lot of trouble," he concluded.

Conservative professors are also very displeased with the anti-intellectual tendencies of populists inside the Republican Party. The Tea Party, in fact, was widely condemned as a "know-nothing" movement. A political scientist at a liberal arts college spoke for many of his conservative colleagues: "My strong impression is that the Tea Party talks a lot about the Constitution without knowing the constitutional order very well." In a more general way, another subject liked the Tea Party's opposition to big government. "But as a group," he warned, "it doesn't have a particularly well thought out political philosophy." A philosopher at a state university is especially disappointed by the Tea Party's spokespersons. "I want somebody up there who is intelligent, who knows about the issues, who can rule with other people in a reasonable way," he mused. "I don't see . . . the Tea Party candidates doing that." Even some scholars with a generally more positive view of the Tea Party still lamented its anti-intellectualism. As a noted literature professor explained to us, "It doesn't simply have much of a head in terms of intellectual sophistication or smarts or anything." Similarly, a philosopher at a public research university confessed,

> To be perfectly honest with you, I also think a lot of people who self-identify as Tea Partiers are in fact kind of knee jerky, that is to say, kind of America, right or wrong. . . . [I]f you're [going to] talk about why abortion is wrong or if you're going to talk about why we should restrict the way government gets involved in things like marriage contracts, [then] you better have really thoughtful, well-grounded reasons. In other words, part of the problem is these people aren't embarrassed by the stupidity of some of their reasons, and that irritates me.

A less critical political scientist at a liberal arts college nonetheless faulted the Tea Party for its anti-intellectualism as well. "There has to be some kind of respect for actual expertise," he demanded, otherwise the Tea Party cannot possibly understand "the limits" the Constitution "imposes on politics" or how "to get things done within those limits."

While many conservative professors appreciated the Tea Party's opposition to our soaring federal debt, they also faulted the movement for failing to offer thoughtful and serious solutions to the problem. A historian at an esteemed public university wondered: "[W]hat do they want to *cut* exactly? You really have to sit down and tell me what you're *going to* cut." A sociologist at a private university also criticized the Tea Party for neglecting the thorny problem of entitlement reform. As he explained,

> The really hard questions have to do with questions on Social Security, Medicare, and so on. I have not heard many members of the Tea Party forthrightly confront the prospect of who is going to be satisfied with less. Are [Tea Party members] willing to make some sacrifices?

An accomplished political scientist at a private research university expressed the same concern in more general terms. As he put it, the Tea Party is pushing "simplistic answers to complicated problems."

Other conservatives were troubled by the ascent of some of the Tea Party's populist leaders, especially Sarah Palin, Rick Perry, Michele Bachmann, Herman Cain, and Ron Paul. A sociologist at a prominent research university disliked such leaders because they feed liberal prejudices about cultural conservatives. "I just can't stand Sarah Palin," he fumed, "because I think she basically proves them right about us. And that drives me nuts. There is a great Yiddish phrase, *a schande vor de goyim*, which basically means that you're embarrassing us in front of the gentiles." Similarly, a political scientist at a public research university faulted Palin, "because either she chooses not to learn or she [can't] learn." Two words leaped into another professor's mind when he thought of Sarah Palin: "ill-educated and naïve."

Rick Perry, the governor of Texas and 2012 presidential aspirant, was roundly criticized as well. A philosopher and social conservative offered a gentler rebuke than other critics: "He's not an intellectual, let's put it that way. His instincts are all sound, but he was either unable or unwilling to do the kind of homework that he needed to do." An economist at a large public university expressed a franker version of the philosopher's indictment. "Rick Perry is an embarrassment, [he's] an idiot," he decreed. A literature instructor at a large southern university was perhaps more critical still: "He is a blowhard and he's too arrogant, and he's just not sharp."

"I think Rick Perry is not very bright," another of our subjects concurred. "I think he's the dumb Texan."

One literature professor at a state university was initially optimistic about Governor Perry. As he recalled:

> Before I heard Rick Perry speak, I thought, okay, great, this is a governor who has got low unemployment, [and is] probusiness. Then I heard him speak, and I said, 'There is no way he is electable, no way is America going to elect another Texan governor who butchers the English language, right?'

His criticisms of Perry, however, were not limited to his syntactical transgressions. This subject also disapproved of the deeper anti-intellectual tendencies he often found in Tea Party candidates. "I am certainly not a Michele Bachmann, Rick Perry conservative." A Bachmann-Perry conservative, the professor explained, is one who is "knee jerk and programmed through a lens where everything is going to be black and white, with a little bit, but not much complexity to it, not much nuance, and not much sophistication."

Others criticized Michele Bachmann for claiming that the human papillomavirus (HPV) vaccine causes mental retardation. "That's just crazy," said an economist at a liberal arts college. A philosopher at a state college was just as alarmed by Bachmann's demagoguery: "It's one thing to have some intellectual position about whether or not the government should require vaccinations. But what Michele Bachmannn was saying was like deliberately pandering to this antiscience–vaccinations-cause-retardation crowd, which is like completely medieval." Another of our subjects was vexed by Bachmann's repudiation of evolution. "If I have a litmus test that's probably it," he surmised, while still another scholar said, "Michele Bachmann is bit of a kook." An economist at a prestigious private university described Tea Party candidates in similar, albeit more general, terms: "Peculiar, strange. . . . I think they have taken some peculiar views."

Though professors tended to regard Herman Cain somewhat more favorably than Bachmann, he was criticized for his intellectual shortcomings as well. One sociologist attended a local Cain event that drew enthusiastic supporters. "But I was very negative, because the man has not done his homework, he was bumbling, and that's embarrassing. I think conservatives should set a slightly higher standard," he concluded.

Such criticisms were hardly reserved for those candidates on the cultural right. Ron Paul, the champion of libertarianism in the Republican Party, was described in similar terms, especially by those professors who sympathize with free-market ideals. "I wouldn't say he is an idiot," one political scientist damned Paul with faint praise. "He always just strikes me as somebody's crazy uncle," another of our interviewees agreed.

More often, conservative professors criticized Paul for his defense of the gold standard. "I think his views on monetary policy are crazy," an economist at a liberal arts college told us. Another called Paul's position on the gold standard a "ridiculous idea," while a third called it "insane." A less critical economist told us that Paul's monetary views are "a little crazed."

Right-wing professors did not regard anti-intellectualism as a disease of the conservative mind, as so many liberal scholars contended. Instead, they critiqued the Tea Party's intellectual shortcomings in Madisonian terms. As one political scientist told us,

In order to become successful in mass political movements, you have to simplify politics in order to generate slogans that get people mobilized. And when you simplify politics, you are obviously introducing a degree of unreality to what is actually going on, and I've never been comfortable with that.

Even those who generally approved of the Tea Party still tended to harbor similar reservations about populist, mass movements. "On the whole, I think positively of the Tea Party," said a historian at a public research university. Yet "like all populism," he noted, the Tea Party "has its own problems and pathologies." In a similar vein, another historian told us, "The Tea Party is a populist movement, but the thing about populist movements is they often are unsophisticated.... [T]hat was true for William Jennings Bryan in 1896, it was true for Andrew Jackson back in 1828. They're just not sophisticated."

Given such a dim view of populism, conservative professors who actually encountered Tea Party activists were sometimes pleasantly surprised by what they found. A political scientist at a private, teaching-oriented university spoke to Tea Party groups about the American founding and constitutional order. This teacher said he was "shocked" by the intensity of their intellectual curiosity, by their eagerness to absorb what he called the "elemental stuff." "I've been with them for five hours straight. I'm not kidding, they won't let you go," he recalled. A historian at a private university was also "amazed," as he put it, by the intellectual serious-ness of Tea Party activists. "They cared a great deal about history and the Constitution," he told us. "And they didn't just say they cared about history and the Constitution, they were actually reading and trying to figure [it] out." So, although these professors parted from the view that Tea Party activists are zealous know-nothings, they did so only by overcoming their deep suspicion of populist movements by observing them up close.

The antipopulism of conservative professors does not mean that they see no place for mass movements in American democracy. To the contrary, movements like the Tea Party, say many conservative professors, do a pub-lic service by directing elite attention to pressing public problems. Many conservative professors did, in fact, praise the Tea Party for placing such concerns as the national debt and the solvency of entitlement programs at the center of the national agenda. For example, a professor of philosophy at a public university spoke for many other conservatives when he told us, "I think it's good to have people raising these questions." A political scientist agrees. "I think there are some salutary benefits of the Tea Party," he told us. "I think it has changed the topics [and] I think that's good." Similarly, an economist at a state university said, "I think it's great that [reducing deficits is] actually becoming a topic that attracts widespread attention, and a lot of it is because of the Tea Party."

What conservative professors do not want, generally speaking, is for populist movements or their amateurish representatives to become too powerful. Instead, much like the American founders, they hope that sea-soned candidates will "refine and enlarge" the crude sentiments of spirited citizens. Conservative professors, therefore, prefer candidates with "estab-lished reputations" over those amateurs who practice what Madison called the "little arts of popularity."[5]

Thus, in 2012 conservative academics tended to support experienced presidential candidates, especially Tim Pawlenty, Jon Huntsman, Mitch Daniels, Jeb Bush, and Newt Gingrich. Even the youngest candidates in this group—Pawlenty and Huntsman—are hardly political amateurs.

When we asked a historian at a private university why he supported Pawlenty in 2012, he told us, "I like the idea of someone who has actual governing experience in a politically divided state. I think that's a great model.... And then he dropped out, so I kind of have no one that I feel completely comfortable with." A philosopher at a liberal arts college felt the same sense of unease when Huntsman dropped out of the race.

"I really like Jon Huntsman, he's like the academic's Republican," she told us. But now "there is really no one to cheer."

Other professors admired even more seasoned politicians, such as Jeb Bush and Newt Gingrich. "I would have liked to see Jeb Bush," one sociologist said. "He would have been my candidate because he is conservative, he has the experience, and he is thinking about issues. . . . [F]or me, that is the trifecta." Praise for Gingrich was often qualified by concerns about his ethical judgment and temperament. Still, many wondered whether he might be ready for a stint in the White House after all those years in Washington. And they admired his intellect too. "[Sometimes] I think, well, maybe Gingrich actually has changed, sobered up, and became wiser and better," a philosopher told us. "I'd say that of all of the candidates," another reflected, "the one that I am most intellectually in line with is . . . Newt Gingrich. I think he is generating ideas like crazy." A more dubious philosopher told us, "I mean ironically the best guy is Gingrich, but I just don't trust him." Part of Gingrich's appeal to conservative academics, of course, is that he is a former professor of history with a record of thinking in serious ways about steering American politics in a conservative direction.

A handful of conservative professors praised some of the younger Republican stars who will become more seasoned presidential candidates in time, especially Paul Ryan and Marco Rubio. A literature professor at a public university adored Ryan for being "a geeky guy," as she put it, and praised his willingness to confront honestly the coming entitlement crisis, unlike so many other Republicans. "We're just on this roller coaster with the entitlement programs and no one's talking about it," she noted with exasperation. "It's like we live in a crazy world."

One historian believed that amateurish presidential candidates will plague the GOP so long as it continues to accept the plebiscitary nomination process that has been in place since the early 1970s. "I wish that the Republican Party would get together the elites . . . and say, 'This primary system is absurd,'" he remarked, observing that past candidates "who I actually have great respect for, like . . . Grover Cleveland and William McKinley [would] never get nominated now." "McKinley refused to campaign for reelection because he thought it was beneath the dignity of the presidential office," this professor noted approvingly.

When we asked conservative professors to name public figures who were good ambassadors for their brand of conservatism, we assumed that they would name politicians. Instead, professors usually named public intellectuals, such as William F. Buckley, Charles Krauthammer, and Bill Kristol. They often struggled to finger a *single* conservative politician, even when pressed to do so. One sociologist responded: "I'd say I very much like Charles Krauthammer. I like Walter Russell Mead. He may not be as prominent, but [he's] very thoughtful, well grounded, good writing, very sharp." Similarly, a political scientist told us, "I have a lot of respect for Charles Krauthammer. I think he is a brilliant guy. Bill Kristol, I think a lot of him." The one politician this academic praised unequivocally was Bill Frenzel, an intellectual who actually worked in the Brookings Institution after he retired from Congress.

A philosopher at a religious university had an even more difficult time identifying conservative politicians whom he regarded as good ambassadors for his culturally conservative views. "Well, in terms of popular figures, I think William F. Buckley," this philosopher offered. "What about politicians?" we asked. He struggled:

> Politicians? Let's see, Reagan. I think Goldwater. I mean I don't remember. I mean he was before [my time]. You know, in terms of writings, I think Gingrich in terms of his writings is great. I think George Gilder, but then again you see [those I admire] are not politicians, they are intellectuals. Boy, it's difficult to come up with [names]. Oh, Paul Ryan. I actually met him two years ago at [the] Heritage [Foundation] and he gave a wonderful talk and I think he is the real deal. Yeah ... that's about it.

Another philosopher, after pondering the question for some time, responded simply: "Reagan."

Others drew a blank. "God, political figures?" one sociologist asked, clarifying our question. After an extended pause, he responded: "Yeah, I'm not enthusiastic about [many candidates]." This sociologist simply could not identify a single Republican whom he regarded as a good public ambassador for his conservatism. When we asked a sociologist whether any politicians were good ambassadors for his political views, he responded: "I guess I have to say no." "I would style myself as a social conservative," he went on, "but the fact is that many people who would be called social conservatives and politicians I don't much care for. They just strike me as strident and dogmatic and as unpleasant people."

Not all conservative professors, however, believed that "dogmatic and unpleasant people" direct the Republican Party. In fact some conservatives emphasized the Tea Party's willingness to work with the Republican establishment. "I'm glad they're not trying to form a third party," said an economist at a liberal arts college. "They're being practical." A political scientist at a prestigious university concurred with this assessment. "I [especially] like the fact that they stay within the Republican Party, instead of trying to make a third party," he told us. An economist at a prestigious research university also agreed: "I think it's great that they're operating within one of the parties, the Republican Party, rather than spinning off." For these conservatives, our Madisonian political system is working well.

To be sure, some conservative professors expressed far more enthusiasm for the populist currents in the Republican Party. One professor of literature at a public research university, for example, expressed an unreserved support for the Tea Party: "I admire them tremendously.... [they're] not business as usual people, and that's what I like about them, because business as usual in politics means screw the taxpayer." When asked about the Tea Party, a libertarian economist said it helped restore his confidence in America. "I thought we were done for," he recalled, but now "we have [Republican] presidential candidates standing up ... and they were all talking about repeal, like repealing something—that never happened before.... I think it's remarkable." Strong enthusiasts of the Tea Party especially praised the movement for its civility and moderation, not its revolutionary zeal. A literature professor at a state university compared activists in the Tea Party and Occupy Wall Street movements:

> [T]he Tea Party [activists] have organizations, the orderliness, the cleanliness, the picking up their garbage, they go home. They are law-abiding citizens. People say they are mirror images of one another. What images are you looking at? To me they are nothing like that.

Likewise, a historian at a public university acknowledged that although Tea Party activists are "outspoken," they are also "so well behaved." And unlike their counterparts in the Occupy Wall Street movement, this professor added, "they aren't going to leave trash everywhere." A historian at a state university insisted that even the Tea Party's ends were moderate, not just its tactics. "I am baffled by the way the media has portrayed it as a kind of monstrous extreme movement," he told us, noting that the movement's two concerns—"constitutional limits" and the "irresponsible accumulation of debt"—are marks of prudence rather than ideological zealotry. "It's mostly people who are just trying to say, 'Wait, you know, let's be reasonable.'" Likewise, a professor of history at a public university insisted that only a small minority of Tea Party activists were "extremists."

On the one hand, these right-wing populists do not seem all that different from Madisonian conservatives. After all, the populist professors expressed distaste for radical movements too. But, on the other hand, the defenders of the Tea Party rejected most conservatives' sense that *all movements* are prone to rash zealotry, preferring instead to distinguish good movements from the bad.

Support for populism among intellectuals on the right always existed in tension with their long-standing concerns about democracy. When conservative intellectuals began to embrace right-wing populism in the 1960s, it was laid on top of an older, constitutional conservatism. That earlier consensus grew out of conservative intellectuals' efforts to anchor their political philosophy in a viable American tradition. As they looked for a conservative intellectual tradition, argues George Nash, one "dominant theme" emerged. That theme was "anti-majoritarianism," which Nash defines as "the belief that the American political system traditionally stood for and should stand for principles like checks and balances, dispersal of power, [and] limits on the power of majorities."[6] Thus, what we have called the "Madisonian persuasion" is quite similar to what Nash called "anti-majoritarianism"—and was critical to the development of a distinctly conservative intellectual tradition after the Second World War.

Something like the "Madisonian persuasion" also seemed to be prevalent among conservative students at the most elite universities. Sociologists Amy Binder and Kate Wood compared conservative activism on two campuses, which they called Western Flagship and Eastern Elite University. Conservative students at Eastern Elite disapprove of the populist tactics of conservative groups at the less selective campuses like Western Flagship. Such populist tactics include affirmative action bake sales, where the price of brownies is discounted for racial minorities. Elite students are critical of such provocative tactics partly because of the culture of selective universities, which prize deliberative styles of political engagement, but also because it offends their understanding of conservatism itself.[7]

Yet given the populist turn of conservative intellectuals in the 1960s, it is somewhat surprising that our interviews with conservative professors did not uncover more enthusiasm for the Tea Party. Perhaps they hold the Tea Party at arm's length because some of the historical forces that nurtured the conservative populism of the 1960s are now weaker.

Nash emphasizes, for example, that "the trend toward majoritarianism was enormously stimulated by a series of Supreme Court decisions that aroused not just conservative intellectuals, but broad segments of the populace, which right-wingers could now, at long last, cultivate." Thus conservatives were "more confident than ever before that 'the people' could now be reached."[8] Yet as conservatives expanded their influence in powerful political institutions, including the Supreme Court, their temper may have become more anti-majoritarian once again. Today, after all, one is bound to hear just as many complaints about the Court from the left.

Whatever the explanation, many of today's conservative professors are alienated by growing populism inside the Republican Party. Yet, compared with the radical libertarians in their ranks, they are happy partisans.

Libertarian Idealism and Alienation

The professors most disaffected from Republican Party politics were the staunchest devotees of libertarianism. They expressed the most frustration with the modern Republican Party and democracy more generally. Free-market conservatives were both more agitated by the compromises demanded by big-tented parties and hobbled by a sense of political impotency. In fact, many told us that they did not vote at all because political participation was itself irrational, a tendency that is particularly true of the many economists with libertarian commitments. Thus, while free-market conservatives often feel more at home in the academy than social conservatives or neoconservatives, they also experience a deeper sense of political homelessness in the wider society.

The reluctance of libertarian professors to fully embrace the GOP is evident in our survey results (see Tables 2.1 and 2.2). Libertarians are less likely to self-identify as Republicans than self-identified conservative professors, and more likely to support the Libertarian Party. On election days,

Table 2.1 Party Identification of Conservative
and Libertarian Professors

	Rep	Ind	Dem	Lib	Other	N:
Cons	76%	18%	2%	0%	4%	95
Lib	39%	20%	0%	36%	5%	44
N:	89	26	2	16	6	139

Table 2.2 **Voting History of Conservative and Libertarian Professors**

2000	Bush	Gore	Other	Didn't Vote	Ineligible	N:
Cons	80%	4%	6%	4%	5%	96
Lib	52%	5%	16%	16%	11%	44
N:	100	6	13	11	10	140

2004	Bush	Kerry	Other	Didn't Vote	Ineligible	N:
Cons	84%	5%	3%	2%	5%	96
Lib	42%	4%	23%	20%	11%	45
N:	100	7	13	11	10	141

2008	McCain	Obama	Other	Didn't Vote	Ineligible	N:
Cons	79%	8%	4%	5%	3%	96
Lib	39%	18%	20%	11%	11%	44
N:	93	16	13	10	8	140

libertarian professors are also more likely to stay home. One in five did so in 2004, for example. And although not a single libertarian professor we interviewed self-identified as a Democrat, some did occasionally vote that way when they were especially dissatisfied with the Republican Party. Nearly one in five libertarian professors, for example, voted for President Obama in 2008.

Our interviews probed far deeper into the complex relationship between libertarian professors and the GOP. Consider the case of an economist at a state university. She was more sanguine than many of her libertarian colleagues about the Republican Party, believing that it has the potential to become an instrument of libertarians like her. But she has also been disappointed by the power of other factions in the Republican Party: "I get hopeful, and then it's like, 'Oh crap, it's just like business as usual.'" And while this professor accepts that the GOP is the "only avenue right now" for free-market ideals, she is far from hopeful: "The Republican Party is so schizophrenic that it is hard to count on."

Another also remembers feeling hopeful after President George W. Bush was elected in 2000. He recalled, "I was looking at [Bush], and I was like, 'He is the new Reagan. He has these libertarian ideas and with the Republican House and Senate, we will be heading in a good direction.'" But then President Bush increased the size of the federal government by expanding Medicare and pushing for the No Child Left Behind Act, not to mention expensive wars in Iraq and Afghanistan. "Things just didn't turn out that way," he concluded ruefully.

The Bush years were also sobering for a literature professor at a public university. "I felt that [the Iraq War] was incredibly destructive, and that coupled with the unending expansion of the federal government, especially on education—The No Child Left Alone Act, that stuff. And then, of course, the bankrupting of the United States," he continued, drawing his critique of Bush to a close.

One economist at a public university tried to be "hopeful" about the future of the Republican Party, without putting much "faith" in it. But he, too, was badly disappointed by the Bush years. "I've voted for Bush twice, and I was immensely disappointed for eight years."

While other libertarian professors were even less optimistic about the Republican Party, they too accused the GOP of ideological "schizophrenia." For example, an economist at a public university was frustrated by what he perceives as the Tea Party's drift from an emphasis on limited government to an emphasis on social concerns. "Again, one of the problems, I think with these movements," he said, "is that it collects people with differing opinions."

Libertarians, therefore, were far less prone than other conservatives to accept, much less embrace, the moderation and pragmatism that big-tented parties demand. Certainly there are exceptions. An economist told us that he would be "ecstatic" if Republican rule would lead to "a little" reduction in regulations and taxes. But there is little doubt that libertarian professors possess a stronger tendency toward idealism than other conservative intellectuals. They admired Goldwater for insisting that "extremism in the defense of liberty is no vice." The Goldwater revolution, however, never triumphed. That failure has left libertarian professors with a painful sense of the better world that our pluralistic democracy prevents from coming into being. The result is a deep distrust and even withdrawal from political life.

This alienation was exemplified by one economist who appreciates libertarian friends who work inside the Republican Party. "They're hoping that they can sway the Republican Party," he explained, "but I just don't see that happening." So he usually does not vote. "I don't want to give any of these people a mandate to do anything," he told us.

Many other advocates of limited government stay home on election days. "Yeah, I don't vote," confessed an economist at a public university. "I do have a visceral disgust at politics, [so] I don't like the idea of participating in it," he explained. Another of our subjects, a philosopher, shares this disaffection, though he does vote on occasion. "I took a number of cycles off, just not wanting to participate at all," he remembered.

Others were even more alienated. "I have not been registered to vote for more than two decades," admitted a philosopher at a research university. This subject looked like a model of civic virtue compared with some others. "I've never voted," declared one. "I tend to think politicians all tend to be pretty wicked people [and] I think the exercise of political power is the exercise of coercion," he added. For this professor, democratic politics is inherently coercive because it creates winners and losers. His exit from the "wicked" world of politics was reminiscent of pietistic Christian sects that wall themselves off from the evils of secular society.

Like that of some religious believers, libertarians' reluctance to participate is partly rooted in their unwillingness to compromise their ideals. And for most libertarian intellectuals, their classical liberal ideals seem especially endangered by their long-standing rivals: social conservatives. When we asked one about his views on the religious right, one subject responded sharply: "Oh yeah. I hate it. I can't stand it." "I'm very weary of the Republican right," confessed another. "Some of those conservatives who know better than other people the right way to live and so are willing to impose their opinions on others, maybe [they] could learn some things from a more libertarian [perspective]," he suggested. A more tempered attitude was expressed by a historian who allowed, "I don't have much sympathy" for social conservatives. In a similar spirit, a political scientist at a public university revealed, "I wouldn't be friendly to, say, the religious right."

For some, the sway of social conservatives inside the Republican Party has left them with a far deeper sense of political homelessness. A political scientist told us, "I don't feel like I have a party anymore, especially with the social conservative takeover, it's really problematic." Another scholar was just as alienated: "I have no common cause with the social conservatives who want to impose . . . a theocratic social system on us. . . . It means that I don't really have a home."

There were some exceptions, of course. A few libertarians, for example, tolerate prolife advocates in the Republican ranks, largely because they support devolution to the states and oppose a strong federal judiciary. For example, an economist at an elite private university allowed, "I actually think it would be very constructive for the country to let abortion be a state issue, whether that's for constitutional reasons or just because we decide that we want to engage in that kind of federalism." But, in general, libertarians found it difficult to tolerate social conservatives.

Social conservatives, however, are generally tolerant of libertarians and even welcome them as allies against modern liberalism. One notable exception was a political scientist at a liberal arts college. "I don't particularly like the creeping libertarianism in the Republican and conservatives worlds today," he told us, adding that it "is a barely concealed defense of selfishness [that offers] no serious thinking about the moral or cultural foundations of a liberal order." The critique of a historian at a community college went further. "I think the Republican Party is basically the Libertarian Party," he lamented. "The traditionalist conservatives have been completely cast aside." Such critiques and anxieties from the most traditionalist conservatives did not mean that they were opposed to working with free-market conservatives, however. When one was asked about the long-standing alliance between social and economic conservatives in the Republican Party, he conceded, "I'll put up with it. I'll put up with it because I live in an imperfect world." Perhaps their acceptance of political imperfections makes it easier for cultural conservatives to work with libertarians.

In any case, more than the highly imperfect world of politics keeps some libertarians home on election days. The alienation of many libertarians is also driven by the cold calculation that political participation is irrational. Since many disaffected libertarians are economists or subscribe to economic assumptions, they subject many life decisions to cost-benefit analyses, voting included. And voting is irrational, say the economists, since the odds that a single vote will sway an election is essentially zero, while the costs of voting are not negligible.

The great mystery for those guided by economic assumptions is why anyone bothers to vote at all. "I think I voted when I was like eighteen," one libertarian remembered. When we asked why he has not voted in decades, he replied, "It's irrational. It's idiotic ... it's pointless for me to go vote." Another offered a similar defense for his refusal to fulfill what many regard as a basic duty of citizenship: "I think first of all one vote doesn't change the outcome of an election, and that's all I have is one vote." A third libertarian offered a wider defense of his reluctance to participate in politics by insisting that nearly all forms of political engagement were pointless. "I don't think there is really much you can do to influence politics," he told us. "And so ... not only would you become angry [by participating in the political process], you wouldn't be able to influence anything." Even when libertarians do get to the polls, they are often nagged by a sense that they are wasting their time. As one recalled, "I voted occasionally when there's a local issue, knowing [that] I probably won't have any impact anyway."

Thus, libertarians are often trapped between their high principles and a sense of political impotence. They are both less willing to accept the compromises party politics demands and less inclined to think they can collectively steer the Republican Party toward libertarian goals. The gap between their aspirations and the means to achieve those ends leaves libertarian professors with a sharp distaste for party politics.

Disaffection from modern conservatism is also a long-standing tendency of libertarian intellectuals. In 1969 militant libertarians broke from Young Americans for Freedom to form the Society for Individual Liberty. Three years later a group of radical libertarians formed the Libertarian Party, a powerful mark of their alienation from the GOP. Even Ronald Reagan's ascent to power disappointed libertarians more than it did other conservatives. "As the Reagan Revolution passed into history," George Nash observed, "some of its intellectual architects—especially libertarians—wondered what it had really accomplished."[9] Many libertarians denounced Reagan even well before he left office. As early as 1982, Cato president Ed Crane dismissed the Reagan administration as unprincipled. "In the end," Brian Doherty's *Radicals for Capitalism* concluded, "most libertarians were sorely disappointed in Reagan, and given his libertarian pretensions, almost enraged at times."[10] Libertarians were even more disaffected by George W. Bush, especially by his "audacious assertion of executive power in the war on terrorism."[11] This history of false hope may help explain why the economic conservatives we interviewed were not more sanguine about the recent ascendance of libertarian concerns and candidates in the Republican Party.

Not all libertarian intellectuals, of course, have been so reluctant to embrace the GOP. There have always been important exceptions. Milton Friedman spent his life attempting to move the Republican Party closer to libertarian ideals, working in the Nixon and Reagan administrations. But radical libertarians harshly criticized Friedman's compromising quest for incremental change. "Milton Friedman is the Establishment Court's Libertarian," Murray Rothbard charged, "and it's time to call a spade a spade, and a statist a statist." Friedman's statist crimes included his advocacy of the negative income tax and education vouchers. For his part, Friedman accused radical libertarians of "intolerance" and "decried the utopian strain ... that makes them distain the half steps necessary in the direction of less government."[12]

As such criticisms of Friedman should suggest, libertarians have tended toward an obsession with doctrinal purity over incremental change. Such passions are evident in what Brian Doherty has called radical libertarian's "favorite pastime": "[R]eading others out of the movement for various perceived ideological crimes." "Libertarians are a contentious lot," Doherty adds. They delight in "finding the most outrageous and obnoxious position you could take that is theoretically compatible with libertarianism and challenging anyone to disagree." It is a game that the Republican operative Grover Norquist loathes. "A lot of libertarians seem to relish losing, because it proves how pure they are. They seem to think they are winning, if you get into a conversation and get more radical in your position to the point where no one else in the room can agree with you," Norquist opined.[13] For the most radical among them, such intellectual pleasures deliver them finally to anarchism.

Defenders of libertarianism like Brian Doherty insist that it is not a utopian doctrine. Yet even Doherty confesses that libertarianism "sells the promise of a world mankind hasn't yet fully known." For this reason, devotees of classical liberalism have long sought a libertarian Zion, a place where they could build the first society ordered by their radical principles. Libertarian Zionism inspired efforts to build floating sea cities and to purchase lands from third-world dictators. More recently, some called for 20,000 committed libertarians to move en mass to New Hampshire.[14] Given these aspirations and utopian tendencies, any broad political coalition was bound to disappoint radical libertarian intellectuals.

Yet for all their disaffection from the Republican Party, and from American democracy more generally, libertarian professors tend to feel somewhat more at home in their chosen profession than other conservatives. We turn now to the work lives of conservative professors.

PART II

Life in the Progressive University

3

The Bias Debate

WHY ARE CONSERVATIVES so scarce in academia? The question has generated enormous controversy. Thus far the best evidence suggests that discrimination at the point of hiring and promotion certainly does not account for most of the disparity. This is because liberals aspire to become professors in far larger numbers than conservatives. But this fact does not mean that the academy is free of political bias. In fact, much evidence suggests that conservatives are widely stigmatized by their progressive colleagues and that they confront real discrimination, especially those on the cultural right.

This chapter reviews this body of evidence to provide a broad understanding of the institutional environment that conservatives finding waiting for them in academia. In doing so it sets up the chapters that follow, which explore how conservatives navigate academia.

The Academic Mind

One long-standing explanation for the scarcity of conservatives in academia is that right-wing citizens tend to lack the cognitive and psychological traits necessary for high-level thinking. There are many subtle variants to this thesis. But they all point to a constellation of supposedly conservative traits, such as rigidity, parochialism, unimaginativeness, and closed-mindedness. The liberal mind, meanwhile, is said to be characterized by the opposite qualities: flexibility, cosmopolitanism, creativity, and openness. Thus, in this telling, liberals dominate academia because there is something about the cast of the conservative mind that is maladapted to intellectual life.

In *The Academic Mind*, a classic account of professorial politics published in 1958, Paul Lazarsfeld and Wagner Thielens influentially argued that the minds of conservatives were ill-suited to academic life, especially in the social sciences. Because social scientists must "visualize a state of human affairs radically different from that of today," wrote Lazarsfeld and Thielens, "ultimate scholarly accomplishment must depend on a kind of imagination" that is not "consonant with the intellectual mood of the conservative." Professors, continued Lazarsfeld and Thielens, must "have analytical minds which do not automatically accept cultural beliefs, minds willing to entertain unorthodox ideas as to how a modern society can best function." Moved by the enduring spirit of Progressivism, *The Academic Mind* presupposed that the proper end of social science was to engineer a better world by discovering scientific solutions to social problems. As Lazarsfeld and Thielens explained, "It is thus the function of the social scientist to be sensitive to innovation," since such creative social change "is needed now to help society adjust to novel conditions while discarding outmoded patterns."[1] From one point of view, *The Academic Mind* offered a simple tautology: Social science is full of progressives because its mission is progressive, which is a bit like observing that the Catholic Church is full of Catholics. But Lazarsfeld and Thielens also anointed liberals with particular habits of mind properly associated with intellectualism, such as creativity and analytical rigor.

In retrospect it is not so surprising that Lazarsfeld and Thielens associated intellectualism so strongly with liberalism. After all, conservative intellectual life in the 1950s was relatively weak during the postwar years. With only some exaggeration, Lionel Trilling declared in 1950 that in "the United States at this time liberalism is not only the dominant but the sole intellectual tradition."[2] Some right-wing intellectuals even wondered whether there was a usable conservative tradition in an America so dominated by liberalism. Liberal intellectuals, meanwhile, tended to identify conservatism almost entirely with its populist elements, especially McCarthyism. And McCarthyism itself was understood as an irrational campaign, driven entirely by anxieties, fears, and prejudices. Seymour Martin Lipset, for example, blamed the anticommunist campaign on a "puritanical morality" that insists on a "fundamental difference between right and wrong."[3] From "suggestive clinical evidence," Richard Hofstadter attributed movement conservatism to a disease of the political mind, with symptoms that include "restlessness, suspicion, and fear."[4] Trilling, mean-while, believed that American conservatives fail to "express themselves in ideas but only in action or in irritable mental gestures."[5]

Given the paucity of conservative intellectuals and such fashionable indictments of right-wing movements, Lazarsfeld and Thielens may have reasonably doubted whether the academic mind could ever be all that receptive to conservatism. What seems more surprising is the persistence of the Lazarsfeld and Thielens thesis after the remarkable growth and success of a conservative intellectual movement. Unlike in Trilling's 1950s, few students of intellectual history today would say that liberalism is the *sole* intellectual tradition in America. Recently, in fact, liberal philanthropists established new think tanks, such as the Center for American Progress, out of a felt need to better compete with conservatives in the marketplace of ideas.[6]

Nonetheless, many academics still blame the underrepresentation of right-wing thinkers in the professoriate on the cognitive and psychological limitations of conservatives. "The fact that conservatives are more dogmatic, intolerant of ambiguity, rigid and closed-minded, than are liberals, may explain why fewer of them are hired than their more open-minded, flexible colleagues," declared law professor Michael Vitiello. For those who doubt the superiority of the liberal mind, Vitiello invites us to "[i]magine how difficult it would be for Rush Limbaugh to teach in a Law School," where professors must "induce discussion focusing on both sides of the legal issue."[7] Like many other critics of American conservatism, Vitiello does not allow much distinction between populist and intellectual expressions of right-wing ideas. Apparently Berkeley law professor John Yoo and bombastic talk-radio entertainers suffer from similar mental defects.

Others believe that conservatism is such an exotic political persuasion among the professoriate because liberalism is the inevitable conclusion of the truly open-minded. As the philosopher Jere Surber opined in the pages of the *Chronicle*,

> [I]f you actually take the time to look at history and culture, certain conclusions about human nature, society, and economics tend to force themselves on you. History has a trajectory, driven in large part by the desires of underprivileged or oppressed groups to attain parity with the privileged or the oppressor. . . . [Thus], most of those in the liberal arts have concluded that there really isn't any other intellectually respectable way to interpret the broad contours of history

and culture. They are liberal, in other words, by deliberate and reasoned choice, based upon the best available evidence.[8]

Conservatism, in other words, is rejected by the best minds because it is
irrational, or at least far less defensible than liberalism. The philosopher
Michael LaBossiere recently developed a more eccentric version of the thesis that more informed minds gravitate toward liberalism. He believes that
since graduate school serves up a "taste" of poverty, it cultivates greater
sympathy for the disadvantaged. "[I]t certainly makes sense," a confident
LaBossiere theorized, "that such experiences would give a person sympathy for those who are poor—and thus tend to lean them towards liberal
positions on things like food stamps and welfare."[9]

Others single out religious and cultural conservatives as especially ill-
suited to intellectual life. According to political scientist Barry Ames and
his colleagues at the University of Pittsburgh, religious conservatism tends
to cultivate "an absolutist, 'faith-based' allegiance to a particular dogma,
the veracity of which is considered beyond question or argument." "Such
worldviews," Ames and his colleagues explain, "are (again, by definition)
antithetical to the philosophy of science, which promotes reason and evidence as the determinants of truth." "Challenging entrenched dogma," he
concludes "is the essence of science."[10] In their view, religious conservatives oppose the academy's deepest values as a matter of principle.

These are not eccentric examples. The sociologist Neil Gross asked
professors why they think there are so few conservative professors. He
found that a plurality (41%) of professors believe this pattern endures
because "liberals tend to be more open-minded than conservatives, with
open-mindedness a requirement for academic work." (Another 30% say
that the greed of conservatives directs them away from the university.) As
Gross has further shown, such explanations for the dominance of liberals
in the academy rest on weak empirical evidence. There is little evidence,
for example, to support the notion that hostility to the values of science
has much to do with the underrepresentation of conservative professors
in higher education. If that were true, we would not expect conservatives
to be better represented in the most scientific disciplines, such as engineering and physics; nor would we expect liberals to utterly dominate
those fields that are the least scientific, such as literature and anthropology. There is also little evidence that conservatives lack other cognitive
traits that academic work requires, such as creativity or open-mindedness.
"The research that currently exists, suggests that cognitive and personality

factors explain no more than a fraction of the liberalism of American professors," Gross concluded.[11]

Some evidence even undermines this thesis. Psychologist Jesse Graham and his colleagues evaluated how well citizens from across the partisan divide understood one another. To that end they asked subjects to describe how "a typical conservative" or liberal would defend their points of view. They found that conservatives were far better at describing how a typical liberal thinks than liberals were at explaining how a typical conservative thinks.[12]

So why does the myth that conservatives are ill-suited to the life of the mind persist? We think that the myth's persistence has much to do with the scarcity of conservatives in academia. Many academics cannot help but associate right-wing thought exclusively with its familiar populist expressions precisely because they do not encounter thoughtful conservative intellectuals. The refreshingly introspective social psychologist Jonathan Haidt described his shock at discovering compelling conservative ideas for the first time. "As a life-long liberal," Haidt began, "I had always assumed the conservatism = orthodoxy = religion = faith = rejection of science." But while browsing a used-book store, Haidt picked up a copy of Jerry Muller's *Conservatism: An Anthology of Social and Political Thought from David Hume to the Present*. "I started reading Muller's introduction while standing in the aisle," he recalled, "but by the third page I had to sit down on the floor." Haidt was "quite literally floored" by the recognition that "there was a kind of conservatism that could compete against liberalism in the court of social science." And this kind of conservatism was not old-style liberalism that is now better known as libertarianism. It was the Enlightenment conservatism of Hume, Burke, de Tocqueville, and Durkheim. Haidt, channeling Muller, summarized their conservatism as a series of core beliefs:

> Conservatives believe that people are inherently imperfect and are prone to act badly when all constraints and accountability are removed. . . .
>
> [They believe] our reasoning is flawed and prone to overconfidence, so it's dangerous to construct theories based on pure reason, unconstrained by intuition and historical experience. . . .
>
> [They believe] institutions emerge gradually as social facts, which we then respect and even sacralize, but if we strip these institutions of authority and treat them as arbitrary contrivances that exist only

for our benefit, we render them less effective. We then expose ourselves to increased anomie and social disorder.

Haidt did not convert to conservatism, but he did appreciate its insights: "I began to see that [conservatives] had attainted a crucial insight into the sociology of morality that I had *never* encountered before" (our emphasis).[13]

It is difficult to imagine that a prominent conservative professor of Haidt's stature would ever find herself "floored" by, say, Rawlsianism or Marxism. Liberal and leftist ideas dominate intellectual paradigms and discourse far too much in academic life for that to happen. But liberal professors, especially in certain social scientific and humanistic fields, may enjoy long, prosperous careers without ever encountering volumes such as Muller's. And this means that the conservative ideas that they do encounter stream from right-wing radio and Fox News. If this is right, it may be that the causal arrow points in the opposite direction: While varieties of the old Lazarsfeld and Thielens thesis do not explain the dearth of conservatives in the academy, the dearth of conservatives in the academy does explain the enduring power of the Lazarsfeld and Thielens thesis.

Political Bias

The enduring power of Lazarsfeld and Thielens's thesis, however, may have its own consequences. After all, the Lazarsfeld-Thielens thesis does not merely provide an explanation for the paucity of conservatives in higher education. It also provides legitimate reasons for preferring liberal professors in hiring and promotion. If conservative minds are unable to develop into impressive academic minds, then why hire or promote right-wing thinkers? Even if there were no stigma attached to conservatism, we still might suspect that liberals would prefer to hire and promote liberals. If academics prize collegiality and community, as most human beings do, then they will prefer to work with others who hold values they share. And, of course, liberal professors will be attracted to candidates who work on research that is informed by their own normative concerns.[14] In any case, a growing body of evidence suggests that ideological discrimination in hiring, promotion, and publishing is real, though it is far from the most important cause of liberal dominance in higher education.

There is evidence that many liberal professors prefer to hire liberal candidates rather than conservative ones. Yoel Inbar and Joris Lammers's

survey asked social psychologists whether "in choosing two equally qualified job candidates . . . [you] would be inclined to vote for the more liberal
candidate." Approximately 38% of respondents said that they would support the liberal candidate in that situation."[15] In *Compromising Scholarship*,
sociologist George Yancey reported the results of his survey of sociologists,
which asked the following question:

> Assume that your facility is hiring a new professor. Below is a list of
> possible characteristics of this new hire. . . . [I]f you were able to learn
> of these characteristics about a candidate, would you be more or less
> likely to support their hire?

This question, designed to measure social and political biases, was dis-
guised in a larger survey about collegiality. Yancey found that nearly 30%
of sociologists said that if they knew a job seeker was a Republican, they
would be less likely to support his or her candidacy. Sociologists, in fact,
clearly preferred communists to Republicans—a fact that is not so surprising given that approximately a quarter of sociologists self-identify as
Marxists. Evangelicals, fundamentalists, and members of the National Rifle
Association (NRA) faired even worse than Republicans, perhaps because
all of these affiliations are proxies for the cultural and social conservatism
that has been at the heart of the American cultural wars. Meanwhile, sociologists said that an awareness of a candidate's liberal identity would make
them *more likely* to support him or her. Membership in the American Civil
Liberties Union (ACLU), for example, would increase the support of about
30% of sociologists. Sociologists who study marginalized groups were
most likely to express a willingness to discriminate against conservatives
and Christians, perhaps because, as Yancey theorizes, they have "more
deeply ingrained an in-group progressive identity."

Yancey also used a smaller version of the same survey to measure bias
in other academic disciplines. It found that sociologists are not unusual.
Many professors in English, history, anthropology, and political science
also expressed a preference for Democrats over Republicans and Jews over
evangelicals. In fact, more than two-thirds of anthropologists and English
professors said that if they learned a candidate was a fundamentalist, it
would damage his or her job prospects.[16] These findings are consistent
with a recent survey by Gary Tobin and Aryeh Weinberg, which revealed
that 53% of faculty members harbor negative sentiments toward evangelicals. Such feelings are connected to politics, suggest Tobin and Weinberg,

since evangelicals were the only group of religious faculty to have a majority of conservatives.[17]

Yancey suspects that frank expressions of opposition to conservatives
understate the degree of bias, since people are not always reflective about
their biases, and because some academics may want to appear (and even
desire) to be unconcerned with a potential colleague's religious and political views. Yoel Inbar agrees. When asked to reflect on his study with Joris
Lammers, Inbar told the *Washington Times* that their survey questions
"were so blatant that I thought we'd get a much lower rate of agreement."
"Usually you have to be pretty tricky to get people to say they'd discriminate against minorities," he added.[18]

We suspect that political and religious neutrality is often the objective
of professors, as these studies suggest. Most social scientists, after all, say
that the political identity of job candidates *does not matter*. Nonetheless,
there is often a gap between our ideals and behavior. While it is "theoretically possible to have social biases and not allow them to shape our social
actions, most individuals are not able to accomplish this task," Yancey
concludes.[19] Even if only a minority of academics in the social sciences
and humanities do not have any qualms about discriminating against conservatives, right-wing thinkers might face a very challenging work environment. If roughly one out of every three search-committee members is
eager to hire like-minded colleagues, that is no small obstacle to professional advancement.

On the other hand, it is possible that the various political and religious
commitments of candidates tend to be unknown to search committees,
rendering discrimination rare. "It is difficult even to imagine ideological
discrimination occurring at the point of hiring," objected political scientist
Barry Ames and his colleagues at the University of Pittsburgh. As they
explain:

> When a typical department offers an applicant an interview, it
> knows little more than the candidate's gender, educational his-
> tory, and publication record. But it has *no* idea about ideologi-
> cal affiliation unless the candidate deliberately brings it up in
> conversation.[20]

Unlike some ascriptive characteristics, such as sex and race, one's beliefs
are certainly easier to conceal.

Nonetheless, the objection by Ames and his colleagues seems obviously overstated. If one were interested in the politics of a candidate, note Stanley Rothman and his colleagues, they might

> examine her CV, her publications, the reputations of her advisors, references, and granting agencies. Increasingly, personal information can also be gleaned by examining her blog or personal web sites and by Googling her to pick up any stray comment that wandered into the Internet. There are also 'lifestyle' cues that are associated with liberal cosmopolitans, on one hand, and cultural conservatives, on the other, down to the make of car one drives, the clothing one wears, and one's use of language. Such factors often lead to inferences about attitudes and behavior.[21]

We would add that it is hardly unusual for scholarship to contain clues as to the political and moral sympathies of its author. In fact, if you wanted to know the political sympathies of the various authors that have weighed into the controversy over political bias in higher education, their conclusions would serve as a fairly accurate guide. And one can always frame a job description that effectively excludes right-wing candidates, such as by seeking candidates who study gender or racial oppression. Still, Ames and his colleagues make a good point when qualified: In many cases, the political identity of job candidates, especially freshly minted Ph.D.s, will not be known to search committees. This is partly because many research questions are fairly apolitical in nature, even in the social sciences and humanities. It is also because many conservatives conceal their political identities and avoid controversial subfields, as we will see in Chapter Four. Thus, if many conservative professors fly under the ideological radar of their liberal colleagues, as Ames suggests, then there will be less opportunity for discrimination at the point of hiring.

Happily, Stanley Rothman and Robert Lichter moved beyond these theoretical speculations by attempting to measure ideological discrimination in hiring and promotion. They did so by exploring the relationship between the professional achievement of professors (by counting their referred articles, books, chapters, etc.) and their professional advancement (by measuring the quality of their university). They found that professional achievement is far and away the best predictor of professional advancement—a finding that highlights professors' commitment to scholarly excellence. But they also found that social conservatism depresses professional advancement, although support for markets does not. In fact, Rothman and Lichter report that "social ideology explained about one-third as much variation in institutional affiliation as did achievement." Rothman and Lichter therefore offer us mixed support for the theory that conservatives confront professional discrimination. If we accept their findings and interpretations, it seems that libertarians and social conservatives confront very different work environments.[22]

Yet Rothman and Lichter's findings are also consistent with more benign explanations. As Rothman later suggested, conservative professors may be underrepresented at research institutions because they are somewhat more interested in teaching than their liberal peers.[23] This explanation, however, cannot account for the fact that conservatives are especially scarce at liberal-arts colleges.[24] Conservatives might also prefer to work in regions of the country that are less populated by prestigious institutions. "[I]t would not be surprising," speculate Ames and his colleagues, "if conservatives, academic or otherwise, *prefer* to work in smaller, more rural areas" than liberals. Cultural conservative professors might like working in, say, Montgomery or Nashville rather than Cambridge or Palo Alto.[25] Perhaps this tendency alone explains why social conservatives are underplaced, given their academic accomplishments. Similarly, Bruce Smith and his colleagues speculate that Christian faculty might be drawn to less prestigious religious institutions: "Many talented academics with deeply held religious views may turn down offers from highly ranked schools in order to teach at less prestigious institutions because they wish to work at a college that supports their religious faith."[26] There have indeed been striking cases that support Smith's speculation, such as Brad Gregory forsaking Stanford for Notre Dame.[27] Only God could inspire most academics to move from Palo Alto to South Bend. How many other excellent Christian faculty members rejected more prestigious institutions in better climates for their faith is hard to say. We would simply emphasize that working in secular institutions is hardly contrary to the Christian vocation, and in the evangelical world there is a renewed emphasis on engaging secular culture and institutions.[28] And, finally, other work has shown that liberals who go into the academy come from family backgrounds with slightly higher levels of intellectual capital and enter more prestigious doctoral programs at slightly higher rates.[29] Such factors may give liberals a modest professional edge over conservatives with similar publication records.

Skeptics go too far when they insist that the very notion of a glass ceiling for social conservatives is absurd. "[I]n order to buy [the Lichter–Rothman] discrimination hypothesis," say Ames and his associates, "one has to believe that liberal majorities at national research universities systematically engage in *greater* intellectual discrimination than do liberal majorities at liberal arts colleges and regional universities." They conclude, "The absurdity of this conclusion points to the likelihood [of] some mechanism other than intellectual discrimination."[30] Gross raises a similar objection in a far more tempered way: "Even if there is bias against conservative scholars, why should there be more bias at the top?"[31]

It is a good question that has not been adequately answered. One possibility is that elite institutions tend to hire more frequently at the senior level, where prospective job candidates possess more established records and reputations. And because some conservative professors establish records that are colored by their politics (just as some liberals do), it may be more difficult for these right-wing thinkers to climb up the academic ladder. Certainly, it is not unusual for tenured conservatives to complain about the difficulties of drawing the interest of other departments, as we show in Chapter Five. Conservative graduate students, meanwhile, may be drawn to departments with right-wing professors—a possibility that may explain their tendency to enter prestigious graduate programs at slightly lower rates than liberal students. And even a mild tendency toward intellectual ghettoization among conservative graduate students may further limit their intellectual advancement because of the lower pedigree of their graduate institutions, and partly because it marks them as the acolytes of right-wing professors. In any case, it hardly seems "absurd," as Ames and colleagues charge, to entertain the notion that ideological bias *might* make it harder for conservatives to climb to the summits of academia.

Although critics of the Rothman and Lichter study believe that it probably overstates workplace discrimination, it is also possible that it understates ideological bias. This is because Rothman and Lichter's measure of achievement (count of referred articles, books, chapters, etc.) assumes that the publication process is free of bias. There is very good evidence to doubt this assumption. Social psychology has demonstrated the tenacious power of "confirmation bias," which is the tendency of human beings to accept facts, methods, and conclusions that are consistent with their preexisting beliefs. Psychologists Philip Tetlock and Gregory Mitchell remind us that "biased information processing is deeply wired into human nature." This is why, conclude Tetlock and Mitchell, "it is not unusual for investigators committed to a research program to display remarkable ingenuity in neutralizing dissonant findings" and to "turn a blind eye to weaknesses in confirmatory evidence."[32] NYU psychologist Jonathan Haidt agrees. "[E]ach individual reasoner," says Haidt, "is really good at one thing: finding evidence to support the position one already holds, usually for intuitive reasons." Intelligence does not improve our ability to identify good reasons to accept another point of view. "Smart people make really good lawyers and secretaries," Haidt explains, "but they are no better than others at finding reasons on the other side." Haidt believes that this is because our reasoning "evolved not to help us find truth but to help us engage in arguments, persuasion, and manipulation."[33] It seems we are political animals by nature.

Though it is rarely explored, work on confirmation bias has uncovered ideological bias in the peer-review process.[34] In one experiment by Stephen Ceci and his colleagues, human-subject committees were asked to assess research proposals with identical methodological designs. Some intended to measure discrimination in hiring practices against racial minorities, women, short people, and obese job applicants. But one proposal was designed to measure "reverse discrimination"—that is, discrimination against whites that is due to aggressive affirmative action practices. The study found that the "reverse discrimination proposals were the most difficult to get approved," partly because its methodological approach was more scrutinized than in the other bias proposals, even though they all used the same method. Its method was more scrutinized because reviewers were anxious about what the reverse-discrimination study might find. Ceci and his colleagues found that the reviewers of the reverse-discrimination study were far more inclined to offer "explicit political criticisms" like this one: "The findings could set Affirmative Action back 20 years if it came out that women were asked to interview more often for managerial positions than men with a stronger vitae." Ceci and his coauthors conclude that reviewers do sometimes "consider the sociopolitical consequences of the proposed research," a finding that is entirely expected given what we know about human psychology.[35]

Other evidence bolster's Ceci's work. Inbar and Lammers's survey of psychologists found that they expressed a surprisingly candid willingness to discriminate against conservatives. Nearly one in four said that they would be at least somewhat inclined to reject grant proposals that seemed to have a "politically conservative perspective." And nearly one-fifth of psychologists admitted that they would be more inclined to reject articles with conservative points of view. Like Yancey, Inbar and Lammers suspect that their study underestimates political bias both "because respondents were asked directly and because presumably there is a strong norm against discrimination among psychologists." If true, conservative perspectives are at a significant disadvantage. As Inbar and Lammers conclude,

> Given that all academics depend on the opinions of their colleagues—who judge their papers, grants, and job applications—and given that such judgments are typically made by multiple reviewers (most of whom are liberal), this means that outspoken conservatives face a very serious problem.[36]

More qualitative studies further bolster these findings. Political scientist Steven Rhoads, for example, found that scholars who "study sex differences seem convinced that it is hard to get this work funded and the results published." One scholar, in fact, found the publication became so difficult that she dropped her research on sex differences for safer topics.[37]

As Tetlock and Mitchell emphasize, however, ideological bias in the peer review and grant-making process are hardly the only potential obstacles to achievement by conservatives. Even when conservative work is published and funded, they say, it will not be cited as frequently or as reverently as liberal scholarship, if it offends the values and theoretical assumptions of most professors.[38] This observation is almost certainly true, though hard to demonstrate empirically. Does anyone doubt, for example, that Edward Said's work would be cited so frequently and admiringly if right-wing thinkers dominated the academy? What about Judith Butler's, Michel Foucault's, and Richard Rorty's work? Such thought exercises, which could be continued ad infinitum, should remind us of how deeply embedded progressive values are in many disciplines and subfields that claim to be built entirely on norms of scientific objectivity. To imagine, moreover, that the norm of academic objectivity—powerful as it can be—has allowed professors to transcend a biased reasoning process that is deeply rooted in our minds trades on an utterly implausible view of human nature. And this means that Rothman and Lichter's study may understate political bias in higher education.

But it is also the case that some of the largest sources of political bias, such as the way professors' politics shapes the reception of academic work, are probably too difficult to measure with the tools of social science.

This is because such a study would require us to assess the quality and importance of social science independently of our own normative judgments. Our inability to overcome this methodological difficulty offers us yet another reason to suspect that scholarship that is framed by and appeals to progressive values will tend to enjoy more enthusiastic praise than conservative work.

Self-Selection

However much bias conservatives confront in academia, it is not the most important explanation for why they are so badly outnumbered. As other research has shown, those who choose to go to graduate school are disproportionately liberal. In "Left Pipeline," political scientists Matthew Woessner and April Kelly-Woessner drew on a survey of the career plans of college seniors, which showed that liberals are twice as likely as conservatives to aspire to Ph.D. programs.[39] The sociologist Ethan Fosse and his colleagues further found that only 18% of current graduate students self-identify as conservatives. They also found that a graduate education itself does not make Ph.D. students appreciably more liberal. Rather, graduate programs are full of liberals because they attract young people on the left.[40]

Graduate programs also seem to engage in little discrimination against conservative applicants. In another study, Ethan Fosse and his colleagues conducted an experiment that sent fictitious emails from prospective students to graduate school directors. The emails mentioned past volunteer experience on either the Obama or the McCain campaign. Although graduate directors responded somewhat less frequently and more slowly to inquiries from the McCain volunteers, the results were not statistically significant. As Fosse and his colleagues concluded, "[G]iven that much of the political tilt of the professoriate is a function of who goes to graduate school, the fact that we found no significant evidence of political bias toward prospective students . . . means that it is unlikely that discrimination is a major factor accounting for professorial liberalism."[41]

Fosse and his colleagues, however, push matters too far when they insist that their study should create a presumption against the view that there is widespread political bias in higher education more generally.[42] Here they seem to suggest that their study should trump all the others that do find evidence of bias in hiring, promotion, and in the publication process. But they do not provide us with compelling independent reasons for placing such great weight on their study. We think it makes more sense to ask why Fosse and his colleagues did not find evidence of bias when so many others did.

What reasons might account for this lone nonfinding? There are a number of plausible possibilities. First, a simple request for information hardly changes the imbalance of political power inside academia. It costs graduate school directors almost nothing to respond to inquiries by conservative students, which they are accustomed to doing anyway as part of their normal work routines. It is far less consequential than actually offering admission and funding to an openly conservative graduate student, much less promoting, publishing, or awarding a grant to a right-wing scholar. As others have suggested, it may even be in the interest of graduate directors to increase the number of applicants and thus disregard the politics and apparent quality of potential applicants. Speaking from his own experience as a director of graduate studies, George Yancey argued that "it is in [their] interest . . . to maximize the number of students who apply for the program they are overseeing."[43] We would add that this incentive is especially strong in elite graduate programs, which regard low acceptance rates as a sign of their selectivity and high standards.

Regardless of what one makes of this controversy, Fosse and his colleagues make an excellent point: The liberalism of the social sciences and humanities seems to be largely a function of the fact that it is liberals rather than conservatives who are drawn into those fields. Conservatives could change this state of affairs, Fosse and his colleagues seem to suggest, if they simply applied to Ph.D. programs in much greater numbers. We are reminded of Jack Shafer's essay in *Slate*, which advised conservatives to "tug harder on their bootstraps" if they want to improve their representation in the world of journalism.[44]

What is far less clear, however, is *why* liberals gravitate to Ph.D. programs far more than conservatives. Ethan Fosse and Neil Gross do not think it is primarily because conservatives learn as undergraduates that the academy is hostile to their values and ideals. This is because surveys conducted during freshman orientation—well before students become familiar with college classrooms—show that only 20% of students who express an interest in completing a doctorate are conservative.

Why is there such a large discrepancy? Fosse and Gross offer an interesting answer. They say that as the modern university took shape, the job of a professor became politically typed, in much the same way that some professions became typed by sex. As they explain, "Just as men or women may form the aspiration to enter certain fields, because of a perceived fit between the reputations of those fields and their gender identities, so too may educational and occupational choices be shaped by political identity." In other words, just as men avoided nursing because it was not a gender-appropriate choice, conservatives passed on academia because it does not fit their political identity. Fosse and Gross believe that the effect is stronger still in more progressive fields, which "define themselves around left-valenced images of intellectual personhood."[45]

Although we think Fosse and Gross correctly place political identity at the center of their theory, it does not adequately explain why conservatives are so underrepresented in the social sciences and humanities compared with the physical sciences. And it does not explain to our satisfaction why Republicans are well represented in economics, but astonishingly scarce in sociology, history, and literature. To understand why there are so few conservatives in these fields, we think Fosse and Gross's emphasis on political identity should be developed further. Their theory supposes that progressive political identities shape decisions to become an academic primarily because that profession is politically typed, but not because academic labor is itself appealing to liberal aspirations. Yet it may be the case that academic work in the social sciences and humanities is attractive to many liberals because it allows them to live out a progressive vocation. In other words, some fields in the social sciences and humanities appeal to liberals not simply because they seem like an ideologically appropriate choice or fit their "image of intellectual personhood," but also because they promise *labor* that advances liberalism.

There is no question that professorial activism is nourished by many disciplines and subfields in the social sciences and humanities. As Christian Smith argued recently, sociology is far from a mere "scientific study of society"—its animating soul is "driven by spiritual commitments, and serves a spiritual project." By "spiritual" Smith has in mind the "most profound, meaningful, and transcendent visions of human existence." The substance of this spiritual project, moreover, resembles the ends of the American New Left. As Smith describes it, sociology is committed to

> the visionary project of realizing the emancipation, equality, and moral affirmation of all human beings as autonomous, self-directing, individual agents (who should be) out to live their lives as they personally so desire, by constructing their own favored

identities, entering and exiting relationships as they choose, and equally enjoying the gratification of experiential, material, and bodily pleasures.

Undoubtedly some sociologists are committed to a purely scientific study of society, just as some mass-attending Catholics reject the authority of the magisterium. But it is this deeply embedded sacred project, Smith believes, that has shaped the culture of sociology and made it so appealing to generations of social scientists on the left. Without it, in fact, Smith suspects that "the discipline would be a far smaller, drabber, less significant endeavor." And although the project blends different intellectual currents and movements on the left, it is anything but conservative. Because sociology's spiritual project is fundamentally "teleological," as Smith puts it, "it is not about conserving a received inheritance, but in unsettling the status quo." Sociology's spiritual project calls for change that is "systemic, institutional, and sometimes radical." It is, Smith concludes, a "secular salvation story developed out of the modern traditions of Enlightenment, liberalism, Marxism, reformist progressivism, pragmatism, therapeutic culture, sexual liberation, civil rights, feminism, and so on." These same traditions, of course, have shaped the cultures of other disciplines and subfields to varying degrees. "What I describe about sociology," Smith notes, "is also obviously embedded in the intellectual and moral culture of higher education."[46]

It could have been otherwise. Stronger currents from the conservative Enlightenment could have guided and shaped American sociology. If they had, sociology today would rest on different assumptions about human anthropology and the best society. Rather than devote itself to human emancipation and autonomy, a conservative sociology would stress the importance of sustaining strong social institutions, especially families and religion, to guide the wayward tendencies of human beings. It would warn of the dangers of tinkering with long-standing social institutions, given that they serve human needs in ways that we do not and probably cannot fully understand. It would acknowledge the reality of sex differences by emphasizing the importance of domesticating young men who are most prone to violent and reckless behavior. It would accept the reality of goods that are the highest ends of any flourishing human being. And, as Peter Berger has suggested, it would be far more interested in why some nations manage to remain decent given the waywardness of human beings. As Berger put it, "The 'problem' is not social disorganization, but social organization—marriage rather than divorce, law-abidingness rather than crime, racial harmony rather than strife, and so on." "What needs explaining," Berger elaborated, "is those instances in which, amazingly, societies manage to curb and civilize" our common tendency toward "faithlessness, violence, and hate."[47] Had these ideas shaped American sociology, it would have been much more appealing to conservatives and less appealing to liberals, regardless of how professorial labor was politically typed.

Smith's insight therefore might help us understand why conservatives are concentrated in the natural sciences and rarely drawn to the social sciences and humanities. Human beings, after all, do not often desire to be professors in a purely general way, being left only with the bewildering task of choosing from a broad menu of specializations ranging from art history to physics. Instead, they are excited by particular disciplines or subjects, and so they want to become something rather more narrow—they want to study culture or paintings or math. If this is right, then the passions that push some professors into sociology should be quite different than those that inspire geologists or economists. And those passions, as Smith suggests, appeal to far deeper spiritual longings and beliefs than Fosse and Gross's interesting theory of self-selection seems to allow, at least in the case of sociology and other disciplines in which conservatives are especially scarce.

Gross himself seemed to move somewhat closer to our view when he refined his theory of self-selection further in his book on the politics of professors. There Gross agreed that more than political typing was at work: "But above and beyond this [typing effect], liberal students should tend to opt into more liberally-oriented fields and conservatives into more conservatively-oriented ones, *out of an interest in doing intellectual work . . . congruent with their political identity and sensibility*" (our emphasis). This is a step in the right direction. But Gross's emphasis on a congruence between intellectual labor and political identity barely hints at the power of the spiritual project that Smith describes.[48] It is not simply that many progressives feel as if they "fit" in sociology or history or psychology, anymore than Roman cardinals feel like they fit in the Catholic Church or Nancy Pelosi fits in the Democratic Party. Many such laborers are drawn to their respective professions because they allow them to live out a sacred vocation.

If some disciplines and subfields in the social sciences and humanities are epistemic communities that are bound together by a deeper spiritual project, then few conservative intellectuals will be either attracted to or feel welcomed into them. This is why conservative undergraduates tend to be less satisfied with their coursework in the social sciences and humanities than their progressive peers—and why they gravitate to majors in the natural sciences.[49] And it is why conservatives flock to Ph.D. programs in economics in large numbers, but not history, sociology, literature, anthropology, or philosophy.

It is true that the paucity of conservatives in the social sciences and humanities cannot be explained by frequent discrimination in hiring. "[D]iscrimination could play a major causal role," Gross explains, "only if liberals and conservatives were applying like anything in equal numbers to academic jobs." But it does not necessarily follow that the conservatives who do enter the social sciences and humanities rarely confront bias. It simply shows that liberals would constitute a substantial majority of the professoriate *with or without* discrimination.

We are also left wondering what would happen if cultural conservatives suddenly *did* begin applying to many jobs in disciplines like sociology. Would discrimination then "play a major causal role"? Gross seems to venture an answer. "[I]t would be foolish," Gross contends, "for anyone with truly antifeminist sensibilities to become a sociologist."[50] By "truly antifeminist," Gross may have in mind someone with the politics of an Islamic caliphate. But to your typical sociologist, someone with genuinely antifeminist sensibilities would presumably oppose abortion, the divorce revolution, and a genderless world. Yet thoughtful intellectuals, not all of whom would even count themselves as conservatives, defend all of these positions. Thus it seems that cultural conservatives—the defenders of an important intellectual tradition—may have good reasons to stay out of a discipline that is in some large measure devoted to the study of culture. In any case, many conservatives protect themselves from political pressures by selecting disciplines and research questions that are less politicized, as the following chapters show.

Managing Stigma

Regardless of how one interprets the debate over systemic political discrimination in academia, professors on the right must manage the stigma of being a conservative—or what sociologist Erving Goffman called a "spoiled" professional identity. As this chapter showed, many progressives continue to regard conservatives as lacking the requisite intellectual and psychological attributes necessary for high-level intellectual work. Perhaps they make good bankers, marines, or real estate developers, but not academics. Goffman believed that most stigmas operated in this way. As he explained, "We normals develop conceptions, whether objectively grounded or not, as to the sphere of life-activity for which an individual's particular stigma primarily disqualifies him."[51] Therefore, while conservatives may be suited to many careers in the minds of progressive academics, they are not cut out for academia. They lack what Lazarsfeld called an *academic mind*. And so certain political beliefs—especially culturally conservative ones—are not just potentially offensive to liberal professors, they are also both a sign and symptom of a nonacademic mind.

Goffman further argued that a stigmatized person must be especially "self conscious and calculating about the impressions he is making."[52] More recently, a growing sociological literature has explored the coping strategies of stigmatized individuals in the workplace, especially gays and lesbians.[53] The following three chapters extend that research to a right-wing group by showing how conservative professors manage their spoiled identity. That is, these chapters explore the strategies conservative professors use to navigate their professions—and why they succeed or fail.

4

Closeted Conservatives

WE MET OUR first closeted professor in a leafy park, about one mile from his prestigious research-one university. Though we found a secluded spot, our subject was edgy and spoke softly. When the sound of footsteps intruded on our sanctuary, he stopped talking altogether, his eyes darting about. As the sound of footsteps receded into the distance, the promise of anonymity returned and our interview resumed.

Given the drama of this encounter, one might think that he is concealing something scandalous. In truth, this professor is hiding the fact that he is a Republican. It is a secret he guards with great care.

This professor of sociology has been in the closet for the better part of a decade, ever since a successful interview for his first tenure-track job. On that fateful day, two fellow sociologists complained over their dinner about the reelection of George W. Bush in 2004. As the conservative sociologist remembered it, they were "ranting how [the election] was a referendum against the Enlightenment." By such logic, a vote for Bush was tantamount to a vote against the Enlightenment. It was a vote against the very foundational values of higher education itself. And, of course, few ambitious social scientists want to be regarded as an enemy of the university. So, like many before him and since, this professor decided to conceal his political identity, at least until tenure. "I smiled and nodded," he said. "That's what I've been doing the last seven years."

As sociologist Erving Goffman's classic work on stigma anticipated, this scholar's decision to conceal his politics is one way to manage a "spoiled identity."[1] Though we do not know precisely how many closeted conservatives toil away in the academy's shadows, some studies suggest that his management strategy is not unpopular among conservative professors in the social sciences and humanities. One recent survey of the California State University system found that conservatives were far more likely than liberal academics to suppress their political views.[2] A study of social psychologists by Yoel Inbar and Joris Lammers also found that conservative professors were more likely than liberals to hide their opinions because of fear. Inbar and Lammers further concluded that conservatives are wise to conceal their politics since they "experience a significantly more hostile environment" than either progressives or moderates.[3] Other studies found that conservatives are far more likely to perceive hostile work environments as well. Neil Gross and Solon Simmons's survey, for example, found that 81% of conservative professors believe that colleges and universities favor academics with left-wing views. "Our survey shows," conclude Gross and Simmons, "that conservative professors, whether they are outspoken or not, register high levels of dissatisfaction with the current university environment." Even 30% of liberal academics believe that their conservative colleagues labor in unfriendly institutions.[4] One study, however, suggested that these fears are overblown. Stanley Rothman and his colleagues found that while Republican professors in the humanities were more likely to self-censor their political opinions, Democratic professors in the social sciences were actually slightly *more likely* to conceal their political views.[5]

Nearly one-third of professors in the six disciplines we investigated tended to conceal their politics prior to tenure. Though our sample is not representative of all closeted conservative professors, this limitation is inherent to any close study of closeted individuals. If there are closeted conservatives who do not share their political identity with anyone, there is no way we could discover the identity of such individuals, except perhaps in anonymous online forums. Others may be known to only a small number of fellow conservatives, rendering them less likely to be identified through our snowball technique. Others, of whom we knew, refused to "out" themselves or others for the purposes of this book. As one typical informant told us, "a number of [conservatives] I've talked to didn't want to meet" you. While closeted conservatives can be assured that their anonymity is protected in large surveys, our study demanded that their identities be revealed, at least to us. Regardless, we were not interested in discovering the precise percentage of closeted conservatives in the social sciences and humanities. Instead, we sought a deeper understanding of how closeted conservatives comprehend their own behavior and how they navigate their professional worlds.

We found that the decision to closet oneself is not a simple binary decision, demanding perfect transparency or concealment. Instead, conservatives are presented with a range of choices that are periodically revisited in the context of new professional encounters and situations. Some conservatives, for example, are open with a handful of colleagues whom they trust as well as with students, while others conceal only those right-wing opinions that seem most offensive. This finding is consistent with prior research on passing.[6]

Managing information about their identity presents conservatives with other choices. Some conservatives, for example, remain silent during political conversations with colleagues on controversial matters, while others feel they need to affirm liberal commitments to ward off suspicion—a finding consistent with prior work on passing as well.[7] A few closeted professors even challenge the opinions of their liberal colleagues in ways that disguise their conservatism.

Despite such variations, closeted professors never publish in conservative journals of opinion, and they almost always decide to reveal their stigmatized identities—or "come out"—after tenure. Thus, for the vast majority of closeted conservatives, tenure presents a new birth of freedom.

The Gay Model

We use the metaphor of "the closet" for two reasons. First, it succinctly describes the experience of those conservative professors who conceal their political identity in a way that is instantly comprehensible to modern readers. Second, some of the conservatives we interviewed actually identify with the gay experience. Such identification, of course, doesn't mean that the experiences of gays and conservatives are the same. They are not, of course.[8] Nonetheless, the very fact that some conservative professors identify with gays is itself interesting, for it suggests that the gay experience has become so central to how Americans understand social and political oppression that it even helps conservatives make sense of their own experiences.

One such political scientist—whom we call Professor A—is a productive young scholar at a research university. Professor A identifies with the experiences of a gay friend, who came out at thirty years of age. His gay friend once "worried that he might be gay," Professor A told us, and so "he felt like every once in a while he needed to make a heterosexual joke periodically to signal that he was normal, and eventually when he realized who he was, he was a lot more comfortable with it." "I think something kind of like that happened with me gradually," Professor A continued. "I knew that some of my beliefs didn't quite fit the party line, so I felt like I needed to make my heterosexual jokes once in a while. Like, oh, doesn't it suck that we don't have health care."

Professor A, however, stopped denying his repressed political orienta- tion when he moved to a new university that employed a handful of conser- vative political scientists. These new right-wing colleagues drew him out of his self-denial by making it seem respectable to be an unapologetically conservative academic. It was an "empowering" experience, Professor A recalled. Over coffee with his new right-wing confidants, he remembered, he opened up by saying things he "would have never said before." For example, he boldly floated the notion that social security benefits should be far more modest, perhaps just enough to pay for "rice, beans, and an apartment in Lincoln, Nebraska." It was suddenly acceptable, and perhaps a little fun, to be a conservative academic.

Not all cases end quite as happily. Professor B, a prominent full profes- sor, remains closeted even though he enjoys the protections of tenure and has achieved great stature in his discipline. "I am the equivalent of some- one who was gay in Mississippi in 1950," he explained, "That's how com- fortable I feel. I'm looking basically to hide." Professor B remains closeted despite tenure because he hopes his home discipline will see fit to honor his scholarly accomplishments—an aspiration that depends on the good- will of his colleagues. "If I came out, that would finish me," he explained. It is a "big part of my life," a "very emotional thing."

In Professor B's view, remaining safely in the closet requires rank dis- honesty. When asked how he responds to colleagues when they are criti- cal of conservatives, he said, "I join in softly when forced to in a bilateral conversation." After President George W. Bush left office, he recalled, a colleague marveled "I can't believe we're getting someone with a brain finally in the White House." In such situations, Professor B reported, "I just roll my eyes and say 'I agree.'" "If it's a dangerous situation," he added, "I will join in aggressively." He thinks such "dangerous" encoun- ters emerge "when the conversation is becoming more emotive and irrational," such as when President Obama won the Nobel Prize. "I said flattering things," he recalled. He did so to shelter himself from charges of racism.

Years of dishonesty seemed to be taking a toll on Professor B. "I started feeling like a whore," he explained, "which is what you feel like when you're lying to people all the time." "I do try to avoid the conversations, I do try to change the subject. I'll do everything I can to minimize the amount of whoring around I have to do."[9]

Though Professor B is a gregarious and well-connected scholar, he speaks frankly about politics with fewer than a dozen conservative colleagues. At annual meetings he seeks them out. But rather than meet in hotel bars where their right-wing opinions might be overheard, they convene in private hotel rooms. In those small conservative sanctuaries, the liquor and liberal barbs flow freely. It is a radical break from his daily life, where Professor B believes "it is dangerous to even think [a conservative thought] when I'm on campus, because it might come out of my mouth."

For all Professor B's anguish, however, the alternative of "coming out" to unsuspecting colleagues presents its own challenges.[10] Once he received tenure, Professor C revealed his true ideological identity to an intimate, liberal friend. As Professor C remembered it, his friend "responded badly because I hadn't felt I could trust him. He was sort of uncomprehending."

Professor C had been so deeply closeted and distrusting because of his understanding of the dynamics of prejudice. In his view, conservatives, like gays, are easier to accept if their identities are discovered much later in the relationship. As he explained: "How many gay people in the 50s, 60s, 70s would tell you that once someone knew you to be a nice person, [then] they could see your gayness as part of your identity; whereas if they met you gay, [then] that would be the way that they would code you." Thus, to avoid being stereotyped in a negative way, he found it prudent to conceal his offensive characteristics.

He had doubted that his patrons—all of whom were far to his left— would support him as enthusiastically if they knew his politics. This doubt grew out of his own experiences with liberal peers. Professor C said his department chair refused to allow department functions at one popular restaurant in town because its owner was once the chairman of the local Republican Party. He also said that his dissertation chair "had the usual intolerances" of liberal academics. She "thought of George Bush as just a moron," Professor C recalled, and couldn't "believe intelligent people vote for him. You know, not nasty, not vindictive, but just a set of mental habits."

Even Professor C's good friend said things that sent similar signals. In fact, Professor C had tested his friend in years past to see if he assumed good faith on the part of conservatives. After he came out, Professor C reminded his "uncomprehending" friend of conversations that persuaded him to remain closeted. He recalled telling his friend,

> You're not going to remember any of this, but I remember the time when once you and I were talking about an article [in] the *New Republic* and I quoted someone in the Clinton White House for saying ... 'I know that there are people who are going to oppose affirmative action that were not bigoted. I know that theoretical category exists, but I don't know if there really are [such cases]. I've never met one.'

Professor C then recalled his friend "just unthinking reflexively saying 'I agree' and ... a dozen things he had said over time like that, and he didn't remember any of them. And of course he wouldn't." "In the end," he added, "[we] just decided to disagree, not just about politics, but [also] about what had happened there in our relationship. I think we just agreed to not discuss it, to agree to disagree even about that, and to move on."

Their differences, of course, run deeper than mere disagreements over what was said in years past. His friend, Professor C explained, genuinely believes that liberals *do not* "routinely disparage the good faith intentions of conservatives." Professor C recalled challenging his friend on just this point:

> So, all those times when the *New York Times* refers to Republican budgets as mean-spirited, you're telling me that every time you read those words you thought 'Ha, what a strange thing to say.' After all, mean-spirited implies uncaring, not disagreeing about which [solution] will work best to cause growth and social equity. Mean-spirited means you're not a nice person, you don't want to help people.

An incredulous Professor C continued, "You're telling me that every time you read that you thought: What a strange choice of words? I wonder what they could possibly mean by that. Right! I told him 'bullshit! You are used to this discourse.'" For Professor C, deeply rooted liberal assumptions about conservative motives are the crux of the problem for right-wing academics. Liberals, in his view, too often assume that conservatism is driven by bad faith rather than by principled and reasonable differences of opinion.

These professors' especially strong identification with the gay experience makes them somewhat unusual among closeted conservatives. In other respects, however, their different experiences highlight the many choices and dilemmas all closeted conservatives confront. They all had to decide how much of themselves they wanted to keep concealed. It also involved deciding whom to trust and when, if ever, to come out.

Political Taboos

Most closeted professors make distinctions between conservative opinions that must be concealed at every turn and those that are less provocative. For many closeted professors, the most verboten conservative views include those social and cultural ones that are central to America's culture wars. A literature professor at a large public university, for example, told us that he concealed views on abortion as a junior professor. "This was not something you spoke about." Similarly, a junior historian at a state university reported that he would "never" express his views on same-sex marriage. Nor would he even raise the possibility that "men and women are different by nature." Though this historian sometimes "hints" at such views in class, he has never shared them with his colleagues. As he explained, not only do all of his colleagues take the "feminist line," the denial of sex differences is "fundamental to the field" of gender history. Thus this subject's views on gender place him at odds with the aspirations of second-wave feminism as well as the deeper anthropological assumptions of most historians. Conservative opinions regarding economics, on the other hand, strike him as far safer to share with his liberal colleagues. This historian even sometimes hints at his own economic conservatism. As he reported, "periodically I'll [openly] question the government spending so much money." But even on economic issues his comments are always measured and circumspect.

Some professors learned the offensiveness of social conservatism as early as graduate school. One sociologist at a research university was at first open about his opposition to abortion as a student. But this interviewee said he was soon "shocked" by the "venom" he observed spewing forth from professors and fellow students when he expressed prolife views. This sociologist had spent his undergraduate years at a Catholic college where one could "be [for] social justice and prolife," he recalled. "That's the Catholic mix that works." But he discovered that it did not "work" in an elite sociology department. And, so, in this new, less tolerant milieu, he decided to begin "liv[ing] two different lives," at least until tenure.

As we'll see throughout this chapter, graduate school provides an important education to its conservative students. Even as it opens up new intellectual horizons (including conservative ones on occasion), it also shows conservatives where the boundaries of acceptable political discourse lie. And it provides a comparatively safe setting for graduate students to transgress these boundaries before they seek employment and tenure. Graduate programs, in other words, are valuable schools of academic politics.

Social conservatism is perceived as so offensive that some closeted professors even worried that the cultural politics of their spouses might "out" them. One philosopher at a small Catholic college worries that some of her colleagues might discover the identity of her husband, who blogs and pens essays in defense of socially conservative ideas. "I have been very concerned to be discrete because of my husband," she explained. "It would make automatic enemies. . . . He would be viewed as a fascist. . . . That was a major concern." Thus this philosopher keeps her scandalous husband safely under wraps. "[Because] I was very concerned to limit the number of people who knew him, he doesn't show up to school functions," she explained. Our subject tells prying colleagues that her phantom husband "has to watch the children. I generally say, he's a stay-at-home dad, because he is and he works from home." They "usually respond, 'how progressive,'" she recounted with a sly smile.

Keeping one's spouse perfectly concealed is not always so easy. A literature professor at a large public university recalled the day one of his colleagues happened to spot his wife's car, which sports a bumper sticker that reads "Abortion Stops a Beating Heart." Goffman called such identifiers "stigma symbols" because they draw "attention to a debasing identity."[11] According to our subject, reports of this unusual sighting spread rapidly through his department. In short order a colleague confronted him. "Oh well, it's my wife's car," our interviewee recalled replying, before adding, "I would never in a moment think that as a male I could tell my wife what [to do]. . . . She is a very strong and intelligent woman and if she wants to have those [opinions], then she is free to have them."

In a related way, some academics concealed demographic facts about their own background when they might help liberal colleagues infer their political opinions. One English professor stopped wearing crosses—another stigma symbol—even though she described Christianity as "the most important part of my life." Likewise, a Mormon political scientist kept her religious identity a guarded secret because of the church's views on abortion and homosexuality. Sociologist George Yancey's work on academic bias suggests that her decision may be a prudent one. Yancey found that professors in the social sciences and humanities would be less likely to hire a job candidate if they discovered that she was Mormon. This reluctance, moreover, seems to have increased in the wake of Proposition 8, a California amendment that attempted to restrict marriage to heterosexual couples.[12]

Though opposition to racial and gender preferences generally seemed to be more tolerable to liberal colleagues than moral objections to abortion or homosexuality, a junior political scientist disagreed. Because this professor strongly opposes affirmative action, we asked her if she ever shares her convictions with colleagues. She responded sharply: "Oh my God, no, no. This is one thing you have to be closeted about. . . . You cannot say in academia that 'I am against affirmative action.' That part you cannot be open about." When we asked why, she said her colleagues would regard her as an "evil person." Like Professor C in our opening vignette, this political scientist worried that her colleagues would assume bad faith if she openly opposed racial and gender preferences. Her distrust and decision to enter the closet partly grew out of her negative experiences in graduate school, where she recalled other female students branding her a "market-oriented bitch" for holding strong libertarian views.

As this example suggests, other professors even found that support for free markets must be concealed. A political scientist at a public research university discovered to his surprise that free-market ideals could offend liberal academics. While he was still in graduate school—that critical school of academic politics—one of his professors encouraged him to talk less about his economic views. His professor, our subject said, told him to do so because his views were "so far outside the parameters of normal discourse that [they were] disruptive." One historian was also afraid to express libertarian sympathies because she believes her colleagues link such views to racial animus. She was particularly chastened as a graduate student when a group of labor historians transformed a conference into an anti-Bush rally. By the time we identified this historian she was deep in the closet. She was one of the few academics who would not let us record her, and she kept the door to her office shut during the interview even though the halls outside were abandoned.

A few closeted academics also placed conservative foreign policy high on the list of verboten topics, especially support for Israel and the war on terrorism. One political scientist, for example, recalled being sensitized to the dangers of supporting the war on terror in graduate school. When one of this professor's dissertation advisors discovered that he supported the war in Iraq, the advisor informed him that he "was really disturbed" by the news.

Other professors did not think their colleagues would accept them if they confessed their support for the Republican Party. In fact, some of the boldest conservatives—including those who believed that their colleagues were open to certain deviations from liberal orthodoxies—nonetheless said that crossing the party divide is particularly dangerous. As a sociologist from a southern university reported, "It's okay to be a Christian and all that, but it would be the ultimate violation if you voted Republican. I mean only idiots are Republicans." This particular sociologist not only votes for Republicans, he has also contributed to Rick Santorum's presidential campaign. A junior sociologist at a prestigious university expressed concern about how her colleagues might react if they discovered that her sibling was active in Republican Party politics: "I think if they knew I had family involved in [Republican] Party politics, that would possibly hurt me. . . . So that, I definitely don't talk about."

One political scientist at a prominent state university remembered direct evidence of liberal animus toward Republicans. While he was still an assistant professor, a senior colleague reportedly said, "No Republican [will] ever get tenure in this department." When this professor came out as a Republican after tenure by working for the local party, it was troubling. As he recalled,

> A number of my senior colleagues were somewhat shocked and disappointed by that. I think there was the 'oh, if we would have known this ten years ago, we would have made a different hiring choice.' . . . Some people just stopped talking to me [altogether].

He also got invited to fewer social gatherings.

It is perhaps not surprising that conservative professors regard their support for the Republican Party as a particularly sensitive secret. While support for a particular conservative cause can be dismissed as an eccentricity, identification with the Republican Party suggests that one has strayed off the liberal reservation altogether.

Interacting with Liberals

In addition to determining which convictions are most offensive to their colleagues, conservative professors must also decide what to do in situations in which liberal colleagues openly critique and sometimes ridicule their values. For many, the answer is simple: Stay silent. Professors gave responses like these: "I just bite my tongue," "I abstained from views on things," "I learned I should keep my mouth shut," "I'd just let it go," "[I stay] stony faced," "just be quiet," "self-censorship," and "I'll keep relatively quiet." One virtue of silence is that it avoids dishonesty. As a Catholic philosopher explained, "My attitude was to never be deceptive, that's a rule of mine. But I don't owe anybody irrelevant details." Self-censorship, however, can also be a source of frustration to people who enjoy expressing ideas. "I think it's quite absurd that I can't talk about intellectual matters if they touch on conservative issues," said a young political scientist, "It's still nuts to me." Meanwhile, an accomplished historian we interviewed remains vexed by what he regards as his coerced silence years after coming out. "I didn't say anything to these people about my political beliefs," he recalled, "I just knew I couldn't."

Other closeted professors speak up by making a habit of laying out the logic of alternative perspectives in a disinterested way. One jocular political scientist described this method of evasion as the "chicken fuck approach to my politics. . . . At some point, you don't know if you believe it or if you don't believe it, because you're rewiring yourself." He reported mixed results. At one university his cast of mind impressed his interviewees. But at his home research university, he found that his articulation of conservative arguments was usually met with "silence" and "shock." One sociologist we interviewed also played the role of the impartial social scientist partly as a strategy for hiding his politics. "People never know, and you're not lying to them," he reported. A political scientist was even willing to raise questions about the constitutionality of Obamacare. " 'Well, my policy preferences aside, I think the health care bill is unconstitutional,' " she recalled telling one colleague. It is a tactic that allows for some space to raise conservative objections without opposing liberal policy ambitions.

One scholar used the same strategy and generally reported positive reactions from her colleagues. After President Bush's reelection in 2004, depression swept through her department. "They truly, truly don't understand why anybody would support him," she stressed. This sociologist recalled telling her grieving colleagues, "Well, it's half the country. You can't claim that half of the country [consists of] racist haters. That just doesn't hold." It is a gentle rebuke. But it nonetheless directs her colleagues away from their reflexive assumption that conservatism is driven by various primal hatreds. Similarly, when the subject of abortion comes up, she never suggests that it might be intrinsically wrong. Instead, she takes a less confrontational approach by raising aspects of its practice that are likely to trouble her colleagues, such as the high rates of abortion among African Americans. "[T]hey admit that this is not the result of personal preferences, that something has gone wrong."

Yet even this bold scholar appreciates that not every hostile comment toward conservatives should be rebutted. In large groups or in cases in which her colleagues are on a "rampage," she keeps quiet. "I think I've learned to wait for a one-on-one conversation with someone you trust, [rather than engage every] random comment that gets thrown out, [such as] all Republicans are idiots and racists," she added.

This professor, however, believes that it is easier to raise such measured challenges simply because she is a woman in a male-dominated department. "I honestly think it's easier to be a conservative woman in academia than a [conservative] man," she said. "I have this theory that women can get away with wrong. That if I challenge people, they're not going to talk to me as harshly as they would with another man."

Other conservative women, however, emphasized that although they may enjoy relatively charitable treatment from liberal men, they are especially leery of left-wing women. One female philosopher confessed that she particularly feared being fingered as a conservative by feminists since "they have a history of being extremely brutal on women who are conservative." Some men, meanwhile, are particularly fearful of female colleagues as well, especially as they seek employment and tenure. "I hate to say it, but it's women in the academy [who] are . . . much more politicized than men are," said one historian.

Conservatives' anxieties about female colleagues may be a rational adaptation to their professional environments and therefore not the result of misplaced prejudices. George Yancey's study of sociologists found that female sociologists were more likely than their male peers to discriminate against conservative job applicants. "Male sociologists," Yancey found, "had less negative social bias against Republicans, NRA members, evangelicals, mainline Protestants, hunters, and divorced individuals than women." Yancey suggests that part of the explanation for this disparity may include higher levels of liberalism among academic women.[13] In any case, male sociologists seem more politically tolerant than female ones on average.

Other conservative professors felt that they needed to send the correct signals to their colleagues, especially when they feared that their commitment to liberalism was in doubt. A political scientist at a major research university reported that when one is under suspicion of harboring conservative views, "there is an assumption that you are racist, sexist, and homophobic. People have to test you out on those issues, and I went to great lengths to send the proper signals." Such signals take many forms. One historian reported that he would typically make jokes at the expense of conservatives, especially anti-Bush ones. Another historian even published an essay in a liberal journal as an assistant professor, partly to signal the appropriate political views to fellow colleagues. Such constant politicking can tax closeted conservatives. One professor described her interactions with liberal colleagues as "exhausting," since it requires careful "thought and decision making."

Conservatives can feel especially compelled to send liberal signals during job interviews. A political scientist at a Catholic college recalled two interviews when "he had to do a lot of dancing." In one interview, for example, he remembered being asked whether he supported the war on terrorism: "It was pretty clear that they were fishing for political things." At another interview he said that he was asked to share his views on women's rights and whether there were enough women in the department. One historian believed that he suffered from a less transparent fishing expedition during a job interview. He recalled a senior professor discussing the "anticolonial struggles in Africa with a great deal of enthusiasm." When this cause failed to stir a commensurate enthusiasm in our subject, he said, "[It was] a bit of a signal that I wasn't onboard, [and] he picked it up instantly. Most academics are smart people. They are attuned to these kinds of things." Thus, it is hardly surprising that some conservatives feel compelled to lie. "I just deliberately outright lie," a political scientist at an Ivy League university admitted, though "I haven't lied in a while."

A historian at a public research university told us that job hiring is "like dogs sniffing each other." So he was careful not to air any offending conservative scents. "I would never wear bow ties," he offered, as an example. "I might as well put a tattoo on my head, 'Don't hire me.'" Indeed, bow ties scream "cultural conservative" in higher education.[14] They complement what one of our conservative colleagues dubbed "the scrubbed-clean Heritage Foundation look."

Hiding in Plain Sight

Nonetheless, fishing expeditions during job interviews seem to be the exception to the rule. Most conservatives reported that the interview process was entirely apolitical, at least as far as they could discern. Their interviewers were focused on research and teaching. This does not necessarily mean that such interviewers are uninterested in the politics of job candidates. Instead, many closeted professors reported there was not much need for "dancing" or sending the right "signals" since their colleagues simply assumed that they were liberals. And, as we demonstrate shortly, closeted professors eschew research agendas that might send the wrong ideological cues. Thus, as long as conservatives conceal their politics both in their self-presentation and scholarship, many do not face much suspicion.

Closeted conservatives, in other words, are often hiding in plain sight. One professor reported, "I don't say anything I don't believe, but it's amazing how when people take things for granted, it's not that hard [to hide]." And this means that his colleagues do not spend their energy rooting out colleagues suspected of conservatism. Similarly, a sociologist recalled, "It is assumed from everything I've ever heard that I always will vote Democrat. . . . [T]hey don't bring that up because they just know. All sociologists are Democrats." He exaggerates only slightly. According to recent surveys, the percentage of Republicans in sociology is somewhere between 3% and 6%, and probably even less at research universities like our interviewee's.[15] "They rarely gather that I actually have voted Republican," he added. A historian at a state college also emphasized the ease with which he hides from his colleagues: "They just take it for granted . . . most people just assume I'm a liberal." Liberal profiling is sometimes so pervasive that even conservatives who make no special effort to hide their politics are presumed to embrace left-wing politics.

But even though such profiling makes it easier to hide, it is simultaneously a source of irritation. "One of the most frustrating things in academia is that everyone assumes that you are a liberal Democrat," noted a political scientist at a research university. During the 2008 Democratic Party nomination contest he was frequently asked whether he was a supporter of Hillary Clinton or Barack Obama. "The big debate in my department was Hillary or Obama; you're either racist or sexist." We interviewed another closeted subject on the heels of an evening with a liberal colleague. "He spent all of dinner telling me how terrible all the Republicans are. . . . Honest to God," she added with a hint of exasperation, "I just think most of my colleagues have never had a conversation with conservatives." One political scientist recalled a similar frustration after taking a new position as a visiting instructor. After indicating her intention to rent a house in a particular neighborhood, an alarmed colleague warned, "You don't want to live there, everybody who lives there voted for [Bush]." Meanwhile, a historian at a state university recalled an uncomfortable job interview. During the interview, he remembered being warned by a liberal professor about a department member who was the local campus conservative. "[H]e made a face while talking about him," he recalled. Another professor agreed that liberal academics never realize that they are making life so unpleasant for conservatives. They "don't even know they're doing it," he fumed, "because the idea that someone wouldn't agree with [them] is astonishing."

Closeted conservatives do not always find their immersion in liberal departments so unpleasant. "It's fun in that certain Seinfeld absurdity . . . I-can't-believe-this-is-happening sense," a political scientist confessed. "It's sort of fun when you sit around in the department meeting, and the department chair says something about 'ladies first' and some woman in the department freaks out." Her main challenge in such situations is suppressing laughter, not anger.

Another factor that helps many conservative professors hide is simply the solitary nature of academic work, especially in large, research-oriented departments. One professor spoke for many when she reported bluntly, "I don't talk to anybody in my department. There is no community in my department, [which is] probably good for me."

The weakness of academic communities does sometimes make them vulnerable to strong minority factions, such as during the 1960s and 1970s when whole universities were overrun by militant student radicals. Allan Bloom, then a professor at Cornell University, was sensitized to the weakness of his own campus community during those turbulent years. In *The Closing of the American Mind*, Bloom lamented,

[T]he community of scholars proved to be no community at all. There was no solidarity. . . . The university has lost whatever polis-like character it had and has become like the ship on which the passengers are just accidental fellow travelers soon to disembark and go their separate ways.[16]

For many conservatives those radical years represented much that is wrong with today's academy. Yet for those conservatives who must make their way in a modern research university, the very weakness of academic communities renders them easier to navigate. Few desire "polis-like" university communities, even if it leaves the university vulnerable to the sort of factions that Bloom chronicled.[17]

It is also the case that closeted conservatives—like closeted gays—often form their own communities by coming out to one another. Some have suggested that this is often a delicate process that involves "signaling."[18] In one anonymous Web posting, an academic recounted this exchange with another closeted conservative:

> I remember one guy who heard me comment on how some architecture reminded me of something I read in *The Fountainhead,* which was enough to alert him. Later we went out for a drink. I remember the nervous moment (for both of us) where he finally came out and asked me, 'so what are your political/economic beliefs?' I chickened out, tempered, and said, 'well, perhaps more to the center than most academics' and countered, 'what are yours?' Reassured, he was willing to admit to conservative leanings. Then I was willing to admit it too. Then at last we could talk about our true feelings, with it clearly and openly stated that (of course) none of this was ever, ever, ever, to go beyond our own private conversations.[19]

Few conservatives we interviewed reported similar exchanges. This is because young, closeted conservatives tend to come out to those senior colleagues who are already known right-wing academics. Moreover, the vast majority of the academics we interviewed worked in departments with other conservatives, perhaps because right-wing professors are more likely to select disciplines and then be hired in departments with greater political diversity and reputations for political moderation. Our survey reveals that a small minority of conservatives are the only right-wing representatives in their departments (see Table 4.1). Although this finding could be an artifact of our snowball sampling technique, there are also reasons to believe that conservatives are more likely to be hired in departments that are already open to hiring right-wing professors. Thus, conservative academics may not be as isolated as their overall numbers suggest.

Table 4.1 Political Diversity in the
Departments of Conservative Professors

Only Conservative	18%
One Other Conservative	19%
Two or More	63%
N:	135

Other Varieties of Self-Censorship

Silence, obfuscation, and lying in the presence of liberal colleagues hardly represent the most important forms of self-censorship. Closeted professors also refrain from engaging in scholarship that might offend liberal sensibilities. A sociologist at a Catholic university only did "noncontroversial" research projects prior to tenure, while a junior political scientist reported, "I have professionally avoided anything that touches on salient political issues." Another political scientist said that he "would not submit anything to something like *National Review*." Similarly, a sociologist at a major research university lamented, "[T]here are certain things that I'd like to be doing," adding that he would prefer to "draw policy implications from my research" for *National Review*. Meanwhile, a political scientist hopes to "investigate some stereotype about conservatives" after tenure, while a sociologist intends to draw on more phenomenological concepts from Catholic thinkers.

Often the decision to avoid conservative intellectual projects begins in graduate school. A historian at a state college decided against writing a dissertation about the history of supply-side economics because it might mark him as a conservative. As he put it, "I guess there was some cowardice on my part." Though she would have preferred to study Middle East politics in graduate school, a political scientist decided that her Zionism would prove too offensive to political scientists in that particular subfield. "I didn't do the Israeli-Palestinian issue, which was the thing I wanted to do." So she chose a far less politicized dissertation topic instead.

Reluctance to publish conservative opinions is hardly the only self-imposed restriction on political liberty. When closeted assistant professors reflected on the possibilities of post-tenure liberty, they often hoped to engage in other forms of political expression. For some, tenure will free them to engage in curricular battles. "I [will] feel more free to be on important committees," one philosopher forecasted, and "to advocate for a curricular point of view," especially with respect to "Catholic-identity" issues. Others imagined that they would become less isolated from conservative students on campus. "I'll be friendlier with some of the conservatives on campus publicly," a historian suspected. Others hope to become more involved in Republican Party politics. One political scientist, for example, emphasized that he would "feel free to take a more active role" in the GOP, perhaps as an advisor to a presidential candidate. Tenure also promises more trivial freedoms. "I was thinking of putting up a picture of Margaret Thatcher [on my office door]," one philosopher mused.

Our survey demonstrates that such self-censorship was not uncommon. We asked our subjects whether they were reluctant to engage in various forms of political expression because they feared the reactions of their colleagues (see Table 4.2). Roughly one-quarter of all of the conservative

Table 4.2 Self-Censorship That Is Due to Fear of Colleagues

Have you refrained from	
Including information on CV that might identify one as a conservative or libertarian	36% ($N = 138$)
Writing an editorial that reveals political views	27% ($N = 139$)
Donating or volunteering for conservative causes	16% ($N = 140$)
Publishing in conservative or libertarian journals	16% ($N = 140$)
Donating or volunteering for GOP or Libertarian Party	15% ($N = 141$)
Applying for grants from conservative or libertarian foundations	11% ($N = 139$)
Censorship Index	
Engaged in at least one form of self-censorship	46% ($N = 140$)
Engaged in three or more forms of self-censorship	20% ($N = 140$)

professors we interviewed said that they have at times been reluctant to publish things that reveal their political opinions. We also assessed other varieties of self-censorship, including conservatives' willingness to give to political causes and parties. Smaller minorities expressed a reluctance to engage in these sorts of activities, perhaps because they are easier to do anonymously. Nonetheless, some 46% of all the academics we interviewed had engaged in at least one of the six forms of self-censorship. Meanwhile, a small, but not insubstantial, minority reported practicing at least three forms of self-censorship.

Some professors get around this problem by blogging for a conservative website under a pseudonym. A historian at a state college revealed that he does so to conceal his political identity. "I don't want to come up on a Google search," he said. Blogging, meanwhile, provides "an outlet" for his pent-up political passions. An assistant professor of philosophy also blogged under a pseudonym because he believed that such essays would really "piss off" fellow colleagues.

Other professors, however, reported that they were more open about their views in the classroom than in faculty lounges or in their written work. Classrooms are relatively protected from their colleagues' view. Such liberty was not universally felt. A political scientist at a research university, for example, refused to assign libertarian thinker Friedrich Hayek in his political economy class before he was tenured. As a junior professor, this scholar also recalled that he was more reticent to articulate conservative positions, such as right-wing critiques of the minimum wage. He did so because he feared that this might invite charges of conservatism from his students. Such accusations might further show up in students' anonymous teaching evaluations, thereby exposing him as a conservative and marring his teaching record.

Although this topic is addressed in a more thoroughgoing way in the following chapters, we found hardly a trace of any of these anxieties among economists. *Only one* economist out of the twenty-eight we surveyed reported that he tended to conceal his politics prior to tenure (see Table 4.3). And many economists seemed surprised that other social scientists would ever feel compelled to censor themselves. In one poignant case, an amazed and slightly disturbed economist asked us whether we had found *any* professors who engaged in self-censorship.

Older professors also rarely reported concealing their politics prior to tenure (see Table 4.4). This may be because the academy has become more

Table 4.3 Professors Who Concealed
Their Politics Prior to Tenure by
Discipline

Political Science	46% ($N = 35$)
Sociology	42% ($N = 12$)
History	42% ($N = 26$)
Literature	32% ($N = 22$)
Philosophy	15% ($N = 13$)
Economics	4% ($N = 28$)

Table 4.4 Professors Who Concealed
Their Politics Prior to Tenure by Age

25–44	46% ($N = 39$)
45–64	33% ($N = 67$)
65 and over	7% ($N = 30$)

hostile to right-wing views or simply because the campaign against liberal bias has heightened the anxiety of conservative professors. These correlations could also be an artifact of our nonprobability sample.

Tenure

We did encounter professors who remained closeted after tenure, either because they sought disciplinary honors or because they sought employment in more prestigious universities. Others waited until they were promoted to full professor. "I had to wait from entering academia in 1992 until I became a full professor in 2010," a disgruntled historian told us. "That's how long I had to keep my views to myself." But such cases were rare.

Most professors who were closeted as assistants came out after tenure. One political scientist, for example, got involved in local Republican politics in an advisory capacity. As he put it, "I wanted to meet like-minded people, to let my hair down a little bit." Even his dress changed. He started sporting cowboy hats and boots. For a time, he posted Web photos of himself instructing his teenage son on how to fire a shotgun. He also started attending conferences organized by Christians in political science as well as ditching the national political science conference for important rodeos. He had come out, in other words, not as some refined country club Republican, but as a rugged, evangelical conservative with a full-blown red-state lifestyle. No wonder his colleagues were surprised.

Another political scientist came out by publishing a river of essays in conservative journals that had been dammed up for years. It was quite a flood. By our count, he authored twenty-two essays in conservative journals of opinion during his first four years as an associate professor. This professor was so eager to get out of the closet that his first conservative essay was in the publishing pipeline as his tenure case was being decided. Beyond such popular writings, his primary research agenda was reshaped as well. His current book project challenges liberal critiques of American conservatives, a sharp departure from his intentionally apolitical first book. Tenure, in short, was liberating, perhaps more so than even he could have foreseen: "It was only much later that I realized how alienating [being closeted] had been in the philosophical sense internally."

Most closeted professors do not overhaul their research agenda to that extent. But conservative professors do often change their behavior, particularly by expressing their opinion more freely. One sociologist, for example, engages in controversial topics now, especially regarding the nature and fluidity of gay identities. As he explained, with a note of mischief, "I don't mind causing trouble now." Likewise, a literature professor at a research university turned his attention to libertarian authors. "I would not have written scholarly articles about Ayn Rand before tenure," he said.

Certainly there are risks and costs associated with being an outspoken conservative, as the next chapter shows. But the job security offered by tenure means that those conservatives with such protections are far freer with their tongue and pen. What is more, closeted conservatives often point to their colleagues' power over tenure as one of the central reasons that they concealed their political identities. We asked a philosopher at an elite university why he was closeted prior to tenure. His succinct response spoke for many closeted conservatives: "Fear." "[I realized that] a tenure decision would be made, and just having experienced the general attitude of academics," he added. A political scientist explained his closeted behavior in similar terms: "I needed tenure. . . . To me, there was no upside, only downside, only risks." A sociologist, meanwhile, blamed his closeted behavior on a "profound risk aversion" prior to tenure.

It is likely that many conservatives are needlessly risk averse prior to tenure. Even some closeted professors believed that they would have been tenured even if their colleagues knew their politics. One professor, for

Table 4.5 Fairness of the Hiring Process

Do you think you would have been hired to your first tenure-track job had your political views been well known in the department?

1. Yes	45%
2. No	14%
3. Hard to say	34%
4. Not applicable	7%
N:	138

instance, said that he "probably would have still gotten tenure," had he been open about his conservatism. Others wondered whether they would have been hired at all. "I think that I may have still gotten the job if they knew I was a conservative, but I wouldn't have been hired unanimously by the department," a philosopher surmised. Some were even more uncertain. "Would my tenure decision have been harder?" a political scientist asked. "I don't know."

Our survey asked professors whether they think they would have been hired to their first tenure-track job had their political views been known (see Table 4.5). A plurality of professors reported that knowledge of their conservatism would have been entirely inconsequential, though those academics were disproportionately found in economics. In fact, *not a single* economist we interviewed said that he or she would not have been hired if his or her politics were known. But others were uncertain. Approximately one-third of professors in our sample replied that it was "hard to say," while a smaller minority believed that they would not have been hired.

Evidence from the psychological sciences suggests that closeted behavior is the prudent course, at least until conservatives can befriend their colleagues. As Jonathan Haidt concluded in *The Righteous Mind*, it is easier for partisans to listen to and comprehend their political opponents when there is "affection, admiration, or a desire to please" the other. It seems that friendship is the key to cultivating a more open and understanding relationships across moral divides. As Haidt advises,

> [If] you really want to open your mind, open your heart first. If you can have at least one friendly interaction with a member of the 'other' group, you'll find it easier to listen to what they're saying.[20]

Thus Professor C in our opening vignette may have been too cautious by not confiding in his friend. But he did intuit an important psychological insight by befriending his liberal academic peers before coming out as a conservative. Had he announced his conservatism shortly after meeting them, it may have proved more difficult to cultivate those same friendships as well as puncture his peers' stereotypes about right-wing citizens.

What about Closeted Political Minorities on the Left?

It is likely that there are some closeted academics on the left. They may be found in those rare departments dominated by conservatives. More commonly, those on the far left, especially Marxists, may hide their politics from their center-left colleagues. Or they may feel threatened by David Horowitz's campaign and other right-wing efforts to scandalize the radicalism of higher education. Neil Gross and Solon Simmons found that nearly 30% of Marxists said they sought advice on "how to avoid getting into trouble at their college or university for their views about national politics." "This serves as a reminder," conclude Gross and Simmons, "that while conservatives in academe may feel themselves to be marginalized, [Roger] Kimball's 'tenured radicals' are not hegemonic."[21]

Nonetheless, Marxists are still more likely to find a welcoming home in the academy. Gross and Simmons's survey shows that there are approximately three times the number of Marxists as Republicans in the social sciences.[22] George Yancey's work also suggests that there is greater bias against conservatives than even "communists," though both groups fare poorly compared with liberals. Sociologists, anthropologists, historians, philosophers, and literature professors are more likely to prefer hiring a "communist" to hiring an NRA member. Only political scientists (economists were not surveyed) were marginally more likely to prefer hiring an NRA member to hiring a communist. Republicans fared somewhat better, with only sociologists, anthropologists, and literati clearly preferring communists. But as Yancey's findings make clear, support for hiring Republicans is far lower if it is discovered that the job applicant is also an evangelical or advocate for gun rights.[23]

Had Yancey assessed bias against "Marxists" rather than against "communists," we suspect that these differences would have been starker. Thus the extant evidence suggests that conservatives are both scarcer and confront greater political bias than do Marxists, and perhaps communists as well.

In addition, most of those who lament the plight of the far academic left tend to highlight dangers that bombard university sanctuaries from *the outside*.[24] In doing so, they celebrate the university as an imperfect haven from a hostile, right-wing America. The university may resist those politicized influences more or less well in different eras, but it is still a redoubt against conservative campaigns. During the McCarthy era, for example, most of the political pressures came from outside the ivory tower. Paul Lazarsfeld and Wagner Thielens's classic study on academic freedom during the McCarthy era found that "the professoriate feel safer on the campus than outside its walls."[25] Conservatives, on the other hand, find that these threats are inverted: They must worry about dangers lurking *within* the university. Pressures from the outside political community, meanwhile, are comparatively few, since conservatives' own views tend to be fairly mainstream. There is no left-wing analog to David Horowitz, anxiously chronicling the radicalism of conservative professors. Thus, conservatives fear the university itself, the very institution that stands for academic and intellectual freedom.

There is another asymmetry between right-of-center academics and those on the far left, such as Marxists or communists. Though we certainly do not condone the practice, to discriminate against such individuals is to marginalize those who are genuinely far outside the mainstream of American political discourse. A closer—albeit imperfect—analog to bias against either Marxists or communists on the academic right is not discrimination against Republicans; it is bias against fascists or monarchists. Since the university is supposed to prepare its students for lives as citizens, it strikes us as something altogether worse to exclude perspectives that are at the very center of our national discourse and controversies.

Insofar as moderately liberal professors do conceal their politics, they may be most prevalent at those fundamentalist and evangelical colleges where Protestant theology and conservative politics are consciously bundled together. For instance, at Liberty University—founded by Jerry Falwell in 1971—a professor who expressed political liberalism would almost certainly signal theological apostasy to her colleagues.[26] And theological deviation from Protestant fundamentalism, if discovered, would justify her termination. More generally, professors who labor in religious institutions that require them to affirm certain theological doctrines are always aware that their employment depends on their *beliefs*. At evangelical Wheaton

College, for example, a professor was recently fired for entering the Catholic Church.[27] Given this vulnerability, some professors at religious institutions may conceal their liberal political convictions, even if they are only weakly associated with theological doctrines that their universities reject.

In any case, we must leave it to others to investigate intellectual minorities on the left. We now turn our attention to those open conservatives who confront a different set of choices and challenges.

Open Conservatism and Its Challenges

OUR FIRST INTERVIEWS brought us to a paradise for right-wing academics. Its edenic campus sprawls up a mountain just above a seaside town, where the ocean sweeps out to the horizon and dominates every vista. Although liberals predominate in the faculty at this particular university, some major islands within it are inhabited by various species of right-wing academics. As we peered out over the mountains and blue waters, we began to suspect that with protected sanctuaries like this one, the plight of conservative academics could not be all that bad.

When "I came here I had to pinch myself," said a political scientist we call Professor E. His early career had been spent in a New England liberal-arts college where he was a maligned figure. "It was distorting of my personality," he said. "I didn't even realize it [at the time]. It's almost like being in a car wreck. Your initial response is adrenaline to get through it."

His stint in New England, however, actually began well. Though Professor E possessed hawkish views on foreign policy, he was hired and tenured in the 1990s. Wedged between the end of the Cold War and the war on terrorism, it was a decade in which foreign policy controversies were less salient on university campuses. During those placid years, Professor E was even courted by a liberal department at another college, partly because he was a conservative. At the time he was impressed by the academy's tolerance toward conservatives.

Professor E's perspective changed after he became an outspoken defender of America's war on terror in the wake of the carnage on September 11, 2001. He became "a lightning rod," E recalled, after participating in a post–9/11 teach-in that was attended by some 1,400 students and faculty members. As Professor E remembered that fateful day: "[The other professors] were expiating our sins, 'this was hubris, we deserved it,' all of that. I gave an opposite presentation, [and it] gave me widespread notoriety." In a New England college town he called "Cuba with bad weather," Professor E became the village conservative. The local media turned to him when it sought a defender of the war or the Bush administration. "I gave myself in jest the nickname Dr. Evil," he added.

Professor E became a local pariah after the teach-in. He was excluded from events and shunned in public. "When I walked in" a local market, he remembered, "they'd let me go right to the front of the line, because they and I wanted this miserable experience to end as rapidly as possible." The environment was so chilly that Professor E pulled his children out of the public schools and enrolled them in the local Catholic school. "The atmosphere for my children was much better [in the parochial school], much more welcoming, much more accepting of them."

At work, life was little better. A member of the English department distributed a circular that accused Professor E of training Nazis. There were also a "series of swastikas put on my door," he remembered. E was less troubled by the swastikas, since they were the handiwork of "one crank kid." Instead, he was vexed by the university's uneven policies toward harassment. As he put it,

> It didn't seem to trouble them beyond the level of a nuisance, and I was the nuisance that was bringing it up. I mentioned more than once that had this been a woman of color, if this had been a gay person, and there had been a comparable symbol on the door multiple times, you folks would have brought in consultants, et cetera.

Making matters worse, Professor E reported that he was among the lowest-paid faculty members despite having an excellent publishing and teaching record. His penurious compensation was so well known that it became a subject of local humor. One student, E recalled, boasted "that he got more Bar Mitzvah money than I got in salary."

To an unusual degree this professor's career captures the full range of work environments open conservatives find waiting for them in the liberal academy. It also underscores what a difficult task it is to assess such disparate professional experiences. On the one hand, universities are often remarkably tolerant places, as the following chapter emphasizes. And this means that the academy is generally not the political hothouse Professor E found in New England. On the other hand, many of E's complaints—an icy working environment, unfair wages, and belligerent colleagues—are familiar to many conservative academics, especially those who write about controversial political issues.

This chapter explores the strategies openly conservative academics like Professor E use to navigate their profession. And it further reflects on why some approaches succeed, while others fail.

Varieties of Professional Engagement

In this section we outline three styles conservatives use to manage social conflict with their progressive colleagues: *assimilative, evasive,* and *combative.* The dominant strategy conservative professors adopt is an *assimilative* one. Those who embrace this style attempt to puncture liberal stereotypes about themselves and other conservatives by presenting themselves as thoughtful and temperate university citizens. An assimilative strategy is similar to what some scholars call "normalizing." "Those who normalize," noted Judith Clair and her colleagues, "attempt to assimilate into local organizational culture [and] behave in accordance with the norms of the organization." "The invisible social identity is subtly acknowledged," they explained, "but its significance and stigma are minimized."[1] For many conservatives, however, assimilating does not simply involve fitting in—it is often more subversive than that. Every successful act of assimilation, after all, undermines the notion that conservatives are unfit for academia.

The assimilative style is often a powerful one in the university, partly because its small scale encourages friendship across political divides. We know that partisan passions are muted even in politicized institutions, such as the United States Senate, when there are opportunities for friendship. As political scientist Ross Baker has emphasized, the smallness of the Senate mutes partisan passions by allowing its members "to get to know one another and so take the measure of colleagues as individuals."[2] A similar dynamic is at work in many academic departments where conservatives often make distinctions between good "cosmopolitan liberals," as one professor put it, and those prone to ideological tribalism. Conservative professors often enjoy close relationships with these more cosmopolitan peers.

Some of the conservatives we interviewed believe that they are accepted by many of their colleagues despite their politics simply because they are civil and friendly. "There's a lot to be said for just being well-liked," one political scientist said. "I think that's part of how I get along in the academy." When we asked a philosopher at a state college whether his colleagues were more troubled by difficult personalities than by conservatives, he responded, "I think at the end of the day, yeah, absolutely. I think if you're a schmuck people aren't going to want you there."

Conservatives even occasionally reported close friendships with colleagues far to their left. "I love my colleagues, we love each other very much," said one literature professor in a public teaching college. He is even teased in a friendly way for his conservatism. "They might come and joke with me and say 'oh, I heard you're in love with Michele Bachmann' or 'you're in love with Sarah Palin.'" Likewise, a professor of history reported that his "best friend" at his research university is a leftist historian. When his friend introduces our interviewee to others, he sometimes says, "'meet my friend, [he's] a right-wing fanatic.'" "I don't mind him saying it," our subject explained, "because he knows it's not true." A political scientist reported a similar playfulness with her department chair. Thanks to his direct dealings with academic assessment regimes—a farce to academics everywhere—her chair quipped, "'this is almost enough to make me a Republican.'"

Some seemingly unlikely conservatives praise their liberal colleagues. Consider the case of a conservative-libertarian in a far-left literature department, even by the discipline's standards. By his own account, he has certainly not always been treated fairly by his colleagues. And yet our subject also praised many of his leftist colleagues and the university he has labored in nearly all his professional life. "I have had many wonderful relationships with many people who were very far, far to the left in my department," he volunteered. "But, you know, every population has a certain population of mean people. Some of the meanest people I have ever known have been libertarians." This professor's great affection for many of his colleagues seemed to color his view of the university as a whole. With great emotion he told us,

> This university has really given me my life. It's a very wonderful place. Almost everybody in it I have enjoyed and they contributed in magnificent ways to our society.... It's a privilege to be here. It's an honor.

It is not the sort of testimony one would expect from reading *Tenured Radicals*.

Other right-wing scholars feel obliged to become assertive ambassadors for conservatives, particularly since liberal academics have such little
exposure to citizens on the political right. A sociologist at a research university mused, "I think it is helpful [to be a good department citizen], but
it's helpful especially for people in my position to be as constructive as
I can be. So I guess my reputation would be a constructive conservative."
One literature professor praised the example of Robert George, an affable,
yet outspoken, conservative professor of politics at Princeton University.
"He smiles, he laughs, he's genial, he's friendly," our interviewee noted
admiringly. "So, the ability to stand up and be forthright without being
aggressive, without being unpleasant, I think, goes a long way." Similarly,
a philosopher at a teaching college believes it is important to demonstrate
through his moderate and thoughtful example that "he's not some freak . . .
that he doesn't fit the caricature that you might have of [a conservative]."

Libertarians generally found it easier to find common political ground
with their colleagues than did foreign policy hawks or social conservatives. "Being a libertarian means that some of the views that I have actually jibe with the prevailing orthodoxy," said a philosopher at a regional
state college. "So, like when same-sex marriage debates come up, I'm on
the right side of that issue, as far as my colleagues are concerned," he
added. "I'm probably less weird to them than a . . . party-line Republican
conservative, because so many of the things that I would say are going to
fit with their worldview, but just enough doesn't fit for them to think that
it's interesting."

Conservative academics, however, often suspected that their assimilative style would not work everywhere. These conservatives believed that
life is rather unpleasant for their fellow right-wing academics in other
departments, universities, or disciplines. One sociologist was typical of
such conservatives. "I would distinguish between my department and the
discipline," he began. He then explained:

> So I am quite happy locally with the way we run our business, fairly
> happy with the way the university [operates], though I have some
> misgivings about that, but very unhappy with the national disci-
> pline, which I think took a hard left turn. Its recent leadership has
> been very, very left, left-left.

When we asked a historian of the ancient world whether his positive
experiences in the academy meant that it was a more tolerant place than

conservatives appreciate, he responded sharply: "No, but it is entirely a question of your discipline and the good fortune of the department you end up in. I have been enormously fortunate, because of the constitution of the departments that I ended up in." A libertarian philosopher agreed. "Despite what I was saying before about our departmental culture of openness, I do know that [discrimination] happens in other departments," he warned. This subject also considered other disciplines less tolerant than philosophy. "If you are in ... the sociology department or in the history department, you would be worried about getting your head handed to you." Meanwhile, an economist who works in a department dominated by libertarians acknowledged, "I realize it's sort of a cocoon here."

The tendency of some conservatives to believe that they are on some strange tolerant island in a sea of perilous dangers has been confirmed by more systematic surveys as well. Bruce Smith and his colleague found that while 60% of very conservative professors think liberals enjoy an advantage in hiring and promotion, only 25% believe their *own department* prefers to hire or promote progressives.[3] Another sign of conservatives' relative discontent with the wider discipline is their reluctance to attend national conferences.

When conservatives are relatively happy with their home institution, it may be because they gravitate to more welcoming disciplines and because they are often hired in more accepting departments. Given the scarcity of conservatives in academia, one of the most remarkable findings from the survey by Smith and his colleagues is that some 26% of "very conservative" and 34% of "moderately conservative" professors say that ideological homogeneity is not a problem at their university because it is already politically diverse. Thus, more than one in four conservative professors believe that they are laboring in a pluralistic work setting.[4] As the last chapter showed, this may be because most of the conservatives in our sample worked in relatively pluralistic departments. In fact, more than 60% of the professors we interviewed said that there were at least two other conservative members in their department. "There [are] actually a lot more of us than you think," one political scientist reported. "I think academia actually gets a bad rap for not being intellectually diverse enough, which is not a conception that a lot of my conservative friends have—they say it's all a bunch of liberals. It's not as bad as they think it is," he maintained.

Other professors tended to evade conversations with their progressive colleagues, either because they found them unpleasant or simply because of the atomized culture of their university. Goffman identified this *evasive*

strategy in his work on stigma as well. The "anticipation of [mixed] con-
tacts," Goffman noted, will sometimes "lead normals and the stigmatized
to arrange life so as to avoid them."[5] Academia is certainly an institution
that accommodates such arrangements, as the previous chapter suggested. Just as the solitary nature of academic work renders it easier for
closeted academics to fly under the radar undetected, it also limits social
pressures on outspoken conservatives. The most significant expression
of the evasive style is reflected in the tendency of conservatives to enter
comparatively moderate subfields and disciplines, which the following
chapter shows.

But now we turn to evasiveness in everyday work life. Consider the
case of one historian at a public research university. "I really don't hang
out to kibitz or shoot the breeze with people," he pronounced. "I work
hard." So does a literature professor at a private research university.
"I generally don't speak to my colleagues," he said. "I generally show up
and teach, and [then] I leave." Another literature professor informed us
that he doesn't "sit around and engage" in political conversations with his
liberal colleagues. "We have a polite agreement that we're not going to try
to change each other's minds about those sorts of things."

The independence and solitariness of academic life mean that most
social relationships are chosen, especially in big departments and
universities. "We don't actually talk a lot of politics," one political scientist
acknowledged. These days he drives into campus only twice during a typical
week. "At most I'll say hello to one faculty member and I won't see anyone
else," he told us. He attributed such infrequent and transient encounters
with colleagues to his campus's "weaker sense of intellectual community."
A historian, meanwhile, told us, "We're a big department, and so there's no
there, there. We're so anxious not to have meetings. There's formally one
party a year, [but] nobody goes to [it]. [Thus], the only people one deals with
[are] basically one's personal friends." He underscored the weakness of his
department community through a revealing anecdote:

> [A]n indication of the weirdness of contemporary academic life is
> that there are plenty of members of my department I don't know. I'll
> be in the departmental office and there will be someone asking the
> secretary something. I'll turn to the secretary and say, 'Who's that?'

Therefore conservative academics may not always feel part of the "club,"
as one scholar put it, but the very informality of social ties in the academy

also means that tolerance is probably easier to practice on both sides of the partisan divide. In any case, many conservatives are free to form their own workplace ties largely according to their own preferences.

For other professors evasion is a *submerged* style.[6] That is, evasion is a subordinate tactic that emerges only in particular contexts. A common example is the avoidance of larger disciplinary gatherings. "I tend to avoid going to political science meetings," a political scientist told us. When we asked why, he reported, "I think the main thing is there's a certain sort of contempt for your views. If you defend the other side, [some will ask] 'What's wrong with him? He used to be a good guy, what's happened to him?'" An even more disenchanted professor of literature confessed,

> I quit the MLA [Modern Language Association], I don't know, 25 years ago. I have no confidence at all in MLA. It's a completely politicized organization. And [it draws] the worst people in the profession. They're like people from the Department of Education, which is where they belong.

A less acerbic professor at a research university in the Northeast is hardly less disaffected from his colleagues in sociology. "I haven't been a member of the American Sociological Association [ASA] for decades, because it's so politicized," he told us. "I don't know when I went to the last one. It might have been in the early '80s or late '70s." Thus the last time this professor saw the inside of an ASA meeting might have been during the Carter administration.

Nearly all conservatives find evasion appealing at least on occasion. Even affable professors bite their tongue when they are feeling especially exasperated with their progressive colleagues. "There were times when I was silent, because you just can't go to the ocean and say 'I'm going to stop the waves today,'" said one literature professor.

Conservative professors more often complain that it is their liberal colleagues who practice evasion.[7] This was particularly true of cultural conservatives. Consider the case of a devout Catholic, a troubling eccentricity at the Catholic university where he teaches. When he informs colleagues that he agrees with everything the pope says, they blanch. "You're not supposed to have that opinion at a Catholic university, where there is a big tradition of dissent," he noted. This professor finds that it is especially difficult to engage his liberal colleagues on the same-sex marriage controversy. "It's like talking to a blank wall. . . . It's really hard to have a rational conversation." As he sees it, the problem is twofold. First, he observed, "[T]here is a fairly large propensity for academics to be dismissive of conservative views. To say a strong conservative political opinion with conviction in an academic gathering is analogous to uttering an obscenity. It is just out of place." Second, he found that few of his fellow sociologists have encountered thoughtful conservatives, especially on cultural issues: "A number of academics seemed to never have met an articulate, conservative person on some of these [social] issues."

The academics we interviewed with outspoken prolife views encountered similar campus environments. A literature professor at a large state university lamented that some of his colleagues shun him. "[Y]ou're not greeted, your greeting isn't returned in the hall, graduate students are urged not to work with you," he explained. Though he is not certain, this professor attributes his chilly work environment to his prolife convictions. As he put it, "I can tell they're appalled by my prolife sentiments and ideas. I'm known as that crazy guy who prays in front of the abortion clinic." This professor finds it somewhat odd that his particular perspective on human equality alienates his colleagues. "You know, they won't wear shoe leather, because they respect animal life, but somehow because I'm insisting on respecting unborn human life, I'm strange."

A political scientist at a prestigious research university is also committed to the prolife cause. Despite his mild manner and apolitical research agenda, he too struggles to engage colleagues on the abortion issue. "That's the one where you run into trouble, and where people can't believe you're saying what you're saying," he observed. Now that this professor is known on campus as a prolife advocate, some colleagues avoid him. "If some people saw me coming, they'd walk the other way," he lamented. This political scientist attributes his colleagues' reactions to "the totality of the information cocoon that they live in," which he thinks inhibits their consideration of other perspectives.

Another socially conservative professor also feels like a social pariah at her research university, where she teaches literature. "It's very chilly" at work, she told us, explaining further: "I mean there are some who pretty much don't say 'hi' in the hallway. It was just really odd for me, because I'm generally a friendly person and it really is jarring to me, but I've just gotten used to it." And when another literature professor was appointed to a prestigious post in the Bush administration, he recalled, "[Colleagues] I've known for years stopped speaking to me."

A literature professor at a public research university even lost a tennis partner on account of his conservative views. His former partner harbored political aspirations on campus, and therefore needed broad support among leftist and progressive colleagues. When our subject asked his then-partner whether there was something political about playing tennis, he remembered receiving this reply: " 'No, it's you. In other words, in order for me to move ahead with my Marxist friends and be successful on the campus, I have to not play tennis with you.' "

Although most conservative academics eagerly find ways to get along with their colleagues by either engaging or avoiding them, a minority delights in their contrarianism. They practice a *combative* style, though it is usually a submerged one. Goffman anticipated this style as well, since he noted that some among the stigmatized will find "hostile bravado" appealing.[8] It most resembles what sociologists Binder and Wood called "highbrow provocation," since it is expressed in "words and ideas" rather than through actions.[9]

We interviewed a prominent political scientist who clearly enjoys scandalizing his liberal colleagues on occasion. He told us: "[T]he French have this phrase, *épater le bourgeois*," which roughly translated means to shock or astonish the bourgeoisie. "So the liberals are the bourgeoisie of American academia, and it's kind of fun and easy . . . they make an easy target, so unthoughtful."

Others shared this subject's taste for provocation. When his liberal colleagues used a departmental list-serve to promote rallies for Democratic politicians, one literature professor complained and accused them of breaking federal law. As he fumed, "To my knowledge that's illegal, because it's using state resources for partisan political purposes and every time I would point it out, I would take shit for it because I was spoiling the Democratic fun. How could anyone object?" Similarly, when we asked a philosopher at a state university whether he believed there were any advantages to being a conservative, he responded unambiguously: "Fun, it's clearly just fun . . . for me to say things to people that shock them. They think, 'How could you possibly think that?' " A more mild-mannered political scientist agreed. "It's sort of fun," he mused with a wry smile. "There's an element of challenge, there's an element of being a dissenter, [and] sometimes there's even an element of being the skunk at the picnic."

Though such conservatives delight in unsettling their colleagues, they also think their combativeness is appreciated on at least some occasions. After one prominent historian launched a campaign against speech codes on his campus, he was pleasantly surprised by the "num-ber of faculty who would walk up . . . and whisper, 'I'm glad you're doing what you're doing' or 'I wish I had your taste for confrontation.'" Similarly, a political scientist remembered that liberal colleagues were not all that unsympathetic to his vocal critiques of affirmative action. "They all thought that I was sort of right," he gathered, "but then they didn't want to join me."

Some readers may be surprised that only a few of the professors we interviewed are drawn to the combative style, especially since their tac-tics sometimes draw wide media attention. Recently, for example, John McAdams, a political scientist at Marquette University, was suspended for publicly criticizing a teaching assistant for the way she handled a discus-sion of gay marriage with a conservative student. McAdams accused the teaching assistant of behaving like a "typical" liberal for trying to "shut up" students with politically incorrect views. After his suspension, McAdams then accused Marquette of treating him like a "potential terrorist."[10] In general, however, we found very few conservatives with his taste for confrontation.

More frequently, conservatives complained about combative progres-sive colleagues. A historian at a major state university recalled strong reactions from colleagues for opposing what he bluntly called "an affir-mative action hire." One nonplussed colleague reportedly pulled him aside after the department meeting and challenged him: "[D]o you know what you said?" Yet another colleague simply took to calling him "a fas-cist." At times our subject wondered, "Why am I talking about that, what is wrong with me?" And, as the years passed, he embraced an evasive style by retreating into his work. "I stopped going to those meetings," he recalled. A Jewish historian at a regional state college received similar treatment when he advocated for political diversity on a university panel on reparations. When the controversy hit the local papers, he recalled that a colleague "called me a racist, while another one called me a Nazi and a Klansman." Another historian remembered offending his colleagues when he gave a statement against affirmative action in a department meeting. "It really rattled some people [and] a few people denounced me," he told us.

Sometimes even subtler suggestions trigger hostile reactions. A pro-fessor who identifies as a gay, Christian libertarian and teaches literature at a prominent state university recalled that he once suggested that his department might be able to increase its enrollments by teaching authors like Jane Austen. One colleague, this professor recalled, "got very upset, [and said] that this was just a way of catering to the [gender] prejudices that students learned in high school, and after that she never spoke to me at all."

Such views are sometimes expressed by the university administration through its commitment to diversity. A philosopher reported on one university workshop, directed by a "very well-meaning, earnest person." As our subject recalled, she informed her academic participants:

> 'We are committed to diversity and pluralism, we just want to discourage conservative views.' And then she made it clear that by conservative, she meant racist and sexist. If that's actually your operational definition of conservatism, you could see why conservatives might want to stay in the closet.

And, of course, some right-wing academics say that they entered the closet precisely because their liberal colleagues tended to equate conservatism with racism and sexism.

Other academics emphasized the difficulties of overcoming the stigma of being a Republican in what is arguably the most Democratic profession in America. "I don't know how many meetings I've been at where people have made comments or jokes about conservatives and Republicans," a political scientist complained. "I find that so offensive." And a literature professor said that when she spoke out in defense of the Bush administration, her colleagues "looked at me like I was mentally ill."

Notably, economists are almost entirely immune from these sorts of irritations, except when they engage colleagues outside their own discipline. One economist, who teaches at a prestigious university, recalled a colleague who "said something disparaging about the Republicans," before apologizing:

> 'Oh, I'm so sorry. I forget you're a Republican.' And [then] she looked at me, and the way she looked was like I had some sort of mental defect. But you don't get that in the economics department [since it is] far more balanced.

Another economist took an interest in a campus reading group organized by his progressive colleagues. "I was not welcome there," he remembered with disappointment.

Politics of Hiring, Promotion, and Publishing

Though conservatives sometimes fret face-to-face encounters with progressive colleagues, they are far more worried about what liberals do in the privacy of the peer-review process and hiring committees. It is these confidential contexts that allow for more serious forms of bias, conservatives say, especially when their work reflects right-wing interests and perspectives. And because conservatives often have no personal connection to progressives in these contexts, they feel more handicapped by stigma.

Many conservative professors, for example, reported that it is difficult to attract interest from other universities once one is known as a conservative thinker. One very productive historian at a research university confessed that he had "occasionally applied for other jobs" and thought "this kind of whiff of conservatism about me . . . made me unattractive, [but] I'm not sure about that." If this historian emits a "whiff" of conservatism, another of our subjects exudes a strong pungent odor. After this professor accepted a post in the Bush administration, he believed that any hope of finding other employment was dashed. "That was an act of such publicity, that I knew it would really eliminate my mobility," he acknowledged. During that same period, he also "decided to come out of the Austrian closet," as he put it, by publishing an essay that reflected those economic views.

A more circumspect historian at a research university believes that the mobility of conservatives tends to be limited, albeit because of a more subtle process. He began by observing that conservatives tend to gravitate to less trendy and less politicized subfields, such as military history, religious history, and ancient history. Thus, in his view, conservatives are often excluded from top departments because they do not seek specialists in subfields that are popular among conservatives. As he explained, "If you advertise a job for an ancient historian, you've already made a political decision, because you've not advertised a job, for example, for a historian of Afro-American culture or of gender studies or whatever. The jobs that someone like me could not get because of his politics are probably jobs that will never exist."

And because outside offers are the main way academics get significant pay raises, open conservatives complain that they receive lower wages than their liberal peers. A prominent historian at a prestigious university told us that when he requested raises, his employers always countered with what he called a "good market response." They said, " 'Well, we don't see any bidding wars for you.'" To which this interviewee responded, "[B]idding wars? Are you kidding?" A literature professor agrees: "You don't make as much money, because ... the only thing that gets you raises is counteroffers and I've never gotten them." Having established reputations as conservatives, these professors feel as if they have become unemployable. Nonetheless, these conservatives do not attribute the pay gap between themselves and their liberal peers to a conscious effort to punish conservatives.

Others were less sure. "I was nominated for a professorship a couple years back, and didn't get it," a socially conservative literature professor said. "I'm told by one of my colleagues who has an inside track on information that my prolife activity had been a negative factor." Another literature professor was actually courted by a prestigious department before he admitted to harboring conservative views. "I said, 'yes, please consider me,'" our interviewee remembered. But this professor then informed his suitors that he was a conservative. "People obviously distanced themselves very soon after that," he lamented. "[B]ut there was at least one of them who said, 'Hey, it might be a good idea to have somebody that is different from what we are and so forth.'" A very outspoken conservative at a research university echoed these concerns. "I'm much ... much more underpaid compared to other people in [my university] with a similar record," he emphasized. "I've been nominated for a chair several times, [but they have] been shut down."

A productive historian at a regional state college is paid less today because he was denied an early promotion to full professor, which he believes was motivated by partisan prejudices. "I ended up with a historian and two people from our Social Sciences Department on my [promotion] committee," he recalled. The faculty members from the Social Sciences Department voted against promotion. "And the reason they gave, was that a chapter from one of my books had been [re]published on a conservative website," our subject told us. One scholar on the committee argued that faculty should not be evaluated with political criteria, but he was outvoted. This embittered historian protested: "[E]very time I get a paycheck, I am paid less because of those two leftists. I'm being penalized every two weeks for the rest of my career for my political views."

Not all burning grievances smolder into old age. One historian got so fed up with the pay gap between himself and his liberal peers that he did something about it. "I made up my own file for a pay raise. I wrote two or three letters to fine scholars in the field and asked them to write letters for me and I went to the chairman," he recalled. The gambit worked.

Some systematic evidence suggests that conservatives' professional mobility is harmed by their politics. As noted in Chapter Three, a study by Stanley Rothman and Robert Lichter found that social conservatives teach at less prestigious colleges and universities than their publication record would predict.[11]

In any case, it was striking to hear so many conservatives make a critique of markets that is typically made by the progressives. Liberals, after all, are usually the ones to point out the ways in which markets are corrupted by human prejudices. Conservatives, meanwhile, have tended to downplay those concerns.

Other conservatives complained that the hiring and tenure processes are driven by political concerns. As one prominent historian told us, "I do believe there are political litmus tests for hiring. I've seen them. I think it's disgraceful." He said that one of his graduate students, a religious conservative, is still employed at a small teaching college even though he authored many books published by prestigious presses. Two of his former student's books even won the same award—an achievement he believes has yet to be replicated. "It's astonishing that he doesn't have offers from the Ivies, the flagships, Berkeley, or Stanford," this historian fumed. "If he had done intellectually what he's done and were on the left, he'd be one of the prized people in American history."

A philosopher at a public flagship university thought that he observed similar bias against right-wing Christians in his own department. "At least twice in my experience, I thought it was pretty clear that the best candidate was a [conservative] Christian, and in both cases they narrowly lost our final vote, and I think that was a factor," he explained. A literature professor echoed the same concern: "We had a colleague here who had a wonderful record when he came up with tenure, [but he] barely scraped by because he was an Orthodox Jew and political conservative."

An accomplished sociologist at a top research university recalled stirring controversy when he was considered for a job in a more prestigious department. "That was very contentious," he said. "Some of the grad students had ascertained that I was more conservative, and they wrote a letter to the department chair protesting my consideration for a position." During his interview with graduate students, he recalled, "I was peppered with hostile questions about my views on family matters," a strange departure from their usual obsequiousness in the presence of senior scholars.

This lobby developed, this subject believes, because the graduate students suspected him of opposing same-sex marriage. As he explained, "The irony is that I've never said or written anything as a scholar about gay marriage. Nevertheless, if you are concerned with marriage, concerned with the health of the family, you are instantly suspected of being opposed to gay marriage."

Similarly, a historian at a private university recalled some testy interviews, which he attributes to his conservatism. "I could feel it, I could feel that there were already people who walked into the room who were against me," he said. During one job interview, this subject remembered a faculty member who asked why he would write about a subject that had nothing to do with social justice. His background also raised suspicions, particularly since he attended an evangelical college as an undergraduate. Professors, he said, asked probing questions about his religious background. As he remembered it, "In some ways [they were] innocent questions, but they had an edge to them."

Other conservative professors attributed their struggles on the job market to their interest in topics that progressives tend to find uninspiring. Consider the case of one historian of Latin America at a public research university. "I wrote a dissertation on middle-class white guys [when] the big deal [at that time] was not just gender and stuff like that, but the so-called agency of subaltern peoples," he remembered. The historian does not believe that his work branded him as a conservative: "I just don't think they saw it as a radical dissertation." It is a problem that seems worse in literature, where the spread of leftist theoretical perspectives is even more advanced. One literature professor we interviewed, for example, has become a permanent adjunct despite penning over one hundred essays. Nonetheless, he does not blame his professional failures on the political prejudices of his progressive colleagues, at least not primarily. "I once went to a professor," he recalled, "and I said 'Look, could you look at [my vita] and tell me if there's anything wrong with it.'" This is how our subject remembers his response: "He looked and said, 'No there's nothing wrong with it. It's just not exciting. . . . It was a nice resume for 1940.' . . . So, at that point, I started to say 'Oh the hell with it.'"

One way to help prevent the hiring of conservative thinkers in the first place is to exclude them from hiring committees. "I haven't been on a search committee for a permanent member of our department in thirty years," a literature professor told us. "I used to protest about that from time to time." This professor believes that his exclusion from search committees is quite extraordinary given his seniority and publishing record. "I mean I've been on the search committee for the president of the university," he added. Likewise, a historian reported that he had even been excluded from searches in his own particular subfield in American history. "That's the kind of slighting that would just go on," he lamented.

Others with very strong publishing records believe that they barely cleared the tenure bar because of their political orientation. For a time one professor's conservative politics escaped his colleagues. "I had really long hair and had informal manners and so forth, [and] they knew so little about people on the right that I think they couldn't figure it out," he conjectured. But eventually they did. He remembers those struggles:

> It became a problem with some people . . . when I was up for tenure because by that time they've realized that I wasn't a Marxist. . . . As a matter of fact, I was a pretty traditional member and had actually refused to sign at least one [progressive] petition, and that really pissed [them] off. . . . So a bunch of them voted against me.

A remarkably productive political scientist at a small Catholic college also believes that he was nearly denied tenure on account of his politics. By his estimate, some 40% of the full professors in his university either abstained or voted against him. The vote still irritates him all these years later. "The same people who talk incessantly about the need to create and maintain an atmosphere of diversity in higher education are interested in eliminating intellectual diversity," he inveighed.

Some other professors, meanwhile, believe that they were denied tenure on account of their politics. "I think the consensus was that in my case, politics entered into it a lot," said a historian at an elite research university. "There was a sort of outcry," he noted, "and apparently people still talk about it" decades after the fact. His case was bolstered by the investigative work of a student journalist who discovered a suspicious letter. As our interviewee recalled, "One day there appeared in my cubbyhole of my letterbox a blank envelope with a Xerox of the letter which had this particular professor's signature. It accused me of being an appalling Euro-centric conservative." In particular, the letter writer was troubled that he told his students that North Korea should be blamed for the Korean War. An unusually aggrieved economist reported that he too discovered "a total smoking gun" when he was denied tenure at a research university. According to this professor, there was a "scandalous report" in his tenure

file that said " 'this guy is one of them,' kind of thing and at great length."
As his case became a major scandal, he left for a far less prestigious and
more teaching-oriented college.

A sociologist—whom we will call Professor F—was similarly jaded
by his trying tenure experience. Professor F was an unusually productive
scholar for an assistant professor in a top-fifty sociology department. He
published a widely acclaimed book with one of the best university presses
in sociology and published articles in three of the leading journals in
sociology within his subfield. He also raised large grants for his research.
By such metrics Professor F had easily outpaced other recently tenured
professors in his department. Yet F's department voted against his tenure. He appealed, but the dean sided with the judgment of the sociology
department.

Some of Professor F's more politicized department members, however,
made one fatal mistake: They slipped some of F's popular writings in conservative magazines into his tenure file before his case was reviewed by
the dean. That was the bit of evidence he needed to make compelling legal
threats against the university. "I think that actually was my saving grace,"
a relieved Professor F proclaimed. "That was their big mistake." "I think
the Provost's office was aware that this whole case could blow up in their
face," he surmised. The Provost then awarded Professor F tenure, over-
ruling the dean and sociology department. Some department liberals also
came to Professor F's defense. As F recalled, one was so troubled by the
process that he confided, " 'I'm not supposed to break up confidentiality
here, but this process is outrageous. Your religion, your politics entered
into the discussion for tenure and basically a lot of extraneous things that
were not relevant to [your] performance were questioned.' " According to
F, the department was not hostile to faculty members with strong political
views, since a Marxist was recently promoted to full professor. "What was
a bar to tenure in my department was holding more conservative views,"
Professor F argued. "That was the real truth of the matter."

Such cases are a reminder that some outspoken conservatives believe,
at least initially, that they will be treated fairly in academia, even by their
most left-wing colleagues. Otherwise at least some of these conservatives
would have followed the example of their closeted peers by being more
cautious and circumspect. Professor F recounted his own innocence: "I
went through the tenure process and I thought I would get it without
much difficulty [because of my publishing record]." When F learned his
tenure was denied, he recalled, "I was shocked." Only in retrospect does

Professor F regard his decision to write occasional essays for conservative journals an imprudent one. A very productive political scientist at a small teaching college also did not expect such a difficult tenure battle. As he reflected on his youthful innocence, "I really thought that if one spoke in a civil way [and] introduced points of view that were underrepresented in the academy, that you would get some credit for that. You don't get any credit for that." A literature professor at a research university experienced a similar transformation. "My naive assumption as an assistant professor was that departments like dissent," he recalled. "I believed that's what the academy was all about, and so when I started arguing for things, I didn't realize that people are going to not like me." Likewise, a historian had become more disillusioned by his experiences. "I often say that if I'd known the depth of the politicization of academia, I might have gone in a different direction, but I didn't know," he told us.

Such scholars changed their assessment of the academy's tolerance only *after* they had been working in the university for some time. It is their experiences in the academy rather than isolation in some right-wing media bubble that soured them on academic life. And some scholars became so jaded that they even discouraged conservative undergraduates from pursuing an academic career. In fact, more than one-fifth of the conservative professors we interviewed said that they had done so (see Table 5.1).

One political scientist became so disenchanted with life in the university that he has since left it altogether. When we interviewed him, he was already quite troubled by his experiences. According to this professor, some of his colleagues accused him of being too conservative in the classroom. For his annual review, he told us, they combed through hundreds of

Table 5.1 Mentoring Conservative Undergraduates

Have you ever discouraged conservative or libertarian undergraduates from pursuing academic careers because of concerns over political bias in higher education?	
Yes, I have discouraged students at times	22%
No, I have always encouraged students	63%
The subject has never come up	15%
N:	139

his teaching evaluations looking for complaints of bias. He responded by conducting a formal content analysis of hundreds of course evaluations. Our subject's analysis found that 80% of the evaluations never mentioned politics; 16% said he was balanced; and 4% said he was biased, though in different ways. In the face of such hard evidence, he said that his antagonists then accused him of being unapproachable. Though we can offer no independent assessment of his content analysis, his many reviews on *rate-my-professor.com* demonstrate that he was an unusually popular professor. With nearly one hundred reviews, he is rated a 4.3 (out of a possible 5), a mark that places him well above the university average. He also won a distinguished teaching award. In any case, this interviewee believes that even if he did express political opinions in class, his colleagues still should have rushed to his defense. "Isn't that what academic freedom is actually supposed to be for?" he asked rhetorically. "Everyone should have been rallying for my rights."

Other conservatives complained about the peer-review process. An accomplished historian at a religious university offered one of the most thoughtful assessments of the challenges academic publishing presents to conservative professors:

> I think it's a more acute problem with the journals than it is with the [book] presses, because I think the presses tend to be market driven. And so they're not going to turn down books because they are written from a certain ideological, political, or religious perspective when they know that that's an untapped market.... With the journals, I don't think they have to think about those kinds of things, they're not money-making operations. So, I think they tend to be much more ideologically driven.

In his assessment, however, even journal publishing is fair to conservative authors so long as their articles do not reflect right-wing interests or perspectives. "I think it would be very, very hard to get something [conservative] published in your standard [history] journals.... [For example,] if you did an article on the sanctity of life in early America, I think that would not get published," he surmised.

According to this historian, the problem for conservative authors is twofold. First, they do not really know what is happening inside editorial meetings or in the minds of reviewers. Second, there may also be a lack of self-awareness among the liberal reviewers and editors that discriminate. Thus, for *both* liberals and conservatives alike, academic bias is difficult to detect. He explained it this way:

> The problem is that you can never prove this, right, you can never get behind the scenes in the editorial board discussions. Because I would imagine that if they were faced with a piece [on the sanctity of life in early America], they would not have an overt discussion about why it's not accepted. [Instead, they would say] 'Well this is not up to scholarly standards, this is not historiographically correct, this is not something that we're interested in right now,' and I mean they may not even be conscious about why they're rejecting something.

A sociologist at a research university on the West Coast came to a similar perspective on the peer-review process through an accidental experiment. Originally he wrote an article with findings that affirmed a progressive critique of an important American institution. "People loved that version of the paper," he remembered. Its findings were even prominently featured in *Contexts*, a journal of the ASA that attempts to disseminate sociological knowledge to a wider audience. However, he then discovered a coding error. "I fixed the coding error and the effect goes away," he said. With the correct results, he could not get his article published, despite many attempts. As he explained, "When people liked the result, they overlooked its [methodological limitations]; when people didn't like the result, they started to look for problems in it. It should have always not been a problem or always been a problem."

In a more general way, a historian echoed this sociologist's concern. "Too much work is judged by its political implications . . . than by its compelling intellectual force," he said. And like many other conservative professors, he suspects that liberals are usually unaware of their political judgments. As this subject explained, "I don't think this is conscious. I don't think there's a conscious bad faith going on. I think when people read things they wish to politically sympathize with, it adds brightness points."

A political scientist agreed with this more charitable interpretation of liberal bias. "I just think it's just a natural process, [it is] human nature," he told us, "They're more inclined to support those who agree with them and oppose those who don't." Peer reviewers are not driven by dark prejudices; they are just human.

One scholar, however, suggested that a more nefarious process is at work, at least in some institutions. Professor E, the political scientist in our opening vignette, called the process "corrupt" because of a handful of liberal gatekeepers. Professor E, for example, criticized Stephen Walt, coauthor of the controversial *Israel Lobby* and editor of a series on security affairs at Cornell University Press. He fumed, "Nothing that [Walt] disagrees with gets published at Cornell. And, of course, he'll say it's because no one obtains his Olympian standard of excellence, which always just happens to coincide with his conclusion." Professor E also believes a similar "cabal of people" controls the *Journal of International Security*.

Conservative anxieties about the peer-review process were not soothed by a recent scandal surrounding the work of Mark Regnerus (his real name), a sociologist at the University of Texas. Regnerus published an article in *Social Science Research* that came to an unpopular conclusion.[12] It found that children who were raised by parents who participated in same-sex relationships fared worse than children brought up in intact, heterosexual families. The response was extraordinary. As the ink dried on Professor Regnerus's article, the review process at *Social Science Research* came under intense scrutiny. A letter signed by some two hundred scholars questioned both the "scholarly merit" of Regnerus's work as well as the "process by which this paper was submitted, reviewed, and accepted for publication." These concerns were related, since the journal's critics, mostly sociologists and psychologists, concluded that the article's flaws indicated deeper problems with the review process. As the letter explained, "there are substantial concerns about the merits of this paper, and these concerns should have been identified through a thorough and rigorous peer review process." Critics concluded, in fact, that nothing less than the very "integrity of the peer review process" at *Social Science Research* was at stake.[13]

The journal's liberal editor and gay-marriage supporter, Jim Wright, was alarmed by the attack. To address his critics, Wright solicited an audit of the peer-review process that led to the publication of Regnerus's article. Wright also asked the auditor to investigate the publication of a less controversial review essay on the limitations of prior research on gay parenting by Loren Marks, a professor of family studies at Louisiana State University.[14] Everything was turned over to a special auditor, including private correspondence and the anonymous peer reviews.[15]

Wright needed professional cover, and that meant selecting an auditor with credibility among the journal's many concerned critics. And so

Wright tapped Darren Sherkat, a *Social Science Research* editorial board member and intemperate critic of conservative social scientists. In fact, before he was deputized as auditor, Sherkat had used his blog to refer to Professor Regnerus as a "big mouthpiece for the religious right." Professor Sherkat further speculated on what Bristol Palin would think of Regnerus's research on the hook-up culture: "I'm sure she'd also like Mark's stuff on how women are all whores and they hate sex, and women who have sex devalue other women because all women are whores! I just love that." Included in this same post, Sherkat featured a picture of a rat caught in a trap while being mounted from behind by another rodent, presumably to further demonstrate the depth of his animus for Regnerus and other like-minded social scientists.[16]

Sherkat concluded that the Regnerus article should not have been published. As he explained to the *Chronicle of Higher Education*, "It's bullshit."[17] The audit itself was less blunt. It expressed concern that "three of the six reviewers [for Regnerus's and Marks's articles] are bona fide conservatives." Such "comfortable conservatives," the audit continued, might have ignored these articles' shortcomings because of their "ideological blinders." Thus, Sherkat concluded that the editor should have "made sure that the reviewers were more diverse in their political perspectives." It was an odd conclusion given that the editor solicited an unusually balanced cast of reviewers, with half on the political right. In effect, Sherkat seemed to be saying just the opposite: The reviewers were too ideologically diverse. Moreover, Sherkat acknowledged that the three nonconservative reviewers "can accurately be described as social science superstars." These "superstars" all recommended publication of Marks's and Regnerus's papers, just like their conservative counterparts. Despite unanimity across such a pluralistic and distinguished group of reviewers, Professor Sherkat concluded, "Obviously, the reviewers did not do a good job."[18]

Sherkat's audit brimmed with other curious claims. For example, he insisted that, given that the issue of gay parenting was such an "important and contentious issue," Regnerus should have used higher-quality data than is commonly used in "other peer-reviewed studies."[19] Yet Regnerus's data were arguably better than the data used in nearly all the prior studies on gay parenting, which depended on small, nonrepresentative samples. Paul Amato, a distinguished scholar and chair of the family section of the ASA, even praised Regnerus's study for its methodological sophistication, since it was "better situated than virtually all previous studies to detect differences between these [different family] groups in the population."[20]

Likewise, the economist Douglas Allen concluded, "If the Regnerus study is to be thrown out, then practically everything else in the field has to go with it."[21] An irritated Christian Smith, a sociologist at the University of Notre Dame, also came to Regnerus's defense. "His sample was a clear improvement over those used by most previous studies on this topic," Smith opined in the pages of *The Chronicle Review*. Smith, who identifies as a political moderate, further blamed the whole controversy on rank partisanship: "In today's political climate, and particularly in the discipline of sociology—dominated as it is by a progressive orthodoxy—what Regnerus did is unacceptable. It makes him a heretic, a traitor—and so he must be thrown under the bus."[22]

Understandably, the implications of Regnerus study were troubling to the many academics who regard the legalization of same-sex marriage a matter of basic justice, especially in a highly polarized political context in which progressives are actively working for marriage equality. But in the rush to judgment, many critics ignored the fact that the implications of Regnerus's study were far from obvious. Regnerus found that instability was a common characteristic of same-sex relationships, which we know tends to have bad effects on children. Some supporters have argued that because marriage encourages stable relationships, gays and lesbians should be entitled to benefit from such marital goods.

To be sure, there were reasonable criticisms of Regnerus's study. But such critiques are a sign of a healthy debate, not a fatal flaw in Regnerus's work, much less the review process at *Social Science Research*. Happily, Jim Wright was a broad-minded-enough editor to appreciate the importance of this intellectual controversy, which is why the interesting theoretical and methodical debates generated by the Regernus and Marks papers were continued in the pages of *Social Science Review*.[23] One pointed critique by Simon Cheng and Brian Powell argued that Regnerus's conclusions were "so fragile ... that they are due primarily to the methodological choices made by [him]." But like other fair-minded critics, they also gave Regnerus credit for collecting data that are "rich" and "complicated."[24]

Professor Sherkat's audit did make one important observation about the review process. When "you generally like a paper," Sherkat noted, "you may not bother pointing out what you think are minor flaws (even if those flaws are not minor)." Sherkat roughly described a common and well-supported psychological phenomenon that social scientists call confirmation bias. But had Sherkat followed the implications of his own argument, he should be worried about the treatment of right-wing colleagues, especially given the fact that conservatives are badly outnumbered by liberals in the social sciences and humanities. And Sherkat might not have exempted the campaign against Regnerus—including his audit—from his insight into human nature.

Scott Rose, a gay rights activist, launched the second front of the campaign against Regnerus. Rose filed a scientific misconduct complaint that charged him with violating the University of Texas's policy against academic dishonesty. The letter was laced with charges that reflected the political passions of its author. For example, it claimed that Regnerus's consultation with a BYU professor about his research design is "akin to asking the Ku Klux Klan to design a study about Jews."[25] Despite such rash claims, the University of Texas launched an investigation. Officials from the university's Information Technology Services' security office confiscated Regnerus's six computers and thousands of emails. An outside consultant described these events in his report to the university's Research Integrity Office:

> On receiving the allegations from Mr. Rose, the Research Integrity Officer notified Dr. Regnerus of them by email and personal meeting in July 2012, followed by an immediate sequestration (by the Security Office of the University's Information Technology Services) of all four of his laptops and two desktop computers for copying of the files, said to contain all the materials related to the questioned study. Also sequestered were 42,000 of his emails on the University system.

Then an "inquiry panel" was convened, which consisted of four university professors with expertise in the social sciences.[26] An independent consultant was also brought in to oversee the process. After a two-month investigation, the Research Integrity Office could not find a solitary piece of evidence to substantiate Rose's claims. It concluded, "None of the allegations put forth by Mr. Rose were substantiated either by physical data, written materials, or by information provided during the interviews.... Mr. Rose believed that the Regnerus research was seriously flawed and inferred that there must be scientific misconduct. However, there is no evidence to support that inference."[27] This exoneration, however, did not stop Regnerus's own department chair from issuing a public statement that said his work was "fundamentally flawed on conceptual and methodological grounds."[28]

As trying as such attacks were for Mark Regnerus, the worst effects of the scandal could be the signals it sends to more reticent academics. It reminds all scholars that publishing certain findings may not be worth the professional price. It reminds cultural conservatives to stay out of sociology. And it may tell those clandestine conservatives who labor away in the ivory tower's shadows that they are wise to stay right where they are—in the closet. Sociologist Christian Smith also wonders how the Regnerus scandal will affect the institution of peer review. "Prospective reviewers," Smith warned, "now know that their professional evaluations of the merits of scholarly papers they are asked to review are now in principle in doubt and are, in fact, subject to external questioning, reconsideration, and possible exposure by individuals appointed to audit them."[29]

Some professors we interviewed believe that the pressures to conform are powerful in the academy, even if scholars like Regnerus were not occasionally persecuted for stepping out of line. In this view, these social pressures develop as early as graduate school and continue through the formative years of one's career. As one literature professor explained,

> Most faculty members are timid people. . . . They've been graduate students, and [being a] graduate student is instruction in subservience. That's just what happens. Then, they go a couple of years in the job market, finally something comes through and they're so thankful. They are thankful and they've got to get that golden day of tenure. So, you spend five more years being collegial, getting along, doing the work that you think needs to be done. Then you get tenure. Now, after fifteen years of acculturation into cowardice and furtiveness, suddenly you're thirty-eight years old and now you're going to be [bold]—that doesn't happen. It doesn't happen. People are tired. They have kids. They've got bills to pay. They want life to be nice.

This professor understands that untenured conservatives must "keep [their] head bent," but he also wonders, "How many of them just continue on the same way?" After all, they have made their careers by acquiescing to liberal colleagues, by catering to the sensibilities of advisors, reviewers, and senior colleagues. "So, you're constantly thinking about the judgment of others, and this is the formula for conformity," he opined. Yet he also believes that some conservatives recoil from these pressures since they don't "worry about the mean looks of . . . colleagues up and down the hallway." A prominent historian expressed this concern in nearly the same way:

> If you hide what you believe to get a Ph.D. and say to yourself, 'When I get a job,' then to get a job, you hide yourself. Then you get a job and you say, 'Well, to get tenure, let me wait till I get tenure,' and then it's 'I don't want to be an associate professor all my life, let me wait till I get a full professor,' then it's 'Let me wait till I get a chair.'

"It always gets deferred, and dishonesty with yourself and the world and your colleagues becomes a habit," he lamented.

Professor E—the political scientist from our opening vignette—agrees with these indictments of higher education, particularly since he believes that the academy is not populated by especially courageous thinkers. "To be quite blunt, you don't want academics in your landing craft at Omaha Beach. So, for the more timid or faint of heart, there are a lot of barriers to entry and pressure to [conform]," he asserted. In E's view, such pressures are particularly powerful when a contentious political idea is at stake, such as the merits of the Bush Doctrine. In such cases, it is difficult for the typical graduate student to take on the liberal academic establishment. To do so, he added, is akin to "criticizing the College of Cardinals at the maximum point of papal claims to supremacy." Here again conservative academics echo a standard left-wing argument, since it is usually the left that expresses concern about the power of social institutions to cultivate deference to authority and conformity, while the right tends to regard such institutions more favorably.

Many conservatives do not share the rebellious identity and spirit of Professor E. But as the next chapter shows, such scholars often do not think they are sheep either. Instead, they believe that disciplinary pressures benefit their scholarship and keep the political impulses of their colleagues in their proper place.

6

The Limits of Liberalism

ON A BEAUTIFUL August weekend in Denver, Colorado, thousands of sociologists gathered together for their national conference, an annual migration that they have practiced now for more than a century. Organized around the theme of "Real Utopias," the Denver conference of the ASA resembled a right-wing parody of academia. According to the Marxist president of the ASA, Erik Olin Wright, building utopias in this world requires sociologists who can "elaborate utopian ideals that are grounded in the real potentials of humanity." One of Wright's presidential panels asked, "What Does it Mean to be a Progressive in the 21st Century?" And the lead plenary session on "Equality" featured a "30-minute spoken word performance on social justice" by performers from the First Wave Hip Hop and Urban Arts learning community from the University of Wisconsin. The conference also included an "all genre" jam session.[1] And for those hoping to usher in a genderless utopia, the bathrooms in the Denver Convention Center were marked with signs that read "Unisex."

As Wright was lining up progressive performers for the Denver convention, economists were gathering for their annual conference in Chicago's cold winter. The scene at the American Economic Association's (AEA) meeting could not have been more different from that engineered by Professor Wright. There were no instructions on how to be a modern progressive, no unisex bathrooms, no performances or jam sessions on behalf of equality, and no Marxist president. The AEA did have a presidential address that year. However, it was titled "The Nature of Liquidity Provision," a subject that one would hardly describe as revolutionary.[2] In fact, liquidity provision is probably a topic of greater interest to the Koch brothers than to the typical sociologist.

The Chicago meeting of the AEA should remind us that the progressive hegemony over the social sciences and humanities is far from absolute. Economics is not merely the only social science discipline in which conservatives are well represented—it is also increasingly unified by assumptions and insights that are friendly to conservative points of view. As movements in the sixties and seventies pushed other disciplines leftward, economics tacked right. It did so partly because of the failures of those same equity-minded thinkers to manage the economy well, a development that renewed many economists' respect for markets. Given these developments, we should hardly be surprised that conservative professors tend to gravitate toward economics far more frequently than toward any other discipline in the social sciences and humanities. They also rarely consider themselves a stigmatized minority.[3]

But even in the other humanistic and social scientific disciplines, conservatives gravitate toward intellectual spaces that are relatively insulated from liberal passions. In these relatively safe spaces, the deepest divides are often primarily intellectual in nature, though they are sometimes connected to politics in more subtle ways. In these intellectual divisions, many conservatives find common ground with colleagues to their left. Conservative philosophers, for example, unite with liberal colleagues in the "analytic" tradition against "continental" theory. Traditionalists in history tend to resist disciplinary fads, whatever their politics. Meanwhile, defenders of the humanities, whether liberal or conservative in their politics, rally together to fight curricular battles, especially by defending "great books." And in political science, wars over methodology divide the discipline more deeply than partisanship. Thus, some conservative professors thrive, despite their numbers, because they share with their liberal colleagues a common intellectual orientation that is more important than their political differences.

While many conservatives find tolerant academic niches that are free of political pressures, a few say that their politics actually helped them intellectually, and sometimes even professionally. This is because conservatism sometimes allows academics to identify novel questions and interpretations, and because right-wing professors have managed to colonize a handful of departments. As our chronicle of Professor E's professional odyssey in the last chapter should remind us, there are, in fact, some important islands of conservatism in academia. This chapter therefore focuses on the limits of liberalism by highlighting the different ways in which conservatives thrive in academia.

Economics: The Moderate Social Science

Economics is odd. Surveys of faculty consistently show that economists are far more likely to be on the right than professors of any other discipline in the humanities and social sciences. According to recent surveys, the partisanship of economists mirrors the broader American public, with roughly equal proportions of Republicans and Democrats (see Table 6.1). Unlike the public, however, the discipline of economics is not plagued by partisan polarization. Those who study economics share common theoretical assumptions and methodological approaches that tend to moderate their partisan differences. For these reasons, the economists we interviewed do not feel discriminated against, nor do they ever feel the need to hide their political views.

Many conservative economists we interviewed emphasized a commitment to scientific rigor. As an economist at a prestigious university put it, "[politics is] just not what we're focused on that much." He explained:

We're more focused on, 'Did you ask interesting questions? Did you do the model well? Did you understand the method?' . . . It's a science thing. People's view of the science may be affected by their underlying values, but there is a common language, a common framework, a common methodology.

Table 6.1 Partisanship in Six Disciplines

	Smith and Others			Gross and Simmons		
	(R)	(I)	(D)	(R)	(I)	(D)
Economics	33	33	33	29	37	34
Political Science	16	36	48	6	44	50
Philosophy	10	30	60	—	—	—
History	8	29	63	4	17	79
Literature	6	21	74	2	47	51
Sociology	3	26	72	6	45	49

Source: Bruce L. R. Smith, Jeremy D. Mayer, and A. Lee Fritschler, *Closed Minds? Politics and Ideology on American Campuses* (Washington, DC: Brookings Institution Press, 2008), 77–78; Neil Gross and Solon Simmons, "The Social and Political Views of American Professors," Working Paper, September 24, 2007, 34.

This professor said that his work environment was so depoliticized that he was a colleague of Ben Bernanke for fifteen years without knowing his partisan affiliation. "I didn't find out until he was selected to be on [George W. Bush's] Council of Economic Advisors that he was a Republican," he recalled. "I just didn't know.... [F]ifteen years in the same department and it had never come up."

Others echoed this general account. An economist at an Ivy League University contrasted the depoliticizing effects of the quantitative methods that dominate economics with the softer, more qualitative approaches that are more prevalent in other disciplines. Economists cannot "spin stories," as he put it, because "the math, the modeling rubs your face in what you're doing and if the thing doesn't hold together, the math just blows up on you." Another economist at an elite research university also stressed the way methodological and technical concerns depoliticize the discipline. "If you picked up any of the leading journals, you would have no idea what anyone's politics were by looking at the articles," he informed us. "That means that unless I talk to people about their politics, I don't even know what they are." Given the remoteness of politics to many economists' identities, it is not surprising that this professor told us, "I don't think of myself as conservative economist, I think of myself as an economist."

Because the professional identities of economists are sometimes stripped of their deeper values and ideals, the discipline can seem harshly careerist and meritocratic. An economist at a private research university explained the fierce side of economics in blunt terms: "They don't care about you. They care about your publications. If you're a communist, or anarchist, libertarian, we don't care. If you can hit the [*Journal of Political Economy*], you are going to get tenure here. That's the sole currency of the realm." Nothing else seems to matter.

Many of the core theoretical insights of economics, moreover, tend to at least cultivate an openness to free-market principles, such as the efficiency of even imperfect markets, opportunity costs, marginalism, cost-benefit analyses, incentives, externalities, and the limits of the state's ability to direct and manage the economy. None of these ideas demand allegiance to the politics of a Milton Friedman, of course. But these ideas do make it difficult to accept Marxism, and they at least grant someone with Friedman's politics a hearing. Above all, perhaps, the core economic concepts like incentives and efficiency constrain equity-minded economists by requiring them to reckon with the practical limits of their own egalitarian ideals.

Many conservative economists seemed at home in their discipline as they explained the compatibility of economic assumptions and insights with their politics. One told us,

> Almost every economist is sympathetic to the view that government actions can have unintended consequences. You may or may not think the unintended consequences are worse than the disease you're trying to cure, but every economist is open to the notion that we should think both about the benefit side of interventions and about the cost side.

In this way, he believes that economics brings scholars "halfway toward . . . the consequentialist libertarian perspective. . . . So there is nothing in the . . . DNA of economics that makes them hostile to libertarians. . . . [I]t's totally open."

Others agreed. A professor at a regional public university believes that his discipline's foundational assumptions and insights moderate economists with a progressive bent. As he noted with appreciation, "I think that even Keynesian economists will admit that markets generate usually the outcomes we want or the outcomes that we think are the best, [and] that market failures are the exceptions, not the rule." A second economist recalled the conservatism of his graduate education this way: "Economics just kind of pounds into you the notion of opportunity cost, that there are no free lunches. And that builds an inherent conservatism into people, because you're trying to think about opportunity costs, you're trying to think about unintended consequences." A third offered a similar, if more tempered, assessment: "I think almost all economists have some respect for the properties of the invisible hand, Adam Smith, and so forth." Certainly one could not draw the same blanket conclusion of many other disciplines in the social sciences and humanities.

Perhaps the most telling reminder of the broad intellectual consensus that reigns in economics was hearing conservative economists praise Paul Krugman, the social democratic voice of the *New York Times*. The conservative economists we interviewed not only praised his skill as an economist, but also declared that they agree with his scholarly work. One professor, for example, called Krugman a "great economist" and said his articles on trade have "good economics in there, based on time-tested, market-based ideas." Another even confessed, "[I]n many respects there is not much difference between Paul Krugman and me." Krugman would agree, he said, "[that] markets do a damn good job of allocating resources and generating opportunity and prosperity, and even protecting our free-doms." This economist suspected that he and Krugman disagree only "on the ability of government to come in ... [and] improve upon some of the more glaring errors of markets."

Likewise, it is not unusual for leftist economists to identify substantial common ground with economists far to their right. Herb Gintis, who founded the Union for Radical Economists in 1968, found much to agree with in a 2008 review of Thomas Sowell's *Basic Economics*. Despite disagreeing with some of Sowell's emphases, he still recommended Sowell's book: "*Basic Economics* comes pretty close to being a neutral exposition of what economists know about running the economy. There is no statement of fact, no statement of economic principle in this book with which I disagree, even though my background is from the Left, and I have never voted for a Republican in my life, and Sowell is the arch-conservative guru of Hoover Institution fame."[4]

This broad intellectual consensus among economists has enjoyed strong institutional support, especially by the National Bureau of Economic Research (NBER), an organization explicitly devoted to supporting economic research regardless of ideology. According to an economist at a prestigious university, the NBER promotes "fusion in the economics profession" by serving "as a facilitating device for top economists from a variety of ideological persuasions to interact....I think it's been very useful and very productive for the economic profession." On a personal note, he added that NBER conferences have created an intellectual space for him to exchange ideas with prominent scholars to his left. A further indication of the NBER's ideological neutrality is the fact that Martin Feldstein of Harvard was its director for twenty-seven years, even though he served as Ronald Reagan's chairman of economic advisors and has done significant work on the harmful effects of high marginal tax rates on economic growth. It is almost impossible to imagine a conservative leading such a significant organization for so long a tenure in any other discipline in the social sciences or humanities.

This tolerance matters. Unlike so many of their right-wing colleagues in other disciplines, conservative economists feel no sense of being victims of ideological bias. One economist, for example, reported that he has "always been treated well in academia" despite his free-market enthusiasms. He acknowledges that there may be discrimination against conservatives in other disciplines, but not in economics. He rejected the view that conservative economists face discrimination in emphatic terms: "It's just wrong."

Nearly without exception, economists echoed the same unqualified praise for their discipline's tolerance. An economist at a large state university reported that he was easily tenured even though "they all knew I was very free-market libertarian, [but] I was publishing in the right places, [and] that's what mattered." Similarly, an economist at a state university found his home discipline a welcoming one. "I haven't borne any costs personally," he said. This economist reported a tolerant work environment even though he acknowledged that his research might "seem to suggest the benefits of free markets and less government interference." Another economist reported, "I think economics is a fairly tolerant discipline. We like talking with one another, and don't want to cast one another out." And they enjoy conversing because economists share a similar theoretical and methodological orientation, whatever their political differences. This is why *only one* economist reported concealing his politics prior to tenure.

While many economists seem surprisingly parochial in their innocence of the politicization of other disciplines, some appreciate the discipline's insulation from radical political movements. For example, an economist who teaches at a large public university emphasized the isolation of economics from the political currents that wash over other disciplines. "I mean, you can only find two or three people in my faculty who'd know what postmodernism is," he estimated. What economists do share, in this subject's account, is a common allegiance to "ruling paradigms." "[A]nd to us, they're ruling paradigms in the profession, they are not ideologies."

In fact, many conservative economists believe that their discipline has become *more tolerant* of scholars who harbor free-market ideals since the 1960s and 1970s. The regulatory experiments of that era helped to revive economists' traditional appreciation of markets. Steven Rhoads highlighted this unintended consequence of Great Society liberalism in *The Economist's View of the World*. In that study Rhoads observed that "many economists' skepticism about government's ability to improve much upon the performance of imperfect markets comes from their recent experience with economic regulation and antitrust policy."[5] The Nobel Prize winners in economics during the 1970s and 1980s also reflected this renewed appreciation for markets. Prominent libertarian thinkers were honored with the award in those decades, including Milton Friedman, Friedrich Hayek, George Stigler, and James Buchanan.

Many conservative economists are grateful for the rightward turn in economics and the pioneers that led the way, such as Buchanan and Friedman. "Today, I would say, [economics is] vastly more open," one professor told us. "If we were in the 1940s or 1950s [and] if you were not an avowed Keynesian, you were not allowed to teach at any university," he said. There were some exceptions, he allowed. In that era the redoubts of classical economics included Hillsdale, Grove City College, and, importantly, the University of Chicago, which our interviewee described as "the only other place that offered a glimmer of hope out of that darkness of Keynesian dominance." But today *even* Berkeley—that former bastion and enduring symbol of professorial liberalism—is producing Ph.D.s whom conservative economists admire. One economist confessed that he would be "delighted to hire somebody coming out of Berkeley, if we could possibly attract one here. But, you know, thirty to forty years ago, they were left-wing loonies."

Conservatives have not destroyed Keynesianism, of course. Today's Keynesians are just much less sanguine about the ability of the state to direct economic growth. As one prominent economist explained, they used to believe that central planners could "fine tune" the economy, but Keynesians "don't spout that stuff today." And while Keynesians do believe that the state could theoretically intervene effectively, they recognize that the political process often frustrates their prescriptions.

Even in the era of Keynesian dominance, however, economists were more moderate in their politics than their colleagues in other social sciences were. As Everett Carl Ladd and Seymour Martin Lipset's classic work on the academy noted, "economics [is] located on the conservative side of the human behavior disciplines."[6] In 1959 George Stigler also emphasized the relative conservatism of economists compared to other professors and the "educated classes generally." Stigler acknowledged that the discipline had been blown leftward by the "strong wind" of New Deal liberalism, but he nonetheless found it "remarkable" that economics "shall not be contributing to the wind."[7] Stigler's insights seem prophetic in light of the reticence of economists to embrace various egalitarian economics policies in the 1970s. "It is striking," reflected Steven Rhoads, "that there is almost no support for any of these price control measures even among the most equity-conscious economists."[8]

Precisely why economics dampened enthusiasm for such prescriptions is less clear. Stigler believed that the conservatism of economists is best explained by their empirical findings, which are grounded in the most advanced methods. In his view, a radical left orientation is difficult to maintain after one studies economics:

> It becomes impossible ... to believe that a small group of selfish capitalists dictates the main outlines of the allocation of resources and the determination of outputs. It becomes impossible for him to believe that men of good will can by their individual actions stem inflation or that it is possible to impose changes on any one market or industry without causing problems in other markets or industries. He cannot unblushingly repeat slogans such as 'production for use rather than for profit.' He cannot believe that a change in the form of social organization will eliminate basic economic problems.[9]

Perhaps the intellectual foundations of the discipline, which are usually traced to Adam Smith's *The Wealth of Nations*, are simply too well laid for the discipline to drift far to the left. As an economist at a public research university explained, the history of the discipline has shown that it was "hard to expunge" a deep respect for markets from economics, even in the wake of the Great Depression. Another economist made the same point by recalling memories of student radicalism in Students for a Democratic Society (SDS) during the 1960s. In his telling, the economics majors who participated in SDS were always more tempered in their radicalism than their comrades from other disciplines. He recalled,

> It was very funny to observe the meetings, because there would be students from other departments who'd say things like, 'Well everything should be free.' These economics radicals [would then reply], 'Well maybe that's not such a good idea.'

And, of course, history has shown that markets tend to function remarkably well, especially when compared with their alternatives. Today even social scientists who are hardly conservatives, such as Jonathan Haidt, suggest that if one gives any thought to the way markets work, it is difficult to find them anything less than "miraculous."[10]

Table 6.2 Self-Identified Libertarians
by Discipline

	Libertarians	N
Economics	77%	30
Philosophy	29%	14
Literature	26%	23
Political Science	22%	37
History	19%	26
Sociology	0%	12
N:		142

Table 6.3 Support for Same-Sex Marriage by Discipline

	Favor	Oppose	Don't' Know	N
Economics	79%	10%	10%	29
Philosophy	36%	64%	0%	14
History	32%	64%	4%	25
Political Science	24%	68%	8%	37
Literature	17%	74%	9%	23
Sociology	17%	67%	17%	12
N:				140

But if economic training moderates even SDS radicals, it may also undermine support for social conservatism. Most of the economists we interviewed were libertarians who expressed outright hostility to cultural conservatives. In fact, nearly 80% of the economists we interviewed self-identified as libertarians (see Table 6.2). And while large majorities opposed same-sex marriage in every other discipline we surveyed, only 10% of the economists did likewise (see Table 6.3). This may be because libertarians are especially attracted to the discipline of economics. An education in economics might also cultivate libertarianism, since it teaches students to demoralize choices through an emphasis on consumer sovereignty and the subjectivity of value. As an economist at a private university in the South explained, "whether you buy a Snickers bar or Milky Way isn't a matter of right and wrong. It's just a subjective choice, because somebody likes caramel or something." Whatever the causes, conservative economists tend to see most choices, whether they are chocolate bars or heroin, as simply different lifestyle choices. And so economics is a discipline in which social conservatives seem as scarce as Marxists.

To be sure, some of the most radical libertarian economists labor outside the discipline's mainstream. But this is not due to their politics. It is because they are committed to the beleaguered "Austrian school" of economics, a camp that criticizes the mainstream for its scientism. According to Austrians, the most significant aspects of economic life are far too complex to be modeled or understood through the methods of modern social science. This orientation, however, makes it difficult for Austrians to develop an active research agenda. As one prominent economist explained,

> The Austrian stuff you hear today seems to me to be pretty much the same Austrian stuff forty years ago or even close to a hundred years ago now. It's correct, but taking it to the next level in academic journals is really hard, because it's really hard to quantify this stuff.

Another economist quipped,

> [S]aying we are going to do our economics and stop using math and statistics is a little like saying we are going to write all our articles in Esperanto. You can have some really good ideas, but you're not going to have many readers.

The result is that Austrians have little new to say to a discipline built around the assumption that economics is a normal science that can incrementally build a body of scientific knowledge.

Austrian economists, however, see the mainstream's methodological orientation, while superficially ideologically neutral, as nonetheless biased toward a status quo that accepts a much larger role for governmental power than they would prefer. As one of the rare Austrian economists at a major research university explained, "[I]f you're not concerned about ideology or policy and you're more concerned about applied mathematics, the default is you basically accept the prevailing ideology." It is a long-standing objection of radical Austrian economists. When George Stigler wrote his influential article on the affinities between conservatism and economics, the Austrian Murray Rothbard offered a characteristically sharp response. While Rothbard acknowledged that economics probably "imposes a rightward shift in ideological belief," he objected to Stigler's thesis because the collection of statistical data serves the needs of the state. "In a free market economy," Rothbard wrote, "the individual business firm has little or no need of statistics. It need only know its prices and costs." The state, however, has different needs. As Rothbard explained,

> [S]tatistics are the bureaucrat's only form of economic knowledge, replacing the intuitive, 'qualitative' knowledge of the entrepreneur. Accordingly, the drive for government intervention, and the drive for more statistics have gone hand in hand.

Worse still, Rothbard objected that the scientism of economics creates an illusion that the government can control the economy so long as it is guided by economic expertise.[11]

Austrians also accuse mainstream scholars of reducing the study of economics to what can be easily measured, thereby excluding more fundamental and philosophical questions. As one professor told us,

> Economics has become an area of applied mathematics with the ideological things taking backstage. So for me as an Austrian, what's more important is the fact that Austrians have wider social, scientific, and philosophical interests.

Another economist lamented what he regarded as the increasing narrowness and triviality of economic research. "You end up focusing on what the streetlight illuminates," and doing so requires one to "forego a lot of the really most relevant considerations in judging policy matters," he observed.

Pockets of leftist economists level similar critiques against the economic mainstream. The economics department at the University of Massachusetts at Amherst, for example, offers a graduate education committed to social justice. Like the libertarian Austrians, the leftists at Amherst feel marginalized by the discipline and accuse it of reducing the study of economics to questions that are easy to quantify. The progressive *Journal of Post Keynesian Economics* is an organ for such criticisms, having been founded in 1978 to address the many important issues that are neglected by the discipline's mainstream. In the journal's second issue, for example, Donald Katzner criticized economists for their lack of interest in "important phenomenon" of special concern to egalitarians, such as the "vague political, social, and psychological pressures" that influence "labor-management disputes" or the fair distribution of income. Although this latter question "cannot even be approached without a theory of 'justice,'" Katzner observed, "'positive' economists take pride in exorcising any such theory on the grounds that what cannot be measured is not 'scientific,' or that value judgments are exogenous."[12]

Katzner's intellectual affinities with the Austrians far to his right highlight two important truths about economics. First, progressives and conservatives are well represented on both sides of this methodological divide. Second, mainstream economics tends to frustrate those scholars with strong ideological and normative orientations, regardless of whether they are on the equity-minded left or libertarian right.

Moderation and Diversity in Other Disciplines

While economics enjoys a broad intellectual consensus, political science is fractured into many competing camps. The late Gabriel Almond compared political science to a school cafeteria in which various cliques dine at their own tables. Reaching for a more cosmopolitan metaphor, Bernard Grofman likened political science to a "dim sum brunch."[13] Allan Bloom, meanwhile, compared political science to a "rather haphazard bazaar with shops kept by a mixed population."[14] Significantly, many of Bloom's shopkeepers are indifferent and sometimes even friendly to conservative points of view. These camps include behaviorism, rational choice, realism, and, of course, Bloom's own Straussianism. Beyond the pluralism, there may also be something about the orientation of the discipline that tends to moderate political scientists. In *The Divided Academy*, Ladd and Lipset accounted for the relative conservatism of political science by pointing to the nature of its subject matter. As they observed,

> Political scientists have occupied themselves with the problems of government and governing, and so have tended to be more exposed to, and hence sympathetic with, the problems and perspectives of politicians who must make hard, pragmatic, expedient, 'half-a-loaf' decisions.[15]

More recently, James Ceaser and Robert Maranto offered a similar explanation. Grappling with the "harsh" problems of terrorism, war, and violent revolutions, they noted, will tend to "sober the mind and produce a highly realistic approach."[16] Whatever the precise causes, the relative tolerance of political science attracts conservatives into its ranks. With the exception of economics, in fact, political science boasts a higher percentage of Republican professors than any other fields in the social sciences and humanities (see Table 6.1).

Though political science remains a pluralistic discipline, behaviorism is now its dominant intellectual tradition. It is a tradition that attempts to apply some of the core principles of logical positivism to the study of politics. Most important, behaviorists strive to conduct value-free inquiries by purging the study of politics of its normative dimensions. Instead of addressing what ought to be done, it investigates the political world as it is. But its aim is not merely to provide more accurate descriptions of political phenomena. Political behaviorists believe that if they dispassionately use the methods of the natural sciences, they will also uncover patterns and regularities in political life. New laws of political behavior might even be discovered. Unearthing these patterns or laws would then allow political scientists to make accurate political predictions.

Given this general orientation, political behaviorists have been especially receptive to the theoretical assumptions and methods of economics, especially rational-choice theory. As Ceaser and Maranto observed, this school of thought originated in the "ideas of political economy that emerged from the libertarian 'Virginia school' of James Buchanan and Gordon Tullock." Most rational-choice thinkers are not devotees of libertarianism, of course. But as Ceaser and Maranto note, economic assumptions tend to cultivate "skepticism of traditional left-of-center approaches to public policy."[17]

Some of our subjects agreed. A political scientist at a research university reflected, "One of the things that rational choice does is that, given the way that collective action occurs, feeling the right way, having the right preferences, is no guarantee that it will produce a policy with good outcomes." And, in any case, actors in politics, he continued, tend to "have motives that are a lot like [corporate executives], they want to get more money and get more power, too." Another political scientist acknowledged that rational-choice theory compels one to place "constraints on what could be done" through public policy by always keeping both costs and benefits in view.

More generally, behaviorists of all stripes emphasize the importance of methodological rigor. One political scientist acknowledges that although he is close with other conservative scholars, they do not discuss politics much. Instead, they talk "a lot of shop," which is to say, they mostly chatter about fairly arcane theoretical and methodological issues in political science. Another recalled how few political discussions he participated in as a graduate student in political science. "It was more about causal processes and that kind of stuff," he said.

Some conservative political scientists believe that quantitative methods not only offer powerful tools for investigating the political world—they also restrain the ideological passions of their progressive colleagues. "I'm a hard-nosed quantitative behavioralist," announced a political scientist at a state university. This subject is "hard-nosed" partly because he has "some sensitivity about being a conservative in a liberal profession." As he put it, "I think it's all the more important that we address things in as objective a way as possible, because if you leave political scientists alone to themselves without strict methods or the rigor of methods, then that allows their biases to run rampant." He also looks askance at Perestroika, a movement in political science that sought to open the discipline to more qualitative approaches, calling it "largely left wing" and "soft" methodologically, a mixture that is hardly accidental in his view. Even some qualitative political scientists appreciate the constraints quantitative methods impose on ideological minds. "It prevents you from saying truly stupid shit," one such scholar acknowledged. "It keeps people more honest than they would otherwise be."

Some conservative political scientists, however, were active in the Perestroika movement precisely because they believe that understanding politics involves deeper normative and philosophical questions that should not be marginalized. "At first you could see that [Perestroika] was New Left, [but] it was immediately clear that there was some basis of an alliance," he recalled. This is because Perestroika's ends were never merely leftist ones. In fact, in one critical sense Perestroika was a conservative movement, since it called the discipline back to its traditional respect for varied approaches to the study of politics. Perestroika was at once revolutionary and old-fashioned. But, of course, if a qualitative revolution ever succeeded in political science, it is not clear the discipline would be friendly to the scholarship of conservative Perestroikans.

As such testimonies might suggest, usually the deepest conflicts in political science are only tangentially related to politics. Even a prominent political scientist well known for his ideological bomb throwing acknowledged this, noting that conservatives in his department usually unite with liberals who share their general approach to political science. A behaviorist

at a public research university reported a similar dynamic in his department. "I think it's much more likely when we split, it will be on methodological grounds," he acknowledged.

We were sensitized to the depth of the methodological cleavage in
political science even before we conducted our first interview. As we were
developing our sample, it quickly became evident that qualitative- and
quantitative-oriented conservatives in political science did not generally
know one another. Qualitative political scientists tended to name other
qualitative scholars, while quantitative scholars usually identified other
quantitative political scientists.

The American Political Science Association (APSA) has responded to
these conflicts by adopting a "federalist" approach that allows factions to
receive formal recognition if they demonstrate appeal. When the panels
of organized factions attract large audiences—at least by the standards of
academic conferences—then they receive additional slots at future conferences. This has helped preserve disciplinary peace with conservatives and
other heterodox movements within the discipline. At every APSA conference, for example, the conservative Claremont Institute has ten to twelve
panels. Smaller and more obscure clusters of conservative scholars, such
as those devoted to the work of German émigré Eric Voegelin, also host
multiple panels.

Because of the relative methodological and political pluralism of political science, it has become something of a default discipline for right-
wing students who might have pursued graduate work in other fields,
especially history, sociology, philosophy, and even literature. Thus, unlike
liberal scholars, conservatives' decisions to specialize in one field rather
than another take place within a relatively constrained set of professional
choices.

But that does not mean that disciplines outside of political science
are inflexibly hostile to conservatives. Even in sociology, where conservatives are much scarcer than in other social sciences, right-wing professors occasionally find common intellectual ground with colleagues
far to their left. One of our subjects recounted a presentation he gave at
the annual meeting of the ASA on the fluidity and mutability of homo-
sexual identities. He concluded his paper by arguing that gay identities
were not simply hardwired; "some element of social construction" was
at work too. The reception was unexpected: "I was pleasantly surprised
that there was a lot of openness, there was a lot of willingness to discuss it. Sociologists, as a rule, if you've got an argument and a data

set, they're willing to listen." And, of course, sociology has traditionally stressed the constructed nature of social reality—a perspective at odds with those arguments generally made on behalf of gay rights. It was this sociological orientation that created space for a more conservative perspective. As our subject explained, "I found openness, because the idea that gay identity is constructed is still pretty well accepted by sociologists." In a more general way, an aging and prominent sociologist said that he still believes that "a scholarly person can succeed" in sociology, even if they are conservative. "There's enough meritocracy that even ... people who are personally deranged [can] nevertheless appreciate scholarship," he observed.

A sociologist who nearly was denied tenure on account of his politics nonetheless regarded quantitative methodologies as an important constraint on partisan minds. He noted, for example, that all quantitative scholars now accept the truth that children fare better in stable, two-parent homes, on average, since "it's clear in the regressions." But that acceptance is not universal. As he explained, "[T]he kind of people who do more qualitative or theoretical work never have to confront a regression equation that may not behave like they hope it would. And so they can kind of construct a world in their own mind," such as one in which "family structure is really unimportant." Sometimes an obsession with methods can become more depoliticized still, even in sociology. As Peter Berger reflected long ago, "it is quite true that some sociologists, especially in America, have become so preoccupied with methodological questions that they have ceased to be interested in society at all."[18]

Although many disciplines in the humanities are no friendlier to conservatives than sociology, right-wing scholars often find particular subfields or theoretical orientations that tend to mute ideological differences. In philosophy, for example, the analytical tradition was often praised by conservative and libertarian philosophers for its emphasis on logical rigor, an orientation that limits the importance of politics. One of our subjects attended UCLA, which is distinguished for its strength in analytical philosophy. He praised the intellectual rigor and integrity of the department: "I think they may have known [about my politics], but they absolutely didn't care. It was a pretty technical place, logic was very highly prized, and so for that reason they had the sense that ... what matters is philosophy." A libertarian philosopher lauded his graduate education in similar terms:

I have to mention that even though my professors in graduate school who were supervising my project weren't particularly committed to the work I was doing intellectually, they were very supportive of the fact that I was doing it.... [M]y main adviser was not a libertarian, but he never gave me a hard time about my project.... [H]e just said, 'Well, if this is the project you're going to do, then you have to write this chapter like this and don't forget to do this.'

And when we asked another philosopher about his experiences seeking employment, he replied, "Politics could [have] come up, I suppose ... but it just never did. What they ask you is what do you think of this theory or how would you explain this or what courses would you teach." A different philosopher made the same point when we inquired about his experiences on the job market. "There really [weren't] any political tests that I could tell," he remembered. "It was really do the arguments work."

One libertarian philosopher at a state university even recalled feeling bewildered as a graduate student when he encountered a concerned conservative historian who urged caution around liberal academics. "I sat there thinking, 'Man, what has happened to you?'" he remembered. "Maybe something did happen ... [but] I think what all my professors [wanted in graduate school], and I think this now about my colleagues, is good arguments. And whatever the conclusions are, it doesn't matter as long as you can provide good arguments," he declared.

Of all the philosophers we interviewed, not one worked in continental philosophy. We do not think this is because there is something about the thinkers in this tradition (such as Husserl or Heidegger) that repels conservatives. To the contrary, there have been some rather deep conservative scholars who were quite engaged in continental political thought, such as Leo Strauss and Eric Voegelin. Instead, it seems that conservatives gravitate toward analytical philosophy partly because its rigor restrains the moral and political passions of progressives. Those conservatives interested in continental theorists, however, sometimes gravitate toward the subfield of political theory in political science—a reminder that it serves as something of a refuge for many conservative thinkers outside economics.

The discipline of history, meanwhile, is no friendlier to conservative perspectives than philosophy—probably less so. As the intellectual historian Peter Novick observed, the study of history "has been relatively untouched by conservative [intellectual] currents."[19] Nonetheless, conservatives have been able to locate a few subfields in history that are largely sheltered from political agendas. One interviewee, for example, said that in ancient history, where he is a specialist, it is difficult to gin up interpretations that speak to today's controversies. "We're all in agreement that those [ancient] societies were politically extremely unpleasant. I mean it doesn't matter what your [political] position is, you rarely approve of things like slavery," he observed. Partly because the study of classical antiquity is so removed from contemporary political concerns and sensibilities, this professor believes that conservatives are drawn to it. As he explained, "If you are conservative, there [are] such huge no-go zones. You can't do huge areas of contemporary or modern history, particularly in American [history], because it's inflected by race." But one can study ancient Greece or Rome, without the risk of getting "fired" for right-wing views. Thus, this subject suspects that "Classics is probably the only realm in humanistic disciplines where there is a political split that reflects the nation as a whole."

One danger of such subfields, aside from the fact that they are unfashionable, is that they can be branded as conservative. An expert in military history reported that his subfield is regarded "as being hopelessly and insufferably on the right and that marks you." But such complaints underscore our point: Some subfields in history are not hostile to conservative academics.

In some cases, professors' common views on the liberal arts mute ideological differences. A professor who teaches political theory at a state research university said that she allies with traditionalists in the literature and philosophy departments to defend a traditional "great books" curriculum. "So even if we might disagree on political matters, we form a kind of united front in terms of . . . our academic values," she told us. Another political theorist was also pleased to find many colleagues to his left that shared his curricular orientation. As he put it, "Not everyone was politically a conservative, but nearly everyone was a kind of great books type, and interested in undergraduate education. . . . We were all interested in acquainting students . . . with great moral questions." And although a literature professor described his department as "eighty to ninety percent" Democratic, he also shares what he called a common "literature orientation" with his colleagues, which includes an opposition to the "political correctness that is widely spread in the other departments."

An appreciation for a traditional liberal arts education also inclines some conservatives to fight right-wing colleagues in economics and other fields that are more pre-professional in their orientation. "Quite frankly, there are people who come from the right who could care less about whether or not students read a certain amount of material or are intro-duced to a certain body of knowledge," noted one historian who teaches at a community college.

In a more personal way, one professor who teaches literature at a private regional university told us about the great intellectual affinity he shared with his Marxist mentor. They shared what this subject described as a similar "aesthetic appreciation," which drew them to similar authors. Still, he was surprised to discover that his mentor was also an avid admirer of G. K. Chesterton, a conservative Catholic and staunch defender of reli-gious orthodoxy. "It turns out he read all of Chesterton's detective work, and he admired Chesterton's work on Dickens," he recounted.

Occasionally the traditionalism of conservatives made for more pecu-liar alliances with leftist professors. For example, one of our subjects once taught at a women's college that considered becoming co-educational. He opposed the effort along with feminists who were committed to the col-lege's women-centered culture.

Professors at less selective institutions, meanwhile, were sometimes united by a common desire to remedy the deep educational deficits of their students. A literature professor from a state teaching college told us, "[W]hat binds us together is the sense that we're trying to do good for the students"—and doing good *does not* mean "empowering" them through radical pedagogies. Instead, everyone in his department generally agrees that their disadvantaged students are more "empowered by literacy" than any meditation on the works of Foucault or Marx. The demands of such basic educational needs sometimes frustrate conservatives. One literature professor reported that he does not bother introducing his students to libertarian ideas. Rather, he labors toward more fundamental objectives, such as helping his students "read a poem intelligently"—a task that he says gets "harder and harder every year." A political scientist at a Catholic college also has trouble engaging his students in political discussions, a failure that he blames on their poor academic preparation. He lamented, "I don't honestly know what they do in [high] school. They don't come to me with any basic understanding of history, not even the sequence of events. They don't come to me with writing skills."

While conservative professors sometimes regret the limits of what they can achieve in the classroom, there is no question that their students' press-ing needs create pedagogical common ground with colleagues to their left. A professor at a regional state college believes that his history syllabi do not look substantially different from his colleagues'. They all assign what he called "standard stuff" with little in the way of "heavily theory-laden" materials. Such content is avoided, he told us, "mainly because I don't think my typical eighteen-year-old freshman would get it. I have to accommodate the quality of [the] student body I am dealing with."

One historian at a research university believes that there are institutional and disciplinary pressures that moderate the humanities and social sciences as a whole—not just pockets within them. He particularly disagreed with Roger Kimball's indictment of the humanities in *Tenured Radicals*. "To claim that university life in the '80s and '90s was all about tenured radicals subverting the minds of the next generation is just obviously false," he declared. Contrary to some conservative critics of higher education, he especially emphasized the ways in which the modern academy tempers political passions. As he observed,

> First of all, the radicals who got tenure were scrupulous about the disciplines. They weren't just propagandists. And that itself has a very deradicalizing effect. Second, getting tenure itself has a very deradicalizing effect because you realize you are in fact part of an establishment and that your job now is to uphold it in its principles and traditions even if you think you're not.

In these respects, this historian regards the academy as a deeply conservative institution.

Of course, this same professor agrees with Kimball that the university can become a haven for political radicals. But he thinks such radicals are the exception to the rule. He recalled,

> When I came [to this university] and I looked around, I thought there are 10 or 12 people here on a faculty of 500 [that were tenured radicals]. But nobody in any of the science departments, nobody in psych, one or two in history, one or two in English, but . . . the scale of the allegation was completely disproportionate to the reality. And Kimball . . . he has got some interesting things to say about particular people, but they really are particular people.

Similarly, an economist at a state university criticized David Horowitz's campaign against political radicalism in higher education. He told us, "I am sure that there are appalling incidents of the kind that Horowitz specializes in highlighting, but it's . . . like the man bites dog stories. These things, they make news."

In a more indirect way, a political scientist at a research university noted the moderating influences of disciplinary expectations and norms. "To conservatives Paul Krugman is possibly the antichrist," he said. And though this interviewee does not venture nearly that far, he agrees that Krugman's editorializing for the *New York Times* is "fiscally crazy." Yet he also told us that Professor Krugman's professional scholarship on trade is "excellent." "It's as good as it gets," he gushed. "He deserved to win the Nobel Prize for that work." Thus, from this scholar's perspective, there are two Paul Krugmans walking about: Krugman the academic is shaped by powerful disciplinary demands that temper his thinking enough to impress conservatives, while Krugman the journalist is an undisciplined liberal hack. Politicization, in other words, happens in institutional contexts *outside the university*, at least in the case of moderate disciplines like economics.

Harvey Mansfield, an outspoken conservative and Harvard political scientist, has also implied that the academic life is less politicized than some conservatives insist. When Mansfield was asked about his conservative students who struggled to get academic jobs, he responded with characteristic mischievousness: "I guess they'll have to go to Washington and run the country."[20] And, indeed, some of his students left relatively arcane intellectual pursuits behind for the hurly-burly world of politics. Just consider Mansfield's most prominent student, Bill Kristol. Kristol's Ph.D. certainly reflected his politics. Journalist Nina Easton called it "a condemnation of activist courts." Yet Easton also reported that most of Kristol's dissertation was not overtly political, noting that most of its "494 pages are devoted to a Straussian-style meditation on what the authors of the *Federalist Papers*—Alexander Hamilton, James Madison, and John Jay—intended when they made their case in support of the U.S. Constitution."[21] Thus Kristol, the academic, was largely consumed with historical and philosophical interests that were at some remove from his politics. But outside the ivory tower's gate, Kristol was free to directly engage political causes, unfettered from the norms and pressures of academic publishing. He became an *untenured* radical.

The sociologist Tom Medvetz made a similar observation in a stronger way in his work on conservative think tanks and intellectuals "inside the Beltway." Working in these networks, Medvetz concludes, "confers on its members certain advantages not available to academic scholars, whose professional closure is more likely to isolate them from public and policy debates." Conservative intellectuals are therefore "shielded from the dangers of 'ivory tower' scholasticism."[22] Aside from the likelihood that Medvetz overstates the distance of the professoriate from political controversies and policy debates (as the next chapter contends), the very isolation of academics from the world outside their narrow intellectual silo can itself contribute to their radicalization. As the conservative intellectual Thomas Sowell noted, unlike financiers and engineers, there are no external standards that restrain, say, deconstructionists. "An engineer whose bridges or buildings collapse is ruined, as is a financier who goes broke," observed Sowell. "But the ultimate test of a deconstructionist's ideas," Sowell concluded, "is whether other deconstructionists find those ideas interesting, original, persuasive, elegant, or ingenious."[23] Likewise, Christian Smith noted recently, "most sociologists have for their professional conversation and debate partners primarily others who are focused on the same things that they are."[24] Nonetheless, scholasticism can isolate academics from contemporary political controversies, as Medvetz rightly emphasizes. That alienation can be frustrating to academics of all political stripes. Cut off even from other liberals in the larger society, many progressive professors do feel sealed behind something like what the sociologist Alvin Gouldner once called "self-barricaded intellectual ghettos."[25]

Some conservative professors we spoke with, meanwhile, wished they could engage in the sort of political editorializing Bill Kristol routinely does. They might do so more regularly if such commentating was not dismissed as mere journalism by their departments. This tendency, too, underscores the apolitical orientation of many academic departments, especially in economics. As one economist complained to us, "So, the publications I have in the [scholarly] journals, that looks great [to my colleagues], but then I have this other stuff on [my c.v.], and they essentially count that as negative." These "other," more popular venues, do not "count" because, as this economist put it, "they don't involve high-power mathematics or high-power econometrics or anything like that."

A few conservative professors found their liberal colleagues so agreeable that they doubted whether political discrimination even exists in higher education, though we found such skeptics primarily in the disciplines of economics and political science. One economist at a prestigious university, for example, believes that more self-interested motives drive conservative complaints. "I think it's just jealousy and frustration," he said. Not one to pull his punches, this economist threw another jab:

> I think it's unwillingness to say, 'He's at Harvard and I'm at South West Kentucky Community College.' It somehow makes you feel better if you say, 'It's because of a grand conspiracy theory,' rather than accepting, 'You know what? Maybe there is someone else who is just smarter than me.'

A political scientist at a research university also thinks that some plaintive right-wing thinkers deserve to wind up in lesser institutions. She observed, "Well, usually, I would say it is the second-raters, the ones who are not careful in terms of their own work or their own thoughts. You really need to be rigorous in your own work." Another economist agreed: "I think that there's a tendency among people, conservatives and libertarians, to exaggerate the extent to which their setbacks are due to their ideology. I mean, we all have our excuses."[26]

Rewards of Conservatism

Some conservatives even believe that they enjoy certain compensating advantages over their liberal peers. Conservatives, for example, told us that their peculiar cast of mind allows them to see the world in a different way. "If you're interested in things that other people aren't interested in, you can come up with a lot of really interesting stuff," one literature professor asserted. Sometimes that means simply identifying neglected topics. For example, one historian we interviewed wrote a dissertation on modern conservatism decades before it became fashionable to do so in history. A sociologist, meanwhile, wrote a book on anti-Americanism—an interesting topic, but hardly one that progressive academics gravitate toward. With apparent sincerity, another professor confessed, "I really do feel sorry for your absolutely conventional liberal scholar." He imagines that it must be difficult to discover something of "incremental additional value" from "within the framework of their thinking." But for a libertarian thinker in political science, it is far less challenging. As he explained, "[It is] very easy to do what is considered new and original in the profession. It's not innovative in the sense that you didn't innovate it, but it's innovative to [the academic] discussion."

Others made similar arguments more concretely. An accomplished historian told us,

> I do think that if you've got a conservative outlook, you're more willing to remember that there's nothing natural about the idea of human equality. In fact, it's actually very easy to make the argument that hierarchy is natural. And I think I can sometimes see that more clearly, partly because of my [working-class] background and partly because of how I've continued to think about things.

A sociologist at a research university also believes that his colleagues' pre-occupation with inequality creates opportunities for conservatives to offer fresh observations. "I mean, how many ways can you talk about inequality?" he wondered. Often inequality is "the only thing [sociologists] can see, [and so] they can't hear all the other interesting cultural things that are going on," he lamented. According to both professors, it is as if progressive academics suffer from an intellectual near-sightedness in which they can see everything in the background unusually well, but not many other objects that sit right under their noses.

Of course, many of our subjects also believe that the expression of distinctly conservative or libertarian perspectives presents its own dangers. Yes, there may be some low-hanging fruit on the tree of knowledge, but those who pick it worry they will be punished by their liberal gods for doing so. It is a risk many choose not to take, especially prior to tenure. But those who do take the gamble mention another reward. Not only does the academy sometimes prize fresh perspectives, outspoken conservatives also believe that it holds them to a higher standard. "I'm constantly challenged, because I'm challenging the prevailing view," one political scientist told us. And that "makes me sharper . . . more rigorous," she concluded. A Catholic philosopher made the same point more bluntly: "You can't be lazy. You can't—you're not going to be cut any slack and so you can't cut yourself any slack. I think that's a real advantage in so far as it makes the work better."

So, while conservatives complain about the unfair peer-review process, they also praise the additional scrutiny their work must endure. It is not necessarily an inconsistent set of beliefs. One accomplished sociologist said the higher review standards are a "good thing" so "long as the end results are fair." In practice, however, it is unlikely that a more scrutinized review process will always lead to the same outcome as a less critical one. Thus the greater intellectual pressures on conservatives are only purchased at some professional cost. Such are the trade-offs of being an outspoken conservative.

Other conservatives report that they benefited from right-wing networks, grants, and fellowships. One libertarian philosopher remembered feeling quite anxious about his job prospects after graduate school. But his anxiety did not last long. As he recalled,

> I was invited to participate in a seminar over the summer and met a senior libertarian political philosopher, hit it off, and he ended up inviting me to apply for a one-year job. That one-year job ended up lasting for three years and really made my career. I don't know if it's true that there really is this . . . hard-core bias against anybody who is not a leftist, but the [libertarian] social networks have been really helpful to my career.

His perspective was not universally shared. One Catholic philosopher told us,

> I know some people might say, 'Well, if you're a conservative in the academy, there are going to be libertarian and conservative organizations that are going to be willing to help you out and so forth and support that view in the academy.' But that's like saying if you have cancer, there's going to be somebody out there who's going to help you find a cure.

**Table 6.4 Right-Wing Professors
in Conservative-Majority Departments**

	Conservative Majority	N:
Economics	36%	25
Philosophy	21%	14
Political Science	17%	30
History	12%	25
Literature	4%	23
Sociology	0%	11
N:		134

"I don't know if I can call it an advantage," he concluded.

Meanwhile, in political science, history, philosophy, and economics, there are conservative departments that tend to hire like-minded scholars (see Table 6.4). Some scholars even go their entire professional careers without ever being a political minority in their own department. In these cases one's conservative politics helps, rather than hinders, one's career. One philosopher we interviewed was hired long ago at a southern university known for its conservatism. As he remembered it, "The fact that I was a very active conservative Republican and had been a military chaplain for a short time influenced the hire. In other words, it wasn't a negative, it was quite positive." He even affirmed that the university president who hired him was explicit about the virtues of his conservatism. "Well most all philosophers are communists," our interviewee remembered the president informing him, "but, since you've been in the military and you're a minister and you worked with the Republican Party, you'll probably fit in here." Another professor suspected that his "libertarian views were actually a selling point" when he was offered a job at a military college. After all, he attested, "I can talk about the Declaration of Independence like I mean it." A political scientist at a Catholic college also believes that he owes his current post in part to his conservatism. "I was hired, strangely, because I was a conservative," he told us. "It was clear that people there wanted to hire someone . . . [with] a conservative and classical liberal perspective."

Sometimes religious institutions are even drawn to cultural conservatives. One philosopher we interviewed was hired in a department that was created to re-Catholicize the college. As he explained, the department's purpose was to stop "the drift in the university and the attenuation of its sense of identity and mission that resulted from the concerted effort to hire non-Catholic faculty." But this project required a new openness to social conservatives, since the college could not claim to represent Catholic ideas without taking seriously conservative views about abortion and marriage.

There is at least one more benefit to being a conservative academic. Because they are small in number, conservative academics find it easier to find their way into conservative media outlets or presidential campaigns than their progressive peers do. "[T]here's one advantage, which is if one is interested in policy jobs, [it is easier to land one]," a prominent economist asserted. This is because, he explained, "the number on my team is smaller than the number on the other team, especially since some of the conservative economists are so disdainful of government that they don't even want to work for it." A political scientist offered a similar observation. When this interviewee came out of the closet, he began reaching out to conservative foundations, magazine editors, and think tanks. He then discovered "a real asymmetry," as he put it. While being a conservative in the academy "was only downgrading," he noted, "within the conservative movement to be a professor at a top-thirty university was a big deal for all the anti-Harvard posturing. So, people answered my calls." If one wants to influence public life from the ivory tower, it is better to be a conservative, say these professors.

This chapter should offer some comfort to those who worry about liberal hegemony in the social sciences and humanities, even as it highlights a limited range of "safe spaces" for conservatives. We now turn to a more difficult question: In what respects does the scarcity of conservatives in the social sciences and humanities matter?

PART III

Should We Care?

7

The Consequences of a Progressive Professoriate

PARTISANS ON THE right and left often suggest that the professoriate is an ideologically inappropriate career choice for conservatives. The previous chapters cast doubt on the assumptions that inform those claims. In this chapter we further present reasons to suppose that more conservatives would be good for the university itself. We do so by identifying some of the negative effects of political homogeneity on students, scholarship, and the integrity of the university itself.

Teaching

The conservative websites Phi Beta Cons and Minding the Campus are devoted to finding fresh campus offenses, especially overtly politicized courses. One recent story nicely illustrates conservative anxieties about classroom indoctrination and why they are misplaced. In 2006, an evangelical Christian named Emily Brooker enrolled in a class at Missouri State University that required all students to lobby the legislature in support of gay adoption. When Emily refused to participate, the School of Social Work charged her with a "Level 3" grievance, the highest-level complaint that can be brought against a student. Emily was then summoned to a hearing before an ethics committee to discuss whether she violated the school's standards. During a two-and-a-half-hour interrogation, committee members asked her whether or not she considered gays and lesbians sinners.

Emily then sued the university for violating her First Amendment rights. Within two weeks the university settled, expunging her record of the grievance, paying her attorneys' fees, waiving tuition for graduate school, and removing the offending professor from administrative duties. Missouri State also investigated the School of Social Work. Investigators reported that it engaged in ideological and religious discrimination, creating a hostile and dysfunctional environment:

> Many students and faculty stated a fear of voicing differing opinions from the instructor or colleague. This was particularly true regarding spiritual and religious matters, however, students voiced fears about questioning faculty regarding assignments or expectations. In fact 'bullying' was used by both students and faculty to characterize specific faculty. It appears that faculty have no history of intellectual discussion/debate. Rather, differing opinions are taken personally and often result in inappropriate discourse.[1]

Conservative activists could hardly have invented a story illustrating so many of their fears of higher education. At *National Review*, Emily's attorney, David French, called her interrogation a "Star Chamber," and said her experience represented the "Final Frontier" of indoctrination. "Here, the university goes beyond censorship, beyond one-sided instruction, and invades the student's most basic right to freedom of conscience," French intoned.[2]

The example of Emily Brooker shows that some professors do try to indoctrinate their students. But it also highlights another fact that conservative activists are inclined to ignore: Ham-fisted efforts to mold the political minds of students tend to fail. In this case Emily did not change her position to accommodate her professors even when they threatened to deny her a diploma. To the contrary, the leftist professors at Missouri State transformed a career-minded student into a conservative activist.

While research on the effects of professorial indoctrination is limited, the evidence supports the conclusion that it does not work very well, and in some cases might even reinforce the very attitudes it is trying to undermine. In *The Diversity Challenge* several psychologists found that diversity programs have almost no effect on the political and racial attitudes of students. "Cultural diversity and multicultural education," they concluded, "simply are not earth-shattering experiences for university students."[3] One study even found that the diversity programs often found on college campuses increased levels of prejudice in students. In fact, aggressive interventions may "incite hostility toward the perceived source of the pressure (i.e., the stigmatized group), or a desire to rebel against prejudice reduction itself."[4] Other research finds that college seniors are more conservative on some economic issues than first-year students. They are moderately less supportive of government efforts to reduce income inequality and guarantee jobs.[5]

And while it is true that college graduates tend to be more liberal than other Americans, recent research suggests that this tendency may have little to do with the liberalism of college courses. A number of studies, for example, find that self-selection largely explains the political differences between college graduates and other citizens.[6] Another study by sociologist Kyle Dodson found that high levels of student engagement with faculty actually tended to moderate the political attitudes of conservative and liberal undergraduates. Meanwhile, less studious students—those who spend more time with their peers in campus activities and organizations than in office hours with their professors—do not moderate. In fact, they tend to move either farther to the left or to the right. Thus, the polarization of student attitudes may be more driven by their peers than by their professors.[7] It is still probably the case that a college education contributes to the liberalization of students in some respects, but the extant evidence does not suggest that anything like widespread indoctrination is taking place.

Why does college not have a more formative influence on the political and moral views of young people? Perhaps because the relationships between students and professors are generally not very close. Students spend relatively little time on their studies, partly because their research-oriented professors tend not to make serious demands on their time. As Jonathan Zimmerman observed, students spend an average of thirteen hours per week studying outside the classroom, while professors spend even less time on teaching, class preparation, advising, and grading.[8] Given this reality, it seems odd to suppose that professors would have a major influence on their students. This conclusion is strengthened by what we now know about human psychology. As Jonathan Haidt has shown, we are not usually persuaded through rational arguments alone. Because human beings are driven by sentiments, a friendship with someone of another political orientation is often necessary to get us to rethink our views.[9] With so little personal contact between professors and students, it would be genuinely surprising if such relationships had a significant influence on either party's political thinking. We agree with the conclusion of Bruce Smith and his colleagues: "The classroom experience is often overwhelmed by the outside influences that buffet the student during the college years, including the mass media and new peer groups that students encounter."[10]

But even if professors and students invested more in undergraduate education, there are two other reasons to suspect that college graduates would not suddenly become appreciably more liberal. First, citizens tend to filter new information through their partisan minds, as research on media effects have shown. This is why media messages tend to reinforce preexisting views rather than transform a conservative partisan into a progressive one.[11] Second, citizens also tend to tune into messages that they already agree with. Just as Republicans prefer to read the *Wall Street Journal* rather than the *New York Times*, many right-wing students tend to select into less politicized majors, thereby avoiding the most leftist professors. Stephen Porter and Paul Umbach, both professors of education, found that conservatives are more likely to choose majors in the natural sciences than in the social sciences and humanities, even after controlling for other variables. In fact, they say students' political views are a "very strong" predictor of major choice, rivaled only by personality traits.[12] Amy Binder and Kate Wood also noted the tendency of conservative students to "choose more 'conservative' courses of study" in their ethnographic study.[13] And, of course, some colleges and universities themselves have distinct political identities. Conservative students, for example, make up a much larger share of the student body at religious colleges than at secular ones.[14] Political self-selection, therefore, takes place well before many freshmen set foot inside their first college classroom. It seems that higher education is hardly immune from the growing political segregation and polarization that is reshaping American democracy.

These forces leave some leftist professors frustrated by a sense of political powerlessness. Donald Lazere, a longtime literature professor, recently lamented his inability to transform conservative students. He blamed their stubbornness on corporate influences. As he explained,

> Students' desperation to get and keep jobs in corporations and professions pressures them into compliance with corporate ideology, so that they tend to be impervious to any liberal deviations that they get in humanities courses.[15]

Others blamed Christianity. Adam Kotsko, a professor at Shimer College, believes that evangelical Christians suffer from a "persecution complex" that shields them from enlightenment. Ultimately, professors should not expect to make much headway with these students, Kotsko says, at least not until "parents and pastors" encourage young evangelicals to find the "courage to speak up against leaders whose extreme views only bring their community into disrepute."[16]

In another case, Snehal Shingavi, an English instructor at Berkeley, became so frustrated by his inability to reeducate conservative students that he discouraged them from taking his class on the Palestinian resistance.[17] Conservatives rightly criticized his intolerance. What they missed, however, was this professor's sense of impotence as a proselytizer of the Palestinian cause. He did not even attempt to "indoctrinate" conservatives—the task seemed too great.

Unlike some right-wing thinkers outside the academy, conservative professors do not believe that their leftist colleagues convert many students to Marxism, postmodernism, radical feminism, or other popular varieties of left-wing thought. But they do often worry about the treatment of conservative students. A philosopher reported that although he felt "fine" as a political minority in his department, "a lot of [conservative] students don't feel fine, because students will frequently report to me that they'll get shut down by other professors when they try to express contrary views." One prominent political scientist also lamented the treatment of his conservative students. "When the history is written of this time, I hope that just how much injustice was done to conservative students will be discovered," he said. He thinks feminist professors have been especially intolerant, observing, "They are the worst. They claim to redress their grievances of millennia; that's what's behind them. So they think that anything they do is right."

More commonly, conservatives simply worry that students of all political persuasions are not exposed to a wide range of right-wing perspectives, which compromises their formation as broadly informed citizens. A philosopher at a community college, for example, lamented that students are not introduced "to the range of views they should be exposed to." When we asked a historian at a regional state college whether the underrepresentation of conservatives in the academy really mattered, his response was unequivocal:

> Absolutely. I think that the absence of conservatives in history departments is a bad thing for the same reason that a lack of conservatives in an English department or sociology department or

political science department [is bad]—mostly because the students
only hear one point of view.

Some conservative professors believe that their progressive colleagues do
not teach right-wing thinkers or points of view simply because they do not
know them. "I think that my colleagues don't know" conservative thinkers,
one sociologist told us. She observed, "They don't read Friedrich Hayek
and they don't read a Jacques Maritain, they don't read them. So, I'm not
sure if they're [excluding conservative voices] on purpose." Other conservatives think that the marginalization of conservative thinkers in college
syllabi was less innocent. A literature professor, for example, insisted that
"it's just not hard" to represent multiple points of view.

Generally speaking, it may be easier for conservative academics to
expose their students to a range of thinkers from across the ideological
spectrum than it is for their progressive colleagues. This is not because
conservatives are more broad-minded. Rather, right-wing academics may
simply be more familiar with ideas on the other side of the political spectrum, since they cannot easily avoid encountering the many streams of
leftist thought that shape their own disciplines and subfields. And, in fact,
quite a few conservative professors told us that their students discerned
their politics simply because they did teach thinkers on the left *and* the
right.

Sociologist Kyle Dodson believes that students are exposed to a range of
conservative intellectuals. How else, Dodson wonders, can we account for
the fact that the most academically engaged liberal students become slightly
more moderate during their college years? As he concluded, "Indeed, it
appears that a critical engagement with a diverse set of ideas—a hallmark
of the college experience—challenges students to reevaluate the strength
of their political convictions."[18] It is certainly possible that the moderation Dodson identifies is driven by changes in economic views. One study
found that students who took introductory economics classes were more
likely to regard free markets as fair.[19] Alternatively, it could be the case that
liberal students simply adjust their political identities slightly because they
use their progressive professors (and the thinkers they assign) as a refer-
ence group. If their professor seems like a "5" on an ordinal scale, some
students may decide that they are a "4" after all.[20]

We suspect that students are rarely exposed to conservative ideas outside the libertarian tradition in a serious way. Consider a study by the late
sociologist Norval Glenn on liberal bias in marriage textbooks. Glenn

concluded that these books are a "national embarrassment" since, among other shortcomings, they are "typically riddled with glaring errors, distortions of research, omissions of important data, and misattributions of scholarship."[21] Also, if liberal professors are good at exposing students to conservative thinkers, why would so many of them continue to dismiss conservatism as a symptom of closed minds or dark prejudices?

In any case, we simply do not know much about either the extent to which students are exposed to conservative thinkers or the psychological mechanisms that cause some students to moderate their political identities. The classroom is a space that remains quite opaque to outside parties—a fact that exacerbates right-wing distrust.

Some progressive thinkers rightly object that an education that excludes conservative ideas and thinkers can nonetheless present a wide range of views. After all, a syllabus that requires one to read Marxist, feminist, and Foucauldian authors certainly offers students distinctive ways of thinking about the world. But graduates who are unfamiliar with right-wing intellectuals are not well prepared to be citizens in a democracy in which half the population sits well to the right of Nancy Pelosi. In fact, that limited exposure might help explain the curious finding that conservative citizens are much better than liberal ones at being able to understand the other side's moral and political reasoning.[22]

Conservatives might also be able to present right-wing ideas in a more compelling way than their liberal colleagues. Steven Hayward, who served as the inaugural visiting professor of conservative thought and policy at the University of Colorado at Boulder, argued that, ideally, actual conservatives would expose students to right-wing ideas.[23] John Stuart Mill addressed the same issue in *On Liberty* 150 years ago. Mill argued that to know your own argument you must first know the argument of your opponents. But to truly know your opponents' arguments, Mill insisted, one "must be able to hear them from persons who actually believe them; who defend them in earnest, and do their utmost for them." Only those who actually believe in an argument, Mill continued, will know them "in their most plausible and persuasive form" and compel others to confront "the whole force of the difficulty which the true view of the subject has to encounter and dispose of, else he will never really possess himself of the portion of truth which meets and removes that difficulty."[24]

Hayward confessed that his own experience teaching John Rawls makes him doubt the capacity of liberals to give conservative ideas a fair hearing. His presentation of Rawls, he believes, must be "inadequate and incomplete" since he is not "passionately committed to Rawls's point of view."[25] Some of the professors we interviewed agreed. "I've had students say to me," one recalled, "that I'm the only professor they've encountered who [has given them] a sympathetic account of Saint Augustine."

As one of us (Shields) has argued elsewhere, we have good reasons to share at least some of Hayward's skepticism about our rational nature. Just consider the defenders of deliberative democracy. Although these thinkers attempt to weigh moral claims without prejudice, they nonetheless present conservative arguments in ways that obscure their rational power.[26] The failures of deliberative democrats, moreover, are entirely predictable if we accept the insights of psychology. "Smart people make really good lawyers," Jonathan Haidt explains, "but they are no better than others at finding reasons on the other side."[27]

Generally speaking, however, conservatives both inside and outside the university have not really considered Hayward's case in a serious way. Perhaps this is because they dislike more extreme versions of Hayward's argument in the context of race and gender (e.g., one needs to be black to teach African American history). In any case, conservatives often insist that professors simply need to start teaching in a fairer and more balanced way. The "basic premise" of the campaign for an academic bill of rights, noted David Horowitz, is that "professors were obliged to behave professionally in the classroom, and that students had a right to expect them to do so."[28] This argument suggests that academia does not actually need more ideational pluralism—it just needs more professionalism. What it does not consider is the limits of professionalism itself. The professors we interviewed obliquely pointed to such limits as well, despite all of their emphasis on fairness and balance. Only a small minority of conservative professors, for example, said that ideology has no influence on their teaching (see Table 7.1).[29]

Table 7.1 Politics and Teaching

Do conservative or libertarian values shape your teaching?	
Yes, significantly	17%
Yes, but only moderately	61%
No, ideology has no influence	22%
N:	140

The university is also one of the only spaces where elites on both sides of the partisan divide could model civic virtues, such as mutual respect. Right-wing students might especially benefit from the example of more conservative professors on their campuses, especially since some are still developing into activists. As Binder and Wood found in their study of conservative campus groups, political activists are "made, not born, as colleges nurture and aggrandize particular forms of conservative student activism."[30] But with hardly any conservative professors on campus, many right-wing students find their way with little elite direction. In fact, young conservatives' alienation from the professoriate may speed their drift toward populism. One closeted professor we interviewed was disappointed when a conservative group invited the bomb-throwing Ann Coulter to campus, though he could understand their desire to do so. "They wanted someone to come in here and say all kinds of outrageous shit, because they are forced to be quiet themselves. It's like [they said] 'now you idiots have to listen to us puke all over you,'" he surmised.

And, finally, some of the conservatives we interviewed also believe they can help with the so-called crisis in the humanities. Over the past forty years humanities majors declined by half. In 2013 the American Academy of Arts and Sciences addressed what it called "the crisis" by offering suggestions for reinvigorating the liberal arts. Ultimately its recommendations never moved beyond platitudes like this one: "[C]ollege and university curricula must also offer the broad-gauged, integrative courses on which liberal education can be grounded, and such foundations need to be offered by compelling teachers."[31] Such empty calls to action offer little guidance and less comfort to liberal-arts faculty members caught in the crisis.

A few conservative literature professors we spoke with are hopeful that the current crisis might compel their leftist colleagues to rethink the virtues of more traditional approaches. One professor at a research university said that literature professors are belatedly recognizing that the politicized battles over literary theory of the 1980s and 1990s were destructive. "At this point," he began, "it's not which language and literature study will survive, but whether it will survive at all. It's time to put aside childish things." Another observed,

[A] lot of older people who might have been edgy and outré twenty years ago are actually coming around [and saying]: 'You know, our bread and butter isn't queer theory. Our bread and butter is

Shakespeare.' That's what people still care about, that's what people respect us for. Maybe twenty-five years ago you could talk in edgy ways about gender theory and people would get excited about it. Now, who cares?

For all the concern over the indoctrination of students, the crisis of the humanities should also remind us that students are hardly passive or powerless. To use Albert Hirschman's influential formulation, students may not wield much power in college classrooms through "voice," but they can "exit"—and have done so by selecting less radicalized courses and majors in large numbers.[32]

Research

Not many observers doubt that the large and growing body of social and humanistic knowledge would look quite different if conservatives dominated the professoriate rather than progressives. Even *Professors and Their Politics*, a recent edited volume built around the refutation of many conservative criticisms of the academy, made no effort to challenge this evident truth.[33] Only 15% of all social scientists, meanwhile, say it is unacceptable for political beliefs to shape professors' research interests.[34] The conservatives we interviewed did not dispute the importance of politics either. More than 70%, in fact, said that politics shapes their own research at least moderately (see Table 7.2).

It is, of course, hard to say precisely how different what we think we know would change if the social sciences and humanities were more pluralistic. Nonetheless, some scholars are beginning to reflect on how the lack of ideological pluralism in the social sciences and humanities shapes human knowledge. Christian Smith, for example, recently described

Table 7.2 Politics and Research

Do conservative or libertarian values shape your research agenda?	
Yes, significantly	26%
Yes, but only moderately	46%
No, ideology has no influence	28%
N:	141

sociology's unconscious spiritual project, which we discussed previously.[35] The same progressive vision shapes other disciplines as well. Deborah Prentice, a psychologist at Princeton, believes that even some of the most technocratic controversies can conceal shared progressive norms. In the case of social psychology, for example, she says that debates "center on how to measure what everyone knows to be true and whether the under-lying psychological mechanisms have been nailed down with sufficient precision. . . . With so much ideological common ground, many of the big questions about what drives human behavior receive little attention."[36]

How might the progressivism described by Smith and Prentice distort our understanding of the social world? Recently a group of six social scien-tists from different political backgrounds—Jose Duarte, Jarret Crawford, Charlotta Stern, Jonathan Haidt, Lee Jussim, and Phil Tetlock—specified ways in which the validity of social psychological knowledge has been undermined by the near absence of conservatives in psychology. In doing so they acknowledged that there are many important research areas that are relatively unaffected by the ideological skew of the academy. Some topics, however, are especially vulnerable to political influences. As they observed,

> The lack of diversity causes problems for the scientific process pri-marily in areas related to the political concerns of the left—areas such as race, gender, stereotyping, environmentalism, power, and inequality—as well as in areas where conservatives themselves are studied.[37]

Although Duarte and his colleagues focused on such problems in the context of psychological knowledge, they provide a useful starting point for thinking about the effects of political homogeneity in other fields. We agree, for example, that many disciplines neglect topics or provide suspect answers to questions that complicate the progressive narrative. Sometimes academics do so by telling the history of the left in either a triumphant way or in a way that leaves no room for conservative contributions to human progress. We set forth three examples: The histories of eugenics, commu-nism, and the civil rights movement. In addition to telling a biased story about the past of liberalism, academics also shore up the progressive nar-rative by discounting evidence that they regard as favorable to conservative perspectives. In making this case, we draw on examples from research on the family, affirmative action, sex differences, abortion, and distributive

justice. Just as Duarte and his colleagues pulled examples from psychology, we can offer only a limited set of cases from research areas that are
most familiar to us. For this reason, we suspect that the cases we cite—as
well as those Duarte and his colleagues fingered—are probably just the tip
of a much larger iceberg.

We begin with the political controversy over eugenics in America—a
topic long neglected by historians even though our eugenics program was
quite advanced, leading to the sterilization of some 65,000 citizens. As the
journalist Harry Bruinius noted recently, "the history of American eugenics
has been in many ways forgotten."[38] Why? Partly because so many progressive heroes lined up in favor of eugenics in the name of scientific progress,
while Catholics opposed it because of the Church's doctrines on the sacred-
ness of human life. It was not until 2013 that anything approaching the full
story of the Church's often successful opposition was told by the Catholic
historian Sharon Leon.[39] In his blurb, the conservative political theorist
Robert George noted with exasperation, "If there is a story long overdue
for telling, surely it is the story of how and why the Catholic Church and
its faithful stood against the eugenics movement at a time when just about
everyone else had gotten on the pro-eugenics bandwagon."

As one of us (Shields) has emphasized elsewhere, neglecting Catholic
opposition and progressive enthusiasm for eugenics simplifies a story
the left tells about our national struggle between the forces of religion
and science. By emphasizing the battle over the teaching of evolution in
public schools rather than the conflict over eugenics, historians elevated
the Scopes Trial as our nation's emblematic struggle between science and
religion.[40] This happened even though the conservative historian Edward
Larson recently showed that the issues of eugenics and teaching evolution were linked in important respects. The textbook under dispute in the
Scopes Trial, for example, espoused scientific racism and social Darwinism.
And these issues were partly responsible for inspiring William Jennings
Bryan's crusade against the teaching of evolution in public schools.[41]

Liberals justifiably take pride in their record on civil rights, especially
after 1964. Liberals were undeniably the heroes of the civil rights movement. But that same pride may lead progressive scholars to tell a story that
is far too tidy and much less interesting than the messier historical reality.

Unlike eugenics, the history of communism has attracted consider-
able scholarly attention—but it is also a history that has been distorted
by the dominance of sympathetic Marxist historians. After the 1970s,
observe the conservative historians John Haynes and Harvey Klehr,

new radical historians in the United States developed a consensus on communism, both in America and Russia. It was a consensus, Haynes and Klehr say, that "took a benign view of communism, arguing that Marixst-Leninism embodied the most idealistic dreams of mankind and that American communists were among the most heroic fighters for social justice." This portrait of communism inspired scholars to brush over evidence of Stalin's murderous brutality and paint the Communist Party USA (CPUSA) as an ordinary political party—one that "embodied the best impulses and values of American democracy." The new historians explained away a growing body of evidence that challenged this rosy view of communism, such as testimony from defectors and refugees. The older and contrary perspective—that the Soviet regime was a murderous totalitarian state and that the CPUSA engaged in espionage that was financed and directed by the Soviet Union—was an idea that met with disbelief and ridiculed by historians. Meanwhile, anticommunism was derided as a paranoid witch hunt. The result, conclude Haynes and Klehr, was a curious mix of "righteous indignation toward Joseph McCarthy and McCarthyism (a slur directed at all anti-communists)" and "cool aloofness toward Joseph Stalin and Stalinism."[42]

This perspective on communism should have been devastated after 1991, when the Soviet Union opened up its archives for the first time. Millions of new documents that showed communism for what is was, both here and abroad, were made available to American historians for the first time.[43] According to Haynes and Klehr, however, only "a few" historians "dealt forthrightly with the new archival resources." Most historians responded with a mix of evasion, silence, and new intellectual contortions, all of which served to minimize the dark realities of communism. These tendencies were especially pronounced among historians of American communism, who continued to insist that anticommunism was an irrational response to a benign movement. "Despite all the new archival evidence of Soviet espionage and American spies," conclude Haynes and Klehr, the benign view of communism "still dominates the academy and the historical establishment." The major American journals in history— the *Journal of American History* and the *American Historical Review*—have refused to publish a single article critical of the new orthodoxy.[44] "In these journals," lament Haynes and Klehr, "there is no debate about American communism and Soviet espionage." The procommunist perspective still "reigns without challenge."[45]

Unlike scholarship on the CPUSA, historians of all political persuasions justifiably praise the civil rights movement. But the near-universal leftism and secularism of academics has distorted our understanding of the movement. For example, it took decades for a single scholar to stress the importance of religion to black activists in the South, preferring instead to describe Christianity as merely part of the cultural flavoring of the civil rights movement. Then, in 2005, David Chappell's groundbreaking work, described by the *Atlantic Monthly* as among the best handful of books on the civil rights movement, unearthed a mountain of evidence that challenged the historical consensus. Chappell's work found that religion was not marginal to the civil rights campaign—it was what made that movement *move*. That is, Chappell showed how an intense revivalist and otherworldly Christianity gave activists the solidarity and confidence that they could prevail over a more powerful enemy. Activists braved the dogs and fire hoses, according to Chappell, because they believed that God was really intervening in history and would protect them from death. "To believe that one is morally right is easy and common," Chappell observed, but "to believe one is going to defeat one's enemies requires rather extraordinary faith."[46]

Chappell emphasized the oddness of this historical oversight. "It now seems very strange," Chappell reflected, "to leave the religion of the protestors out of the picture—to refuse to see their religion as central and distinctive." Indeed, Chappell even described the prevailing secular account of the movement's origins and motives as nothing short of "breathtakingly obtuse."[47]

Why were historians and social scientists "breathtakingly obtuse" for so long? There is probably no single explanation. But a partial explanation may be that academics regard themselves and the civil rights movement as the heirs to a shared progressive worldview that looks askance at religious orthodoxy and celebrates Enlightenment rationalism. Chappell damages this collective identity by showing that the faiths of progressive northerners and southern blacks were fundamentally at odds. The "liberal's animating faith," Chappell observed, "was radically different from that of the southern movement." Liberals believed that the spread of education would eventually subdue the irrational prejudices of white southerners. But as Chappell pointed out, black activists were "driven not by modern liberal faith in human reason, but by older, seemingly more durable, prejudices and superstitions that were rooted in Christian and Jewish myth." The larger implications of Chappell's work are arguably even harder for progressive academics to entertain, especially those who study social movements. "In the age of declining faith in revolution," Chappell concluded, "the tradition of revivalist religion—commonly understood to be the opposite of revolution, indeed the most important form of the opiate of the masses—might supply the raw materials of successful social change in the future."[48]

Academics' Enlightenment faith in the power of reason and education also inclined them to neglect the study of religion outside of the American civil rights movement as well. And because they were guided by the assumption that secularization was a historical inevitability as science and liberal values spread across the globe,[49] social scientists and historians were unprepared to make sense of religious awakenings in the 1970s and 1980s. As Christian Smith observed,

> So, just when sociology was most needed to make good sense of a born-again president, the Iranian revolution, liberation theology, a world-transforming Catholic pope, the religious right, Poland's Catholic Solidarność movement, militant "base communities" in Latin America, the cultural resurgence of American evangelicalism, revolutionary priests in Nicaragua and El Salvador, the spread like wildfire of Pentecostalism in the Global South, the successful theological challenge to South African Apartheid, the church's undermining of Eastern European communism, the growth of militant Islam, the explosion of religion in China, and so many other world-historical events and processes . . . [f]ew in American sociology possessed any of the right conceptual, theoretical, and analytic tools to make sense of what was going on in the world.

Sociologists were unprepared to make sense of these developments, and continued to ignore them for decades. They did so, according to Smith, because sociologists accepted "a simple theoretical dismissal of religion, and so ignored religion as a social fact."[50] Sociologists were hardly alone in this respect. Faith in the inevitable death of religion, noted sociologist Jeffrey Hadden, "is the legacy all social sciences inherited from the Enlightenment."[51] And it was this legacy, after all, that left historians ill-equipped to make sense of the civil rights movement.

Although liberal academics have expressed great interest in the civil rights movement and the subject of race more generally, they were reluctant to discuss the growing breakdown of the black family. Daniel Patrick

Moynihan's report, *The Negro Family*, brought national attention to the problem by highlighting the alarming growth of female-headed households and illegitimacy. After the report was attacked by liberal activists for "blaming the victim," sympathetic progressive academics responded by either trying to minimize the social importance of family structure or, more often, simply ignoring the tragic development of a growing black underclass. As one sociologist told us,

> This is actually my favorite case of why the ideological skew of sociology is intellectually impoverishing to it. Basically, sociology had to be dragged kicking and screaming until it recognized that broken families aren't . . . good thing[s]. It's [as] if you have to spend decades and millions of dollars in NSF grants to convince astronomers that the sun rises in the east.

A recent intellectual history on the Moynihan report by James Patterson largely supports this sociologist's account. As Patterson contends,

> [B]y the late 1970s widespread rejection by liberal scholars of *The Negro Family* had not only perpetuated the great silence that Moynihan had lamented in the late 1960s, it had also hardened into an orthodoxy that virtually excused lower-class black people from much if any responsibility for their difficulties.

The reluctance to take seriously the many benefits of intact families and the cultural causes of poverty softened somewhat in the 1980s as some prominent voices began to speak out, including conservatives, such as Glenn Loury and Charles Murray, and iconoclastic liberals, like William Julius Wilson. Wilson's *The Truly Disadvantaged* took academics to task for failing to conduct serious work on the black underclass. "It emphasized that the failure of liberal scholars and black activists to speak out . . . had dampened serious research into inner-city concerns," Patterson noted.[52]

As the pace of serious research picked up in the 1990s, and as the problems of family instability took their toll on children of all races, the evidence became too difficult to ignore for many, though hardly all, scholars of the family. Some family scholars reluctantly began to appreciate the importance of involved dads and stable marriages. Sara McLanahan, a Princeton sociologist, began researching divorce in the 1970s, with an interest in showing that children faired just as well in single-parent households. But after two decades of research, McLanahan (and her coauthor Gary Sandefur) finally came to the opposite conclusion in the influential book *Growing Up with a Single Parent*:

> If we were asked to design a system for making sure that children's basic needs were met, we would probably come up with something quite similar to the two-parent ideal. Such a design, in theory, would not only ensure that children had access to the time and money of two adults, it also would provide a system of checks and balances that promoted quality parenting. The fact that both parents have a biological connection to the child would increase the likelihood that the parents would identify with the child and be willing to sacrifice for that child, and it would reduce the likelihood that either parent would abuse the child.[53]

McLanahan's own intellectual development is a reminder that it was not simply racial considerations that delayed a serious reckoning with the importance of dads and familial stability—it was also encouraged by feminism's critique of the traditional family.[54]

Progressives' failure to appreciate the importance of intact, two-parent families was not simply driven by racial liberalism and feminism, however. At a deeper intellectual level, American progressives often struggle to see the point of social institutions, both because they appear irrational and because they seem to undermine a spiritual project that prizes autonomy.[55] Culturally conservative intellectuals see the world differently. They have long argued that wayward human beings need some durable social institutions that direct them toward behaviors that are good for them and the wider society.[56] This insight does sometimes lead conservatives to defend institutions that are, in fact, irrational, outdated, and unnecessarily coercive. But given the near absence of conservative perspectives in the social sciences, this tendency was hardly academia's problem.

Scholars have also neglected research on the potential costs of affirmative action. In his groundbreaking article of the effects of affirmative action on Bar passage rates for racial minorities, Richard Sander made a startling observation: "[T]here has never been a comprehensive attempt to assess the relative costs and benefits of racial preferences in any field of higher education." This is so, Sander noted, despite the fact that we have been engaged in "a massive social experiment" that has been guided by the assumption that it will help racial minorities. Sander found evidence that calls this assumption into question. Because of aggressive affirmative action policies, Sander shows that "most black law applicants end up at schools where they will struggle academically." These minority students would be better served by attending less selective law schools where they can compete and learn in an environment tailored to their educational needs and readiness. "Perhaps most remarkably," Sander concluded, "a strong case can be made that in the legal education system as a whole, racial preferences end up producing fewer black lawyers each year than would be produced by a race-blind system."[57]

Sander's is certainly not the final word on this question. Sander's work inspired many criticisms.[58] That is as it should be. What is remarkable is that it took *decades* for a single study to systematically weigh the benefits and costs of such an important and controversial social policy.

Neglect of the costs of social policy more generally is especially pronounced in philosophy departments. While philosophers pay a great deal of attention to libertarian objections to social welfare programs, they have had almost nothing to say to Burkean conservatives who worry that such programs are in one way or another imprudent in practice. As Alex Rajczi, a scholar at Claremont McKenna College, recently observed, the neglect of such conservative objections to the social welfare state represents a "major oversight" in the discipline of philosophy.[59]

Although Rajczi is not persuaded that this oversight is due to the dominance of progressives in philosophy departments, he also suggests that the absence of conservatives might matter. As he reflected,

> I am surprised at the number of philosophers who will say . . . that *of course* a national health system can be made to function in an efficient and fiscally sound way. If one makes those assumptions, then the conservative position may not seem worth addressing at all.[60]

This observation suggests that the dearth of conservative professors does help account for philosophy's lack of interest in conservative critiques of the social welfare state. If philosophy departments were more pluralistic places, then presumably fewer philosophers would simply dismiss conservative arguments as unworthy of consideration.

Sometimes certain progressive commitments even seem to encourage social scientists to ignore large bodies of knowledge that are created by other disciplines. Conservative political scientist Steven Rhoads pointed out that feminists in sociology, history, political science, and women's studies have ignored an impressive corpus of research on sex differences.[61] Sociologist Lloyd Lueptow and his colleagues also observed this tendency recently. As they put it in *Social Forces*, "Especially noteworthy and unsettling is that this large and consistent body of empirical evidence has been almost completely ignored and uninterpreted by students of sex and gender."[62] Scholars of gender ignore this research partly because it complicates their support for a genderless world in which all tasks and interests are shared equally between men and women. One influential feminist even argued that sex differences should become as inconsequential as eye color.[63] More generally, a strong social constructivist perspective has thrived in the social sciences because it renders radical schemes of social transformation more viable. By denaturalizing the social world, Christian Smith explains, it becomes "susceptible to purposeful human transformation through social movements, political programs, reforms, and revolutions," which is why "[n]early all of reality is talked about as if it were socially constructed."[64]

The tendency to ignore discomforting facts is especially evident in the case of abortion law. As prolife Harvard law professor Mary Ann Glendon often emphasizes, *Roe v. Wade* and its companion decision *Doe v. Bolton* created one of the most liberalized abortion laws in the Western world. While most Western democracies restricted abortion to the first trimester, *Roe* and *Doe* permitted abortion through all nine months for any reason a doctor finds compelling. "So far as I know," Glendon testified before the Congress, "there has been no case … in which abortion was denied to a woman on the grounds that it was against the law."[65] But, oddly, few American academics seem to be aware of this basic legal fact. Indeed, even "many law professors," Glendon noted, are unaware of the radicalism of *Roe* and *Doe*.[66] In this way, elites participate in what sociologist James Hunter has called the "mass legal ignorance" that surrounds *Roe*.[67]

In addition to avoiding important topics, resisting conclusions that complicate progressive beliefs, and ignoring important bodies of knowledge, there is a long history of scholarship that mischaracterizes conservatism itself. One research tradition maligns conservatism as a disease of the political mind by attributing it to dark, irrational psychological forces, such as authoritarianism, status anxiety, racism, and sexism. The project of rooting conservatism in dark hatreds and fears has been an eminently interdisciplinary one, including political scientists, historians, sociologists, and psychologists.[68] This tendency has arguably made it more difficult for liberal academics to learn anything from the conservative intellectual tradition. As the conservative political scientist Gerard Alexander recently observed, if right-wing thinkers are thought to suffer from a "psychiatric disorder," why listen to any of them? "To many liberals, this worldview may be appealing," Alexander observed, "but it severely limits our national conversation on critical policy issues."[69] The reduction of conservatism to dark irrational motives by academics also reinforces this same tendency in progressive politicians and journalists. When President Obama famously said conservatives "cling to guns or religion or antipathy to people who aren't like them," there was no pushback from the liberal academy. As Obama correctly described the progressive consensus, "I said something that everybody knows is true."[70]

Given this perspective on conservatism, it is not surprising that many political scientists and historians also blame conservatives for the growth of political polarization.[71] What is more surprising is the sea change in academic attitudes toward the merits of polarization itself. Not so long ago, social scientists longed for a moralized politics in which a principled progressive Democratic Party competed against a more conservative Republican Party. In 1950 the American Political Science Association authored a special report on party reform. It found that American parties suffered from a lack of ideological cohesion, a condition that "slowed the heartbeat of American democracy."[72] That was probably true. Thanks in part to our increasingly polarized parties, turnout in the last three presidential elections has been unusually high by twentieth-century standards. But political scientists in the 1950s wanted more than a newly engaged citizenry—they also presumed that a more ideological party system would benefit progressivism. As political scientists Jacob Hacker and Paul Pierson observed,

> The [APSA] committee implicitly assumed that liberal Democrats would benefits from the hardening of party differences. . . . But the rise of truly national party differences has ultimately redounded not to the benefit of liberal Democrats but of conservative Republicans.[73]

As a consequence, today's progressive academics are often critical of the very partisan polarization that their predecessors desired.[74]

Some might object that conservative scholars engage in politicized research too. That is true. These cases have not been marshaled to show that liberal scholars are more prone to political passions than conservative ones. Rather, we aimed to show that the politicization of these research areas is largely the byproduct of relatively homogenous *groups*, rather than the mischief of particular individuals. Thus, if conservatives dominated the study of, say, race or liberalism, we have every reason to suspect that their work would turn out just as politicized as the extant scholarship on those same subjects. Progressive movements inside academia have also identified important new theories and questions, such as work on gender. The problem is not progressivism. It is the absence of conservatives from many important domains of inquiry.

Others might offer a quite different objection. Even if whole bodies of knowledge are misshapen by the academy's political homogeneity, some critics might wonder if it really matters all that much. After all, mountains of scholarship are left almost entirely unexplored. The articles professors spend months writing for journals will sit in a handful of collections or in cyberspace gathering real or virtual dust. Clayton Christensen of the Harvard Business School gave this description of the traditional research process:

> In academia, you write a paper; you might have a co-author or two. When you're done with a draft, you might submit it to an editor of an academic journal. . . . It takes two or three years to finally get it past these [two or three] reviewers to get published. Then it goes into a well-regarded academic journal and will be read by between eight and 12 people.[75]

We suspect that this description is unobjectionable to most professors. According to one study, 82% of journal articles in the humanities are at most rarely cited, while 32% are never cited.[76] And those numbers are growing higher still.

This objection is true as far as it goes. Yes, most individual authors and publications do not matter very much in and of themselves. But some authors are widely read.[77] In addition, it is difficult to dismiss the significance of whole bodies of knowledge, such as the scholarship on communism or gender. Even when progressive professors are open to presenting students with a more sympathetic treatment of anticommunism in America, it would be easy for them to simply accept the academic consensus: Anticommunism was largely an irrational movement that stirred dark fears. To paraphrase President Obama, that is simply what everybody knows. And, finally, when whole bodies of knowledge lead us away from the best approximations of the truth, they compromise the pursuit of knowledge itself.

In light of these problems, we would like to offer one more reflection on the previous section on teaching. As we stressed earlier, conservatives need not fear the indoctrination of impressionable students at the feet of professorial propagandists. But since professors often hand down politicized bodies of knowledge that concern the very issues that are of special interest to good citizens, students of all political persuasions may leave college ill-prepared to grapple thoughtfully with those same issues. This danger especially threatens the elite students who will go on to shape our culture and politics.

Politics and Policy

The political homogeneity of the social sciences and humanities sometimes tempts professors to abuse their own authority outside the many ivory towers they call home. This is especially the case in legal battles in which academic expertise is granted significant weight and when the conflicts being adjudicated involve those social and cultural issues for which there are few dissenting academic voices. In making this case, we draw on two important controversies that have been central to the American culture wars: abortion and same-sex marriage.

Roe v. Wade was the Court's most controversial decision of the last fifty years. Unlike other decisions, such as *Brown v. Board of Education,* which provoked resistance, time has not lent *Roe* authority or veneration. If anything, the controversy over the Court's ruling has increased and has been the subject of repeated attempts to limit and even overturn it. Critics of *Roe* dislike the sweeping nature of the ruling and its weak constitutional reasoning. *Roe*'s constitutional reasoning is weak partly because it rests on debunked historical claims. Nonetheless, historians organized to defend those same historical myths in their efforts to protect abortion rights.

The prochoice litigants in *Roe* faced a daunting challenge: Because the Constitution provides weak textual support for abortion rights, they needed to demonstrate that they were deeply rooted in Anglo-American legal and political traditions. It was a task that was complicated by the fact that states passed restrictive abortion laws in the nineteenth century. Cyril Means, a New York Law School professor and legal counsel for what was then called the National Association for the Repeal of Abortion Laws (NARAL), rose to these challenges by writing a history purportedly showing that the only purpose of nineteenth-century state restrictions on abortion was to protect the life of the mother.[78] Then in 1971 he wrote another article that said "English and American women enjoyed a common-law liberty to terminate at will an unwanted pregnancy, from the reign of Edward III to that of George III, [a liberty that persisted] in America, from 1607 to 1830." To his credit, Means never hid behind a cloak of academic objectivity. He admitted that the aim of these articles was to provide a historical justification for the Supreme Court to declare abortion a constitutional right.[79]

Despite Means's frank admission, his "scholarship" had its desired political effect. The Court rested the abortion right partly on his historical analysis. In fact, Means was the only historian cited in the majority opinion. Sarah Weddington, the prochoice attorney who litigated *Roe*, also later emphasized the importance of Means's work to her arguments.[80]

Means's claims, however, are false, as even he quietly suggested. Abortion was not a right deeply rooted in the common law; nor were the nineteenth-century abortion laws intended only to protect the lives of women. As conservative political scientist Justin Dyer has shown, the tolerance for abortion prior to quickening in the American colonies and early republic reflected the scientific understanding at the time, not a disregard for unborn human life. "In the absence of scientific understanding," Dyer found, "quickening ... was often the best available evidence for new life (and thus the starting point for any criminal investigation)." When Americans' understanding of embryology improved in the nineteenth century, they acted to eliminate the crude, unscientific emphasis on quickening in state laws by outlawing all abortions. It is also clear that many of the state lawmakers who passed restrictive abortion laws cared about fetal life. "At least seventeen state codes in the nineteenth century," Dyer observed, referred to abortion as "'manslaughter,' 'murder,' or 'assault with intent to murder.'"[81] Nineteenth-century feminists condemned the practice of abortion as immoral too.[82] Thus, "anti-abortion legislation in the mid-nineteenth century was not so much an aberration, but a development," Dyer concluded.[83]

When the Supreme Court revisited *Roe* in *Webster v. Reproductive Health Services* in 1989, historians were offered a golden opportunity to set the historical record straight by correcting Means's patently partisan scholarship. Instead, 281 historians submitted an *amicus* brief that reified this historical legend. "Never before," the brief announced, "have so many professional historians sought to address the Honorable Court in this way." The brief then informed the Court that "nineteenth-century laws restricting access to abortion were not based on a belief that the fetus is a human being" and that "the common law recognized a woman's right to choose abortion."[84] Sylvia Law, who organized the brief, later confessed that there was "a tension between truth-telling and advocacy."[85] Among those who signed the brief was historian James Mohr, the author of a comprehensive history of nineteenth-century abortion law in America. In his scholarship on abortion history, Mohr found that the physicians who were responsible for proposing abortion restrictions "defended the value of human life per se as an absolute." Later Mohr described the brief as a "political document" and admitted that he did not "ultimately consider the brief to be history."[86] The Historians' Brief turned out not to be a work of history at all.

To their credit, when a nearly identical brief was submitted to the Court in *Planned Parenthood v. Casey*, some historians, Mohr included, refused to sign.[87] Sociologist James Davison Hunter later asked some of these historians why they bowed out. One historian, whom Hunter described as a professor at an elite western university, protested: "What I objected to was that historians were signing a document which was making a case for something that they knew nothing about. *Most of the historians signing the thing know nothing about the history of abortion and abortion law in this country*" [emphasis in original].[88] Nonetheless, some 250 professors signed the brief in *Casey*.

Despite its gross inaccuracies, the brief in *Webster* ended up having not only a legal influence, but a scholarly one as well. Ronald Dworkin simply reiterated the historical claims of the brief in his analysis of abortion and euthanasia. In *Life's Dominion* he concluded, "The best historical evidence shows that these [nineteenth-century] laws were adopted not out of concern for fetuses, however, but in large part to protect the health of the mother."[89] Likewise, in her influential book *When Abortion Was a Crime*, historian Leslie Reagan misleads readers when she concludes that the mid-nineteenth-century abortion laws stripped women of an old common-law right.[90] Thus, despite the historically false legal advocacy of the "Historians' Brief," it created a feedback loop into academia whereby its myths linger, misinforming students and scholars. "The new histories," Dyer concluded, "are spun off from deliberately fabricated narratives, and rarely does anyone return to the primary sources."[91]

As the legal battles over abortion quieted, another front in the American culture wars opened, creating new opportunities for professorial activism.

Today academic expertise is playing a starring role in the judicial conflicts over same-sex marriage and adoption. Scholarship on same-sex parenting lies at the center of these conflicts, nearly all of which finds that the children of gay parents do just as well as children raised in different-sex households. These same studies, however, also suffer from serious methodological flaws. In 2013, economist Douglas Allen pointed to three shortcomings of this research. First, he noted, it is "characterized by levels of advocacy, policy endorsement, and awareness of political consequences, that is disproportionate with the strength and substance of the preliminary empirical findings." Second, the literature uses methods that are difficult to replicate. "But most important, almost all of the literature on same-sex parenting (which almost always means lesbian parenting) is based on some combination of weak empirical designs [and] small biased convenience samples," he concluded.[92]

Previously those flaws were considered significant enough for courts to dismiss them as unreliable.[93] But as the movement for gay rights gained momentum, and as academics began asserting a new expert consensus, courts began relying on such troubled scholarship. And academics have given judges little reason to consider the problems that plague research on same-sex parenting. When the American Sociological Association, American Psychological Association, and American Anthropological Association jointly submitted an *amicus* brief in the legal controversy over same-sex marriage, they failed to even mention any of the limits of prior research on same-sex parenting. Instead, the brief suggested that there was no reason to doubt the social-scientific consensus. Citing a statement by the American Psychological Association, the *amicus* brief concluded, "Not a single study has found children of lesbian or gay parenting to be disadvantaged in any significant respect relative to the children of heterosexual parents."[94]

In many respects, the controversy over gay rights should remind us that the values and needs of social science and political movements are at odds. While social-scientific findings are provisional, probabilistic, and slow to develop, political movements require certainty and move fast. These tensions are particularly sharp in this controversy, since we still have so little experience with same-sex parenting. As journalist Andrew Ferguson recently observed, a real understanding of same-sex parenting may still be "scientifically unknowable," and must wait "until gay marriage and child rearing are widespread enough to yield large samples that can be studied according to a rigorous methodology." Conservative scholars Leon Kass and Harvey Mansfield made a similar observation. "Large amounts of data collected over decades," Kass and Mansfield opined, "would be required before any responsible researcher could make meaningful scientific estimates of the effects."[95] But advocates for gay rights both in and outside academia do not feel like they can spare "decades" of time—like most crusaders, they want justice now.

Academics can sometimes leverage their authority to fight the culture wars, but always at the risk of undermining the integrity of their intellectual calling as well as the public trust. When Mohr reflected on the partisan Historians' Brief he confessed, "If we lose credibility as open-minded observers, the power of the opinions we have to offer will be seriously undermined." Thus, when academics misrepresent their own knowledge claims, they may help the cause du jour, but also diminish their power in tomorrow's disagreements. And this means that liberals are advancing their own political goals in a shortsighted way.

Progressive academics might also remember that the answers they give to deeper moral questions should not be determined by empirical evidence. The quality of gay parenting, for example, is an interesting research question perhaps, but it may not be very relevant to whether or not lesbians and gays *should* be allowed to marry or adopt children. As one of us (Dunn) has argued elsewhere, there are dangers when constitutional rights are defined by the shifting outcomes of social science studies.[96] If we collectively decide that marriage is a fundamental right, then who really cares about the results of such research? As James Hunter put it in another context, "This is why the jump from careful scientific work to advocacy strikes one as a bit odd."[97]

Progressive dominance of higher education and the irresponsible advocacy it makes possible also encourages right-wing attacks on the academy. The most recent assaults have been led by conservative governors who have expressed skepticism about the value of "soft disciplines" compared with science, technology, engineering, and math (STEM) fields. In 2011 Rick Scott, the Republican governor of Florida, called for spending more money on STEM majors and cutting funding for the social sciences and humanities. "If I'm going to take money from a citizen to put into education," Scott explained, "I want that money to go to degrees where people can get jobs in this state." "Is it a vital interest of the state to have more anthropologists?" Scott asked rhetorically. "I don't think so."[98]

Two years later the Republican governor of North Carolina, Pat McCrory, argued that public funding for higher education should be more closely attuned to the needs of employers. "I'm a big vocational training advocate," McCrory declared. "I think some of the educational elite have taken over education, where we're offering courses that have no chance of getting people jobs."[99] McCory's rhetoric set the stage for reform in the spring of 2015. After a review of all 237 centers in the University of North Carolina system, the university's Board of Governors voted to close three. One was devoted to the environment and another to voter engagement. The third, and most controversial, was the Center on Poverty, Work, and Opportunity, an outfit run by an outspoken liberal law school professor, Gene Nichol. When the board announced its decision, liberal professors accused it of engaging in a "political crackdown."[100]

While most of these attacks have occurred at the state level, members of Congress have questioned whether the national government should help subsidize research in particular disciplines. In 2013, Senator Tom Coburn, a conservative Republican from Oklahoma, managed to strip National Science Foundation funding from political science projects unless the research promoted the "national security or the economic interests of the United States." Coburn inserted an amendment to a continuing appropriations measure that the Senate unanimously approved. Although the Senate restored funding a year later, the implications for the social sciences of such a successful attack are significant, especially when so many elites from across the political spectrum are questioning the value of a liberal-arts education.[101]

In these cases Republicans have avoided leveling the more divisive charge of liberal bias by simply criticizing the humanities and social sciences as a poor investment. This public good argument helps to insulate Republicans from accusations of rank partisanship by furnishing principled reasons for cutting the social sciences and humanities. Only the naive, however, would believe that Republicans had not considered the fact that their education reforms would erode financial support for an important progressive institution. A similar dynamic can be found in Democratic attacks on the tax-exempt status of white evangelical churches, but not the far more politicized black evangelical congregations. Democrats claim to speak for principle, but they know that using the IRS to frighten right-wing pastors enhances their own political power.[102]

Democrats often protest efforts to gut the humanities and social sciences. One Democratic state senator in North Carolina, for example, rejected Governor McCrory's narrowly utilitarian view of higher education. "Universities are much more than job factories," McCrory urged, "they're also about broadening minds."[103] It is a sensible objection. But it is also unlikely to appease conservative critics, and understandably so. Conservatives, after all, worry that the social sciences and humanities cannot really broaden minds when they are shaped so deeply by one-sided progressive assumptions and aspirations. Given this reality, why not start separating the state from these many secular churches?

In any case, some progressive academics might regard even these modest efforts to weaken the power of the professoriate as an overreaction. But we invite such progressive critics to imagine a world in which social conservatives dominated the academy. Imagine further that these conservative professors helped to persuade the Court in 1973 that human organisms were entitled to a constitutional right to life, protected from the moment of conception. Imagine still further that these right-wing professors used shoddy research to do so. This thought exercise, of course, would provide progressives only a very limited sense of the world that conservative critics of higher education actually find themselves in today. Yet we suspect that it might still be sufficient to sensitize some progressive readers to the legitimacy of conservatives' grievances, however clumsily they are sometimes expressed.

If there was more political diversity in the academy, many of the problems discussed in this chapter would be mitigated. But how might we improve political diversity in the social sciences and humanities? The final chapter asks whether the usual answer to the problem of homogeneity—affirmative action—is the right one.

Epilogue

AFFIRMATIVE ACTION FOR CONSERVATIVES?

UNTIL VERY RECENTLY, affirmative action for conservatives was an idea that would have been floated only jokingly at academic dinner parties. But now the idea enjoys a number of advocates who hail from a range of disciplinary and political backgrounds. In 2012, for example, progressive historian Jonathan Zimmerman authored an editorial in the pages of the *Christian Science Monitor* with this provocative headline: "US Colleges Need Affirmative Action for Conservative Professors."[1] A few years later, a diverse group of social scientists proposed ways to improve the representation of conservatives in the social sciences generally and in psychology in particular. While their suggestions fell short of preferences in hiring and promotion, they nonetheless resembled many traditional affirmative action programs. One reform proposal, for instance, instructed psychologists to "develop strategies to encourage and support research training programs and research conferences to attract, retain, and graduate conservative and other non-liberal doctoral students and early career professionals."[2] Meanwhile, the University of Colorado took the extraordinary step of creating a visiting position in "conservative thought and policy."[3] As these examples make clear, some are beginning to take the idea of affirmative action for conservatives quite seriously. If affirmative action for conservatives ever becomes a reality, its proponents will need to persuade not only their reluctant liberal colleagues, but skeptical conservatives as well.

Ambivalence of Conservatives

Many conservative professors value political diversity in the academy, at least as an ideal. The conservatives we spoke with distinguished political pluralism from racial and gender diversity, which they tend to regard as poor proxies for genuine intellectual diversity. One historian spoke for many fellow conservative professors when he told us, "It seems to me that intellectual diversity is the only thing that matters in academia and that all too often, faculty and administrators want people of different races, ethnicity, and gender thinking the same things." Similarly, another historian distinguished political from racial and gender pluralism by calling the former variety "actual diversity."

And because conservatives believe their progressives colleagues slight "actual" pluralism, liberal praise for diversity is a source of annoyance to many right-wing professors. "They talk about diversity all the time, but there's no intellectual diversity," protested a female historian at a small state college. A literature professor at a teaching college agreed. Academia, he told us, "despises diversity of thought." A female literature professor expressed the same frustration: "There's all of this talk of tolerance and diversity and academia being this place for honest debate, [but] it's exactly the opposite. It's tolerance of all things but conservatives and Christians."

Nonetheless, conservatives do not think that political diversity is important in all disciplines. Their comparatively modest diversity rationale is sometimes lost on liberal critics, who continue to make fundamentally leftist assumptions about the importance of pluralism. Sociologist Neil Gross, for instance, encouraged those who complain about ideological homogeneity to consider the greater political diversity in fields outside the social sciences and humanities. As he put it,

> Do professors in all disciplines agree politically? The answer is no. Invite some anthropologists and professors of engineering to lunch at the faculty club to talk politics and see what happens. . . . What the data show here is that self-identified radicals make up about 8 percent of the professoriate and are concentrated in a select number of social science and humanities fields.

The hard sciences are indeed more pluralistic disciplines. "A more fine-grained analysis," Gross added, "shows that conservatives tend to cluster in fields like accounting, management information, marketing, and electrical engineering."[4]

But conservatives do not care about political pluralism in these fields. If every engineer in the nation believed in Marxism, how many conservatives would protest? They would regard it as a curious social fact. But few would worry that engineering research or teaching was done with a Marxist slant. The same goes for accounting, management information, physics, mathematics, computer science, and chemistry. There are a few pockets of concern in the natural sciences, of course, such as climatology. But generally speaking, conservatives tend to worry almost exclusively about disciplines in the social sciences and humanities because objectivity is an elusive ideal in those fields. As James Ceaser and Robert Maranto note, political philosophy "falls so close to the subject of inquiry [in the social sciences and humanities] that it often cannot help but affect what is taught."[5] This is partly why Everett Carl Ladd and Seymour Martin Lipset referred to the social sciences as *the political sciences* in their classic, *The Divided Academy*.[6] Thus, conservatives and others who worry about intellectual pluralism are hardly comforted by the fact that the left is concentrated in "a select number" of disciplines in the social science and humanities.

Such discomfort highlights just how different conservative concerns are from feminist demands for more female representation among science and engineering faculties. For feminists the underrepresentation of women in the hard sciences matters, even though they do not think that an influx of female professors into astronomy departments would suddenly change our knowledge of dark matter. Their main concern is redressing the long-standing belief that men are better at science. And feminists would presumably not be content if men dominated any field, since it might suggest that women are ill-equipped to study that particular field of inquiry. But for conservatives and others who worry about ideological homogeneity in the social sciences and humanities, "diversity" is defended as a far more qualified good. That is, diversity is only really important in those fields where values and politics fall close to the subject of inquiry. So, if leftists dominated physics and engineering departments, while the sociology and history departments were balanced ideologically, we doubt there would be anything like David Horowitz's campaign against higher education.

Unlike defenders of racial and gender diversity, conservatives also do not believe that political pluralism in the social sciences and humanities needs to be representative of the nation as a whole. As one philosopher at a research university reflected,

> If you're in the situation [that] is thirty [liberals] to zero [conservatives] versus a situation where it is thirty to one, that's a huge difference. Things can be done and said and assumed in one case just with a single dissenter. I would never expect or hope or ask for parity or anything like that, but five percent?

Conservatives, in other words, seem to believe in the significance of a threshold, not proportionality. This is yet another respect in which the defense of political diversity is a much less ambitious one than the usual case for gender or racial diversity. Conservatives believe that a larger minority of right-wing thinkers in a select number of disciplines would address their concerns.

Despite their strong support for political diversity as an ideal, few right-wing professors support affirmative action for conservatives, at least not as a matter of policy. As one sociologist protested the idea:

> I personally think that the only way that we should ever bring up affirmative action for conservatives is the reductio ad absurdum of the diversity rationale, but not as a serious proposal. It's just a fucking nightmare kind of scenario, a cure worse than the disease.

A political scientist at a private research university is just as opposed to affirmative action for conservatives, which he described as "the road to corruption." The practice, he said, "runs against everything that conservatives of my ilk and the academy ought to stand for. I believe in academic excellence, letting the chips fall where they may." Another scholar agreed: "I don't think there should be a rule or regulation for any kind of diversification hiring, whether it's race, ethnicity, religion, sexual orientation, or ideology or partisan affiliation."

Others worried that affirmative action would stigmatize conservatives in the same way that it does racial minorities and women. "So somebody may say, 'Oh yeah, he is a full professor at Harvey Mudd, but you know why he got it,'" one philosopher speculated. The intensity of conservatives' commitment to meritocracy and fear of stigmatization was emphasized by the poignant example of a young female political scientist. When this interviewee discovered that she was the only female to receive a prestigious fellowship in political science, she worried that it was due to tokenism. "I couldn't sleep," she recalled. "That was a nightmare."

Nonetheless, some conservatives expressed support for an affirmative action that promoted political diversity. "I know I'm a minority among conservatives," acknowledged one philosopher, "because most of the conservatives I talk to say, 'no, no, we're against affirmative action of any kind.'" But this scholar supports affirmative action because he believes that even one conservative in a department can make an important difference. An evangelical sociologist at a research university harbors similar views. "What we do for a profession is a communal effort, [and] if we don't have diversity and we get group thinking, we don't find the truth," he asserted.

Our survey also shows that conservative professors often prefer to hire right-wing colleagues. Some 40% of conservative professors told us that they would rather hire someone on the right (see Table E.1) if they were just as qualified as their liberal competitors. Conservative institution building in higher education sometimes even looks suspiciously like programs designed to help women and minorities. Consider the James Madison Program at Princeton University. Founded by the conservative political theorist Robert George, the Madison Program hosts visiting scholars for a year to study constitutional law and political thought. One purpose of the Madison Program that you will not find in its mission statement is the support of conservative intellectuals, especially those who are looking to either land a tenure-track job or earn tenure. The Madison Program supports these professional ends by helping conservative intellectuals transform their dissertations into polished book manuscripts. In this respect the James Madison Program functions like graduate fellowships that are reserved for women and racial minorities. And the James

Table E.1 Hiring Preferences of Conservative Professors

Do you favor the hiring of like-minded conservatives or libertarians in your department over equally qualified liberals?	
Yes, strongly	9%
Yes, but only moderately	31%
No, ideology is irrelevant to hiring decisions	60%
N:	139

Madison Program is hardly the only institution that aids young conservative scholars. The Institute for Humane Studies, Jack Miller Center, and Intercollegiate Studies Institute all offer various kinds of support to conservatives. To be sure, many disciplines remain largely untouched by such efforts, especially psychology, sociology, literature, and anthropology. But they have helped many conservative political scientists, as well as a smattering of philosophers and historians.

The ambivalence of right-wing professors toward an affirmative action that seeks greater political pluralism is shared throughout the conservative movement. Republicans in the Congress and state legislatures have been opposed to pushing affirmative action for conservatives even though they too are concerned about the lack of pluralism in higher education. In 2005, at the peak of the conservative campaign against liberal bias in academia, Congress passed a resolution expressing its sense that viewpoint diversity should be valued in higher education. According to Bruce Smith and his colleagues, Republican leaders conceived the resolution because they wanted to do something without regulating higher education further. "The Republicans could strike a symbolic blow for viewpoint diversity," explained Smith and his colleagues, "without putting Congress in the position of becoming the school board for education." State campaigns foundered on a similar reluctance to push viewpoint diversity.[7]

Republican inaction is hardly surprising, given that there has been no outside push from conservative interest groups and activists. The American Council of Trustees and Alumni (ACTA) is the most well-funded and influential conservative advocacy organization that aims to encourage greater viewpoint diversity in higher education. Yet the ACTA opposes affirmative action for conservatives. Even David Horowitz—the most tireless crusader against liberal bias in higher education—wants state legislatures to urge viewpoint diversity, not mandate it.[8]

We suspect that conservative opposition toward positive measures to increase viewpoint diversity has less to do with a principled commitment to a small regulatory state and more to do with a strong belief in meritocracy. Many conservatives, after all, supported the No Child Left Behind Act, which subjected local schools to federal regulations to an unprecedented degree. And, of course, conservatives have sought to limit the discretion of college admissions' offices by advocating bans on racial and gender preferences. Thus, Republicans have happily meddled in the affairs of schools when it furthered their interests or ideals.

The reluctance of conservatives to mandate viewpoint diversity should prompt us to rethink conservative opposition to racial and gender preferences. Many academics and journalists have long contended that Republican opposition to affirmative action has been opportunistic rather than principled. In this view, the American right's opposition to affirmative action was part of a broad "southern strategy" to solidify their own power by appealing to the public's racist sentiments. Conservative opposition to affirmative action for right-wing professors, however, suggests that their position on racial preferences may be more principled than strategic. After all, conservative elites seem to dislike affirmative action even when they believe that it promotes intellectual diversity and when it promises to weaken the power of the progressive professoriate. Conservatives, in other words, have opposed affirmative action in all its incarnations because they dislike any marketplace in which more qualified applicants lose out to less qualified ones. As one political scientist put it, "I believe in academic excellence."

To be sure, there is something oddly naive about this professor's view, since the assessment of scholarly excellence in the social sciences and humanities is often inescapably shaped by our moral and political sensibilities. It seems that conservatives are sometimes torn between their confidence in an unregulated, meritocratic marketplace and their sense that assessments of excellence in social sciences and humanities are inescapably political.

Rethinking Affirmative Action

While conservatives are caught between their commitment to viewpoint diversity and their principled opposition to affirmative action in all its forms, any serious effort to increase political diversity in higher education would force all of us—and progressives in particular—to confront tensions in the deeper purposes of affirmative action.

Affirmative action has rested on two distinct justifications. It was first conceived as a temporary remedy for past discrimination. President Lyndon Johnson influentially made the case for remedial affirmative action in 1965 when he addressed the graduates of Howard University. "You do not take a person who, for years, has been hobbled by chains and liberate him, bring him up to the starting line of a race and then say, 'you are free to compete with others,' and still justly believe that you have been completely fair," Johnson said.[9] The second justification for affirmative action lays emphasis on the idea that viewpoint diversity should be an enduring goal of any educational institution. In *Regents of the University of California v. Bakke*, Justice Powell, citing an earlier decision, wrote, "The Nation's future depends upon leaders trained through a wide exposure to that robust exchange of ideas which discovers truth 'out of a multitude of tongues.' "[10]

While advocates of affirmative action have rested their case on both justifications, today's proponents of racial and gender preferences usually stress the importance of diversity. As political scientist Benjamin Ginsberg observed, diversity generally ranks among American universities' "very highest priorities." This is why many colleges and universities employ "Chief Diversity Officers," Ginsberg observed, while others hire "diversity consulting firms."[11] The obsession has not been lost on the conservative professors we interviewed. As one conservative professor told us, "To me the overriding, dominant theme—it's almost an ideology—in colleges or the universities today is diversity. . . . This is what you hear endlessly, endlessly—diversity, diversity—it's so important. We have to be more diverse."

Conservative professors present a special challenge to the notion that affirmative action should both increase diversity *and* remedy past discrimination. On the other hand, if we take seriously President Johnson's understanding of affirmative action as a remedy for past discrimination, then, of course, we should not be targeting conservative professors. Not only are conservatives not the victims of historical discrimination, the vast majority of right-wing professors are white males.[12] And because conservative professors are almost always white males, universities that aggressively hire female and minority professors are unlikely to hire many faculty members that are right of center. On the other hand, if the purpose of affirmative action is to cultivate the "robust exchange of ideas," as Justice Powell put it, then conservative professors should be the central targets of diversification efforts. Campuses that seek to hire conservatives in significant numbers, however, will find that doing so comes at the expense of racial and gender diversity. Just take a look at conservative academic institutions, such as Hillsdale College or George Mason's economics department, where there are few female or minority professors.

Advocates of racial and gender preferences might object that the *Bakke* rationale does not oblige them to support affirmative action for conservatives. Some scholars, for example, suggest that we should not conflate political with intellectual diversity. "In the humanities, social sciences, perhaps business," concluded Neil Gross, "it is easier to make a pedagogical case for faculty political diversity—though why, from an educational point of view, political diversity should be privileged instead of intellectual diversity has never been clear to me."[13] Others might object that, as a practical matter, affirmative action for conservatives would make little difference, given that so few are in the academic pipeline in the first place.

One problem with such objections is that they are equally powerful—and probably more so—in the case of gender or racial preferences. A candidate's conservatism can sometimes be a crude proxy for intellectual diversity, but one's gender is often a cruder proxy for viewpoint diversity. Still, the mass entry of women into the social sciences and humanities certainly brought significant intellectual diversity into higher education. More to the point, the problem with the academy is not that it lacks many significant kinds of intellectual diversity, as Gross's objection seems to suggest. Academic disciplines already cultivate an intellectually pluralistic place in many respects. Political scientists tend to see the world very differently from historians, for example. The problem with the academy is that it lacks one significant kind of intellectual diversity. A similar problem undermines the practical objection against affirmative action for conservatives. Yes, it is true that there are not legions of conservative doctorates lingering just outside of the ivory tower's gates. But that is true of blacks and Latinos as well. The larger mission of affirmative action programs attempts to improve such supply problems through various interventions. Thus the *Bakke* rationale obliges its defenders to support affirmative action for conservatives.

Supporters of affirmative action might say that affirmative action should remedy past injustices, not increase diversity. And since the vast majority of conservative professors are white males, we should certainly make no special effort to increase their numbers on college campuses. A reemphasis on remedial justice, however, would compel universities to treat blacks differently from women and Latinos. Our nation, after all, hardly subjected women or Latinos to anything resembling chattel slavery. So, if the point of affirmative action is to create equal opportunity by remedying a legacy of discrimination, then surely blacks deserve far more assistance than women or members of other ethnic minorities.[14] Indeed, women have been so good at competing with men that a number of progressive thinkers have announced the "end of men."[15]

A renewed commitment to remedial justice would also commit today's defenders of racial preferences to the extinction of affirmative action as an ultimate goal. Originally, affirmative action justified temporary race-conscious policies so that we might achieve a fair, color-blind society. The *Bakke* rationale changed that goal by suggesting that universities should never become color-blind, since race would always be a characteristic that enhances diversity. "[T]he diversity rationale," Richard Kahlenberg observed, "neatly disposes of pesky questions of when affirmative action will end."[16]

To be clear, we are not advocating for or against affirmative action for conservatives. We are simply pointing out that if we take ideological affirmative action seriously—as some thinkers are already doing—it raises important problems for defenders of race- and gender-based preferences. In fact, it seems that any coherent defense of affirmative action requires dramatic changes to the way it works in practice. Either it must aim to improve the representation of conservatives or refocus its energies on helping blacks. Alternatively, progressives could abandon affirmative action programs for *all* underrepresented groups on either principled or consequentialists grounds. But that policy reversal would signal the triumph of neoconservatism since progressives would now accept long-standing criticisms of affirmative action.

Some Modest Suggestions

If affirmative action for conservatives turns out to be little more than a provocative idea, how might we improve pluralism in the social sciences and humanities? In light of our findings, we can offer some modest suggestions to liberals and conservatives.

Liberal professors and the administrators of universities should make it clear that they welcome conservative perspectives. Often they do just the opposite. When universities retract invitations to conservative speakers, it simply reinforces the distorted right-wing view of academia. They need to stop such callowness. In their frequent homages to diversity, universities and disciplinary associations should also emphasize their support for political pluralism. Even that modest change might go a long way toward undermining the fear and suspicion conservatives harbor toward academia. Departments might also broaden their hiring by targeting subfields that are neglected and comparatively popular among conservatives, such as the study of religion, business, the military, ancient history, natural law, and the American founding.

Progressive professors might also attempt something their own academic training and ideology disinclines them to do: They could cultivate a measure of distrust in their own reason and impartiality. Undoubtedly some confidence in rationality is essential to the professorial vocation. But when professors' faith in their rational minds is not tempered by an appreciation for what psychologists have called our righteous minds,[17] it will always be difficult to see much point to political pluralism in academia. It also will be easy to slight the struggles of conservatives and trust one's own unerring impartiality. A political scientist we interviewed put it best: "The majority always thinks it's treating the minority well, that's a basic psychological trick we all play on ourselves."

Conservatives outside the university, meanwhile, should be careful not to overstate the intolerance inside its walls. Complaining about professorial radicalism may be one of the few sources of common identity in a rent Republican coalition, but it certainly does not encourage young conservatives to consider a career in academia. Yes, conservatives are correct to some degree—they are widely stigmatized in academia, especially those on the cultural right. That stigmatization is unfair. But as the many examples in this book attest, conservatives can survive and even thrive in the liberal university. Young conservatives, of course, should know the academic landscape well and navigate it carefully. We hope this book helps them do so.

Notes

INTRODUCTION

1. Neil Gross and Solon Simmons, "The Social and Political Views of American Professors," Working Paper, September 24, 2007; Neil Gross, *Why Are Professors Liberal and Why Do Conservatives Care?* (Cambridge, MA: Harvard University Press, 2013), 4, 41–47; Stanley Rothman and S. Robert Lichter, "The Vanishing Conservative—Is There a Glass Ceiling?" in Robert Maranto, Richard E. Redding, and Frederick M. Hess, eds., *The Politically Correct University: Problems, Scope, and Reform* (Washington, DC: AEI Press, 2009), 60–76.

2. Quotation in Everett Carl Ladd and Seymour Martin Lipset, *The Divided Academy: Professors and Politics* (New York: Norton, 1975), 14–36; Paul F. Lazarsfeld and Wagner Thielens, Jr., *The Academic Mind: Social Scientists in a Time of Crisis* (Glencoe, IL: Free Press, 1958), 14, 401–402.

3. See Louis Menand, *The Marketplace of Ideas: Reform and Resistance in the American University* (New York: Norton, 2010); Jonathan Zimmerman, "US Colleges Need Affirmative Action for Conservative Professors," *Christian Science Monitor*, December 13, 2012; Richard E. Redding, "Likes Attract: The Sociopolitical Groupthink of (Social) Psychologists," *Perspectives on Psychological Science*, 7 (2012): 512–515; Jose Duarte et al., "Political Diversity Will Improve Social Psychological Science," *Behavioral and Brain Sciences*, 38, 2015: e130. doi:10.1017/S0140525X14000430.

4. Michael Bloomberg, "Remarks at Harvard's 363rd Commencement Ceremony," May 29, 2014, available at http://www.mikebloomberg.com/index.cfm?objecti d=4D9E60A5-5056-9A3E-D07D6B773CAD46E4.

5. Alan Charles Kors and Harvey A. Silvergate, *The Shadow University: The Betrayal of Liberty on America's Campuses* (New York: HarperPerennial, 1999); David Horowitz, *The Professors: The 101 Most Dangerous Academics in America* (Washington, DC: Regnery Publishing, 2006); Roger Kimball, *Tenured*

Radicals: How Politics Has Corrupted Higher Education, 3rd ed. (Chicago: Ivan R. Dee, 2008); Bruce Bawer, *The Victims' Revolution: The Rise of Identity Studies and the Closing of the Liberal Mind* (New York: Broadside Books, 2012).

6. William F. Buckley, Jr., *God and Man at Yale: The Superstitions of "Academic Freedom,"* 50th Anniversary ed. (Washington, DC: Regnery Gateway, 1986).

7. Ron Radosh, "Affirmative Action for Professors," *Minding the Campus*, December 20, 2012, available at http://www.mindingthecampus.org/2012/12/affirmative_action_for_profess/.

8. Gross, *Why Are Professors Liberal and Why Do Conservatives Care?*, 92–103, 119–120.

9. Lazarsfeld and Thielens, *The Academic Mind*, 148–162.

10. See, for example, Ellen Schrecker, *The Lost Soul of Higher Education: Corporatization, the Assault on Academic Freedom, and the End of the American University* (New York: New Press, 2010), 97–105; Todd Gitlin, "The Academy Shrugged," *The Chronicle of Higher Education* (May 12, 2011), available at http://chronicle.com/blogs/brainstorm/the-academy-shrugged/34965; Benjamin Soskis, "Dirty Money: From Rockefeller to Koch," *The Atlantic*, March 7, 2014; available at http://www.theatlantic.com/business/archive/2014/03/dirty-money-from-rockefeller-to-koch/284244/.

11. To be sure, scholars have done serious work on various movements of conservative intellectuals. But these movements often labor outside America's ivy-covered campuses and are frequently disengaged from its denizens. See, for example, George H. Nash, *The Conservative Intellectual Movement in America*, 30th Anniversary ed. (Wilmington, DE: ISI Books, 2006); Peter Steinfels, *The Neoconservatives: The Men Who are Changing American Politics* (New York: Touchstone Books, 1980); Patrick Allitt, *Catholic Intellectuals and Conservative Politics in America, 1950–1985* (Ithaca, NY: Cornell University Press, 1993); Steven M. Teles, *The Rise of the Conservative Legal Movement: The Battle for Control of the Law* (Princeton, NJ: Princeton University Press, 2008). Scholars have also done excellent work on important intellectual minorities in higher education. Much of this research, however, has focused on religious professors and colleges, especially those with evangelical convictions and missions. See John Schmalzbauer, *People of Faith: Religious Conviction in American Journalism and Higher Education* (Ithaca, NY: Cornell University Press, 2003); Hanna Rosin, *God's Harvard: A Christian College on a Mission to Save America* (Orlando, FL: Mariner Books, 2007); D. Michael Lindsay, *Faith in the Halls of Power: How Evangelicals Joined the American Elite* (New York: Oxford University Press, 2008); Kevin Roose, *The Unlikely Disciple: A Sinner's Semester at America's Holiest University* (New York: Grand Central Publishing, 2009).

12. See, for example, Robert A. Nisbet, *The Degradation of the Academic Dogma, 1945–1970* (New York: Basic Books, 1971); Allan Bloom, *The Closing of the American Mind* (New York: Simon and Schuster, 1987).

13. See, for example, Robert Dahl, *How Democratic Is the American Constitution?* 2nd ed. (New Haven, CT: Yale University Press, 2003); Frances Fox Piven and Richard A. Cloward, *Poor People's Movements: Why They Succeed, How They Fail* (New York: Vintage Books, 1979); James A. Marone, *The Democratic Wish: Popular Participation and the Limits of American Government*, revised ed. (New Haven, CT: Yale University Press, 1998); Risa L. Goluboff, *The Lost Promise of Civil Rights* (Cambridge, MA: Harvard University Press, 2010).

14. Erving Goffman, *Stigma: Notes on the Management of Spoiled Identity* (New York: Simon and Schuster, 1963).

15. For work in this area, see Sherry E. Woods and Karen M. Harbeck, "Living in Two Words: The Identity Management Strategies Used by Lesbian Physical Educators," *Journal of Homosexuality*, 22(3–4), 1992: 141–166; James D. Woods, *The Corporate Closet: The Professional Lives of Gay Men in America* (New York: Free Press, 1993); Gregory M. Herek, "Why Tell if You're Not Asked: Self-Disclosure, Intergroup Contact, and Heterosexuals' Attitudes toward Lesbians and Gay Men," in Gregory M. Herek, Jared B. Jobe, and Ralph M. Carney, eds., *Out in Force: Sexual Orientation and the Military* (Chicago: University of Chicago Press, 1996), 197–225; Donna Chrobot-Mason, Scott B. Button, and Jeannie D. DiClementi, "Sexual Identity Management Strategies: An Exploration of Antecedents and Consequences," *Sex Roles*, 45(5–6), 2001: 321–336.

16. Naomi Schaefer Riley, *Faculty Lounges: And Other Reasons Why You Won't Get the Education You Paid For* (Lantham, MD: Ivan R. Dee, 2011).

17. Some contend that a similar dynamic accounts for why female professors are underrepresented in the hard sciences. See, for example, Nilanjana Dasgupta, "Ingroup Experts and Peers as Social Vaccines Who Inoculate the Self Concept: The Stereotype Inoculation Model," *Psychological Inquiry*, 22(4), 2011: 231–246.

18. Christian Smith, *The Sacred Project of American Sociology* (New York: Oxford University Press, 2014), 1–27, 189–197. For a broadly similar account see Thomas Sowell, *Intellectuals and Society* (New York: Basic Books, 2009), 76–80, 114–116.

19. For an account of this shift in economics, see Steven E. Rhoads, *The Economist's View of the World: Government, Markets, and Public Policy* (New York: Cambridge University Press, 1985).

20. Benjamin I. Page and Robert Y. Shapiro, *The Rational Public: Fifty Years of Trends in Americans' Policy Preferences* (Chicago: University of Chicago Press, 1992). For an excellent account of the libertarian impulse among ordinary, middle-class Americans, see Alan Wolfe, *One Nation, After All* (New York: Penguin Books, 1998).

21. Amy J. Binder and Kate Wood, *Becoming Right: How Campuses Shape Young Conservatives* (Princeton, NJ: Princeton University Press, 2013).

22. Phillip E. Tetlock and Gregory Mitchell, "Why So Few Conservatives and Should We Care?" *Society*, 52(1), 2015: 28–34.

23. Zimmerman, "US Colleges Need Affirmative Action for Conservative Professors"; Duarte et al., "Political Diversity Will Improve Social Psychological Science."

24. Yancey, *Compromising Scholarship*, 49–83, 116–122; Inbar and Lammers, "Political Diversity in Social and Personality Psychology," 496–503.

25. See, for example, James Q. Wilson, "Bowling with Others," *Commentary* (October 2007): 30–33.

26. Gross, *Why Are Professors Liberal and Why Do Conservatives Care?*, 119–120.

27. James W. Ceaser and Robert Maranto, "Why Political Science Is Left but Not Quite PC: Causes of Disunion and Diversity," in Robert Maranto, Richard E. Redding, and Frederick M. Hess, eds., *The Politically Correct University: Problems, Scope, and Reform* (Washington, DC: AEI Press, 2009), 210.

28. Ladd and Lipset, *The Divided Academy*, 93–124.

29. For a treatment of this problem in the context of the discipline of history, see Peter Novick, *The Noble Dream: The "Objectivity Question" and the American Historical Profession* (New York: Cambridge University Press, 1988).

30. For a critical assessment of the growth of these fields, see Benjamin Ginsburg, *The Fall of the Faculty: The Rise of the All Administrative University and Why It Matters* (New York: Oxford University Press, 2011), 97–130.

31. We did so because of our interest in undergraduate education (in the case of law and public policy) and because the professional schools cover subject matter that is similar to the disciplines we included in our study (especially economics and political science).

32. For an understanding of the coalitional nature of modern American conservatism, see Nash, *The Conservative Intellectual Movement in America*; James Ceaser, "Four Heads and One Heart: The Modern Conservative Movement," in Charles W. Dunn, ed., *The Future of Conservatism: Conflict and Consensus in the Post-Reagan Era* (Wilmington, DE: ISI Books, 2007); Sowell, *Intellectuals and Society*, 90–100.

33. On this latter tendency, see Hayek's postscript, "Why I Am Not a Conservative" in Frederick Hayek, *The Constitution of Liberty* (Chicago: University of Chicago Press, 1960), 397–414. For rebuttals see Madsen Pirie, *Why FA Hayek Is a Conservative* (London: Adam Smith Institute, 1987); Jordan Bloom, "Why Hayek Is a Conservative," *American Conservative*, May 8, 2013, available at http://www.theamericanconservative.com/why-hayek-is-a-conservative/.

34. We selected all professors published in the *Intercollegiate Review* and *Claremont Review of Books* between 2000 and 2010.

35. Professors who either rejected a conservative identity or refused to confirm it were excluded from this total. We also excluded professors from our home institutions—Claremont McKenna College and UCCS. And we excluded professors from sectarian, religious colleges that do not grant tenure and require faculty to accept certain Christian dogmas. We did so primarily because we are interested in conservatives within the mainstream of academia. However, we

did include professors who teach at mainstream religious institutions, such as Baylor University and Providence College (see Table I.2).

36. The first dozen interviews were conducted together to improve the reliability of all subsequent interviews.

37. The lone exception is Mark Regnerus, a sociologist who was embroiled in such a public controversy that it made it impossible to conceal his identity.

38. A few professors would not allow us to record them. In such cases we had to rely on our handwritten notes.

39. Stanley Rothman, April Kelly-Woessner, and Matthew Woessner, *The Still Divided Academy: How Competing Visions of Power, Politics, and Diversity Complicate the Mission of Higher Education* (Lanham, MD: Rowman and Littlefield, 2011), 66–71.

40. Alvin W. Gouldner, "Anti-Minotaur: The Myth of Value Free Sociology," *Social Problems*, 9(3), 1962: 199–213.

CHAPTER 1

1. George H. Nash, *The Conservative Intellectual Movement in America*, 30th Anniversary ed. (Wilmington, DE: ISI Books, 2006), 559, 576–577. For a similar, but not identical, typology, see Daniel Disalvo, *Engines of Change: Party Factions in American Politics, 1868-2010* (New York: Oxford University Press, 2012), 44–48.

2. See, for example, Juli Weiner, "Deconstructing Michele Bachmann's Favorite Metaphor," *Vanity Fair*, June 27, 2011, available at http://www.vanityfair.com/online/daily/2011/06/deconstructing-michele-bachmanns-favorite-metaphor.

3. Nash, *The Conservative Intellectual Movement in America*, 505, 541–42, 556, 581.

4. James Ceaser, "Four Heads and One Heart: The Modern Conservative Movement," in Charles W. Dunn, ed., *The Future of Conservatism: Conflict and Consensus in the Post-Reagan Era* (Wilmington, DE: ISI Books, 2007), 21–23. See also Thomas Sowell, *Intellectuals and Society* (New York: Basic Books, 2009), 90–100.

5. Nash, *The Conservative Intellectual Movement in America*, 505.

6. However, we excluded those that identify as liberal-libertarians or "liberaltarians."

7. See Patrick Allitt, *Catholic Intellectuals and Conservative Politics in America, 1950–1985* (Ithaca, NY: Cornell University Press, 1993).

8. According to the Pew Values Survey, 58% of Democrats support tighter restrictions on immigration.

9. See John L. Ashford, Carolyn L. Funk, and John R. Hibbing, "Are Political Orientations Genetically Transmitted?" *American Political Science Review* 99(2), 2005: 153–167; Douglas R. Oxley et al., "Political Attitudes Vary with Psychological Traits," *Science* 321(5896), 2008: 1667–1670; Peter K. Hatemi et al., "A Genome-Wide Analysis of Liberal and Conservative Political Attitudes," *Journal of Politics* 73(1), 2011: 271–285; Kevin Smith et al., "Biology, Ideology, and Epistemology: How Do We Know Political Attitudes Are Inherited and Why Should We Care?" *American Journal of Political Science* 56(1), 2012: 17–33.

10. Daniel K. Williams, *God's Own Party: The Making of the Christian Right* (New York: Oxford University Press, 2010), 153–158, 167–171.
11. Amy J. Binder and Kate Wood, *Becoming Right: How Campuses Shape Young Conservatives* (Princeton, NJ: Princeton University Press, 2013), 40–42.

CHAPTER 2

1. James Ceaser, "Four Heads and One Heart: The Modern Conservative Movement," in Charles W. Dunn, ed., *The Future of Conservatism: Conflict and Consensus in the Post-Reagan Era* (Wilmington, DE: ISI Books, 2007), 21–23.
2. George H. Nash, *The Conservative Intellectual Movement in America*, 30th Anniversary ed. (Wilmington, DE: ISI Books, 2006), 581.
3. Tom Hamburger and Peter Wallsten, *One Party Country: The Republican Plan for Dominance in the 21st Century* (Hoboken, NJ: Wiley, 2006), 11–28.
4. For the best accounts of Madison's constitutionalism, see Joseph M. Bessette, *The Mild Voice of Reason: Deliberative Democracy and American National Government* (Chicago: University of Chicago Press, 1994), 6–39; and George Thomas, *The Madisonian Constitution* (Baltimore, MD: Johns Hopkins University Press, 2008).
5. James Madison, "The Union a Check on Faction," Federalist Paper No. 10, November 22, 1787; James Madison, "The Structure of Government Must Furnish the Proper Checks and Balances between the Different Departments," Federalist Paper No. 51, February 6, 1788.
6. Nash, *The Conservative Intellectual Movement in America*, 390–394, 540–541.
7. Amy J. Binder and Kate Wood, *Becoming Right: How Campuses Shape Young Conservatives* (Princeton, NJ: Princeton University Press, 2013), 1–13, 213–269.
8. Nash, *The Conservative Intellectual Movement in America*, 391–393, 540–541.
9. Nash, *The Conservative Intellectual Movement in America*, 497–500, 566.
10. Brian Doherty, *Radicals for Capitalism: A Freewheeling History of the Modern American Libertarian Movement* (New York: Public Affairs, 2007), 445–447.
11. Nash, *The Conservative Intellectual Movement in America*, 580.
12. Doherty, *Radicals for Capitalism*, 17, 462–469.
13. Doherty, *Radicals for Capitalism*, 19, 534.
14. Doherty, *Radicals for Capitalism*, 3–4, 20, 327–328, 398–404, 476–477, 577–578.

CHAPTER 3

1. Paul F. Lazarsfeld and Wagner Thielens, Jr., *The Academic Mind: Social Scientists in a Time of Crisis* (Glencoe, IL: Free Press, 1958), 148–162.
2. Lionel Trilling, *The Liberal Imagination: Essays on Literature and Society* (New York: New York Book Review Classics, 2008), xv.

3. Seymour Martin Lipset, "The Sources of the Radical Right (1955)," in Daniel Bell, ed., *The Radical Right*, 3rd ed. (New Brunswick, NJ: Transaction Publishers, 2002), 317–319.

4. Richard Hofstadter, "The Psuedo-Conservative Revolt (1955)," in Daniel Bell, ed., *The Radical Right*, 3rd ed. (New Brunswick, NJ: Transaction Publishers, 2002), 75–79. Also see Richard Hofstadter, *The Paranoid Style in American Politics and Other Essays* (Cambridge, MA: Harvard University Press, 1996).

5. Trilling, *The Liberal Imagination*, xv.

6. Matt Bai, *The Argument: Inside the Battle to Remake Democratic Politics* (New York: Penguin Books, 2007), 23–48.

7. Michael Vitiello, "Liberal Bias in the Legal Academy: Overstated and Undervalued," *Mississippi Law Journal* 77(2), 2007: 541–542.

8. Jere P. Surber, "Well, Naturally We're Liberal," *The Chronicle Review*, February 7, 2010, available at http://chronicle.com/article/Well-Naturally-Were-Liberal/63870/.

9. Mike LaBossiere, "Why Do Professors Tend to Be Liberals?" *Talking Philosophy: The Philosophers' Magazine Blog*, December 23, 2013, available at http://blog.talkingphilosophy.com/?p=7707.

10. Barry Ames et al., "Hide the Republicans, the Christians, and the Women: A Response to 'Politics and Professional Advancement among College Faculty'," *The Forum* 3(2), 2005: 1–9.

11. Neil Gross, *Why Are Professors Liberal and Why Do Conservatives Care?* (Cambridge, MA: Harvard University Press, 2013), 92–103, 119–120.

12. Jesse Graham, Brian A. Nosek, and Jonathan Haidt, "The Moral Stereotypes of Liberals and Conservatives: Exaggeration of Differences across the Political Spectrum," *PloS ONE* 7(12), 2012: e50092.

13. Jonathan Haidt, *The Righteous Mind: Why Good People Are Divided by Politics and Religion* (New York: Pantheon Books, 2012), 288–294.

14. These tendencies have been observed in neighborhoods and churches. See James Q. Wilson, "Bowling with Others," *Commentary*, October 2007: 30–33; Robert D. Putnam and David D. Campbell, *American Grace: How Religion Divides and Unites Us* (New York: Simon and Schuster, 2012), 305–306.

15. Yoel Inbar and Joris Lammers, "Political Diversity in Social and Personality Psychology," *Perspectives on Psychological Science* 7(5), 2012: 496–503.

16. George Yancey, *Compromising Scholarship: Religious and Political Bias in American Higher Education* (Waco, TX: Baylor University Press, 2011), 49–83, 116–122.

17. Gary A. Tobin and Aryeh K. Weinberg, *Profiles of the American University, Volume II: Religious Beliefs and Behavior of College Faculty* (San Francisco: Institute for Jewish and Community Research, 2007), 12, 47–49, 81, 86.

18. Emily Esfahani Smith, "Survey Shocker," *Washington Times*, August 1, 2012.

19. Yancey, *Compromising Scholarship*, 139–143.

20. Barry Ames et al., "Hide the Republicans, the Christians, and the Women," 2.

21. Stanley Rothman, S. Robert Lichter, and Neil Nevitte, "Fundamentals and Fundamentalists: A Reply to Ames et al.," *The Forum* 3(2), 2005: 1–10.

22. Stanley Rothman and S. Robert Lichter, "The Vanishing Conservative—Is There a Glass Ceiling?" in Robert Maranto, Richard E. Redding, and Frederick M. Hess, eds., *The Politically Correct University: Problems, Scope, and Reform* (Washington, DC: AEI Press, 2009), 69–75.

23. Stanley Rothman, April Kelly-Woessner, and Matthew Woessner, *The Still Divided Academy: How Competing Visions of Power, Politics, and Diversity Complicate the Mission of Higher Education* (Lanham, MD: Rowman and Littlefield, 2011), 92–95.

24. Simmons and Gross find that while 3.9% of faculty at liberal arts colleges identify as conservatives, some 10.2% of faculty at elite, Ph.D. institutions are on the right. See Neil Gross and Solon Simmons, "The Social and Political Views of American Professors," Working Paper, September 24, 2007, 29.

25. Barry Ames et al., "Hide the Republicans, the Christians, and the Women," 3–4.

26. Bruce L. R. Smith, Jeremy D. Mayer, and A. Lee Fritschler, *Closed Minds? Politics and Ideology on American Campuses* (Washington, DC: Brookings Institution Press, 2008), 192–193.

27. Brad Gregory, "Beyond Either-Or," *The Observer*, February 7 2006, available at http://ndsmcobserver.com/2006/02/beyond-either-or/.

28. D. Michael Lindsay, *Faith in the Halls of Power: How Evangelicals Joined the American Elite* (New York: Oxford University Press, 2007).

29. Gross, *Why Are Professors Liberal and Why Do Conservatives Care?*, 174–176.

30. Ames et al., "Hide the Republicans, the Christians, and the Women," 2–3.

31. Gross, *Why Are Professors Liberal and Why Do Conservatives Care?*, 173–174.

32. Phillip E. Tetlock and Gregory Mitchell, "Why So Few Conservatives and Should We Care?" *Society* 52(1), 2015: 28–34.

33. Haidt, *The Righteous Mind*, 81–91.

34. Stephen Abromowitz et al., "Publish or Politic: Referee Bias in Manuscript Review," *Journal of Applied Social Psychology* 5(3), 1975; Stephen J. Ceci et al., "Human Subject Review, Personal Values, and the Regulation of Social Science Research," *American Psychologist* 40(9), 1985: 994–1002; Inbar and Lammers, "Political Diversity in Social and Personality Psychology," 496–503.

35. Ceci et al., "Human Subject Review, Personal Values, and the Regulation of Social Science Research," 994–1002.

36. Inbar and Lammers, "Political Diversity in Social and Personality Psychology," 496–503.

37. Steven E. Rhoads, *Taking Sex Differences Seriously* (San Francisco: Encounter Books, 2006), 19–21.

38. Tetlock and Mitchell, "Why So Few Conservatives and Should We Care?," 28–34.

39. Matthew Woessner and April Kelly-Woessner, "Left Pipeline: Why Conservatives Don't Get Doctorates," in Robert Maranto, Richard E. Redding, and

Frederick M. Hess, eds., *The Politically Correct University: Problems, Scope, and Reforms* (Washington, DC: AEI Press, 2009), 39.

40. Ethan Fosse, Jeremy Fresse, and Neil Gross, "Political Liberalism and Graduate School Attendance: A Longitudinal Analysis," Working Paper, February 25, 2011.

41. Ethan Fosse, Neil Gross, and Joseph Ma, "Political Bias in the Graduate Admissions Process: A Field Experiment," Working Paper, March 3, 2011. However, an earlier study found some evidence of bias against conservative Protestants in the admissions process. See John D. Gartner, "Antireligious Prejudice in Admissions to Doctoral Programs in Clinical Psychology," *Professional Psychology: Research and Practice* 17(5), 1986: 473–475.

42. Fosse, Gross, and Ma, "Political Bias in the Graduate Admissions Process."

43. George Yancey, "Both/And Instead of Either/Or," *Society* 52(1), 2015: 23–27.

44. Jack Shafer, "The Liberal Media and How to Stop It," *Slate*, October 29, 2008, available at http://www.slate.com/articles/news_and_politics/press_box/2008/10/the_liberal_media_and_how_to_stop_it.html.

45. Ethan Fosse and Neil Gross, "Why Are Professors Liberal?," *Theory and Society* 41(2), 2012: 127–168.

46. Christian Smith, *The Sacred Project of American Sociology* (New York: Oxford University Press, 2014), 1–27, 189–197. It may be, on the other hand, that Smith does not adequately allow for the possibility of subcultures lodged in particular subspecialties. For an interesting discussion of the power and autonomy of subfields, see Christopher Jencks and David Riesman, *The Academic Revolution*, reprint (New Brunswick, NJ: Transaction Publishers, 2002), 523–530.

47. Peter L. Berger, "Sociology: A Disinvitation?" in Stephen Cole, ed., *What's Wrong with Sociology?* (New Brunswick, NJ: Transaction Publishers, 2001), 193–204.

48. Gross, *Why Are Professors Liberal and Why Do Conservatives Care?*, 145–146. In their original essay, Fosse and Gross seem to express a similar, albeit less developed, argument. There they suggested that the subject matter of some social sciences is of special interest to progressives: "Over the course of its twentieth century history, for example, sociology has increasingly defined itself as the study of race, class, and gender inequality—a set of concerns especially important to liberals—and this means that sociology will consistently recruit from a more liberal applicant pool than fields like mechanical engineering." See Fosse and Gross, "Why Are Professors Liberal?," 159.

49. Woessner and Kelly-Woessner, "Left Pipeline," 48–49; Stephen R. Porter and Paul D. Umbach, "College Major Choice: An Analysis of Person-Environment Fit," *Research in Higher Education*, 47(4), 2006: 429–449; Amy J. Binder and Kate Wood, *Becoming Right: How Campuses Shape Young Conservatives* (Princeton, NJ: Princeton University Press, 2013), 151–152.

50. Gross, *Why Are Professors Liberal and Why Do Conservatives Care?*, 149.

51. Erving Goffman, *Stigma: Notes on the Management of Spoiled Identity* (New York: Simon and Schuster, 1963), 48–51.

52. Goffman, *Stigma*, 1–40.
53. See, for example, Sherry E. Woods and Karen M. Harbeck, "Living in Two Worlds: The Identity Management Strategies Used by Lesbian Physical Educators," *Journal of Homosexuality*, 22(3–4), 1992: 141–166; James D. Woods, *The Corporate Closet: The Professional Lives of Gay Men in America* (New York: Free Press, 1993); Gregory M. Herek, "Why Tell If You're Not Asked: Self-Disclosure, Intergroup Contact, and Heterosexuals' Attitudes toward Lesbians and Gay Men," in Gregory M. Herek, Jared B. Jobe, and Ralph M. Carney, eds., *Out in Force: Sexual Orientation and the Military* (Chicago: University of Chicago Press, 1996), 197–225; Donna Chrobot-Mason, Scott B. Button, and Jeannie D. DiClementi, "Sexual Identity Management Strategies: An Exploration of Antecedents and Consequences," *Sex Roles* 45(5–6), 2001: 321–336.

CHAPTER 4

1. Erving Goffman, *Stigma: Notes on the Management of Spoiled Identity* (New York: Simon and Schuster, 1963), 42, 73–91, 100.
2. Nate Honeycutt, "Political Diversity across Academic Disciplines," paper presented at the Western Psychological Association, 2013.
3. Yoel Inbar and Joris Lammers, "Political Diversity in Social and Personality Psychology," *Perspectives on Psychological Science*, 7(5), 2012: 496–503.
4. Neil Gross and Solon Simmons, "The Social and Political Views of American Professors," Working Paper, September 24, 2007, 67–71.
5. Stanley Rothman, April Kelly-Woessner, and Matthew Woessner, *The Still Divided Academy: How Competing Visions of Power, Politics, and Diversity Complicate the Mission of Higher Education* (Lanham, MD: Rowman and Littlefield, 2011), 179–184.
6. Beth E. Schneider, "Coming Out at Work: Bridging the Private/Public Gap," *Work and Occupations*, 13(4), 1986: 463–487; Annette Friskopp and Sharon Silverstein, *Straight Jobs, Gay Lives* (New York: Touchstone, 1996). It was also anticipated by Goffman's theoretical work on passing. "[N]early all matters which are very secret are still known to someone," Goffman noted, "and hence cast a shadow." See Goffman, *Stigma*, 73–74.
7. In his study of gays and lesbians in the military, psychologist Gregory Herek called these "passing" strategies *discretion* and *fabrication*, respectively. Herek also identified a third passing strategy called *concealment*, which involves actively hiding information about one's identity. It is closely related, but not identical, to discretion. See Gregory M. Herek, "Why Tell If You're Not Asked: Self-Disclosure, Intergroup Contact, and Heterosexuals' Attitudes toward Lesbians and Gay Men" in Gregory M. Herek, Jared B. Jobe, and Ralph M. Carney, eds., *Out in Force: Sexual Orientation and the Military* (Chicago: University of Chicago Press, 1996), 197–225. For a similar typology, see James D. Woods, *The Corporate Closet: The Professional Lives of Gay Men in America* (New York: Free Press, 1993).

8. Conservatives, for example, do not have to worry about being rejected by their parents or those they love. Kath Weston, *Families We Choose: Lesbians, Gays, Kinship*, revised ed. (New York: Columbia University Press, 1997), 43–76.

9. Goffman understood that such demoralization is sometimes a consequence of Y's strategy. "And presumably he will suffer feelings of disloyalty and self-contempt when he cannot take action against offensive remarks," Goffman theorized, "especially when he himself finds it dangerous to refrain from joining in this vilification." See Goffman, *Stigma*, 87.

10. Goffman called such confrontations a "showdown." See Goffman, *Stigma*, 85.

11. Goffman, *Stigma*, 43–45, 92–93.

12. George Yancey, *Compromising Scholarship: Religious and Political Bias in American Higher Education* (Waco, TX: Baylor University Press, 2011), 115–117.

13. Yancey, *Compromising Scholarship*, 72–74, 130. Also see Rothman, Kelly-Woessner, and Woessner, *The Still Divided Academy*, 81–83.

14. They are another example of what Goffman called a "stigma symbol." See Goffman, *Stigma*, 43–44.

15. Bruce L. R. Smith, Jeremy D. Mayer, and A. Lee Fritschler, *Closed Minds? Politics and Ideology on American Campuses* (Washington, DC: Brookings Institution Press, 2008), 77–78; Gross and Simmons, "The Social and Political Views of American Professors," 34.

16. Allan Bloom, *The Closing of the American Mind* (New York: Simon and Schuster, 1987), 347–356.

17. For a good discussion of minority tyranny by leftist factions, see Benjamin Ginsburg, *The Fall of the Faculty: The Rise of the All Administrative University and Why It Matters* (New York: Oxford University Press, 2011), 97–130.

18. See, for example, Judith A. Clair, Joy E. Beatty, and Tammy L. Maclean, "Out of Sight, but Not Out of Mind: Managing Invisible Social Identities in the Workplace," *Academy of Management Review*, 30(1), 2005: 78–95.

19. "Bias in Academia, An Email," instapundit.com, February 10, 2011, available at http://pjmedia.com/instapundit/114718/.

20. Jonathan Haidt, *The Righteous Mind: Why Good People Are Divided by Politics and Religion* (New York: Pantheon Books, 2012), 68–69, 309–312.

21. Gross and Simmons, "The Social and Political Views of American Professors," 70–71.

22. Gross and Simmons, "The Social and Political Views of American Professors," 33–41.

23. Yancey, *Compromising Scholarship*, 57–64, 115–122.

24. See, for example, Ellen Schrecker, *The Lost Soul of Higher Education: Corporatization, the Assault on Academic Freedom, and the End of the American University* (New York: New Press, 2010).

25. Paul F. Lazarsfeld and Wagner Thielens, Jr., *The Academic Mind: Social Scientists in a Time of Crisis* (Glencoe, IL: Free Press, 1958), 98–105, 196, 222–225, 232.

26. For discussions of how Protestant theology and conservative politics are linked at fundamentalist colleges, see Hanna Rosin, *God's Harvard: A Christian College on a Mission to Save America* (New York: Mariner Books, 2008); Kevin Roose, *The Unlikely Disciple: A Sinner's Semester at America's Holiest University* (New York: Grand Central Publishing, 2009).

27. Thomas Albert Howard, "L'affaire Hochschild and Evangelical Colleges," *Books and Culture*, May/June 2006: 29–31.

CHAPTER 5

1. Judith A. Clair, Joy E. Beatty, and Tammy L. Maclean, "Out of Sight, but Not Out of Mind: Managing Invisible Social Identities in the Workplace," *Academy of Management Review*, 30(1), 2005: 78–95. Woods's concept of integration is somewhat similar as well. See James D. Woods, *The Corporate Closet: The Professional Lives of Gay Men in America* (New York: Free Press, 1993).

2. Ross K. Baker, *House and Senate*, 4th ed. (New York: Norton, 2008), 60–61.

3. Bruce L. R. Smith, Jeremy D. Meyer, and A. Lee Fritschler, *Closed Minds? Politics and Ideology in American Universities* (Washington, DC: Brookings Institution Press, 2008), 85–91.

4. Smith, Meyer, and Fritschler, *Closed Minds?* 85–91.

5. Erving Goffman, *Stigma: Notes on the Management of Spoiled Identity* (New York: Simon and Schuster, 1963), 12–13.

6. Binder and Wood developed this concept in their work on the political styles of right-wing student groups. Amy J. Binder and Kate Wood, *Becoming Right: How Campuses Shape Young Conservatives* (Princeton, NJ: Princeton University Press, 2012), 3–5.

7. Goffman also assumed that evasion would be in the interest of the dominant group. See Goffman, *Stigma*, 12.

8. Goffman, *Stigma*, 17–18.

9. Binder and Wood, *Becoming Right*, 5, 240–248.

10. Karen Herzog, "MU Prof Banned for Criticizing TA on Gar Marriage Discussion," *Milwaukee Wisconsin Journal Sentinel*, December 17, 2014; Scott Jashik, "Firing a Professor over a Blog Post," *Slate*, February 10, 2015, available at http://www.slate.com/articles/life/inside_higher_ed/2015/02/john_mcadams_marquette_tries_to_fire_tenured_professor_over_blog_post_about.html.

11. Stanley Rothman and S. Robert Lichter, "The Vanishing Conservative—Is There a Glass Ceiling," in Robert Maranto, Richard E. Redding, and Frederick M. Hess, eds., *The Politically Correct University: Problems, Scope, and Reforms* (Washington, DC: AEI Press, 2009), 60–75.

12. Mark Regnerus, "How Different Are the Adult Children of Parents Who Have Same-Sex Relationships: Findings from the New Family Structures Study," *Social Science Research*, 41(4), 2012: 752–770.

13. "Letter to the Editors and Advisory Editors of *Social Science Research*," June 29, 2012, available at http://familyinequality.wordpress.com/2012/06/29/200-researchers-respond-to-regnerus-paper/.

14. See Loren Marks, "Same-Sex Parenting and Children's Outcomes: A Closer Examination of the American Psychological Association's Brief on Lesbian and Gay Parenting," *Social Science Research*, 41(4), 2012: 735–751.

15. Tom Bartlett, "Controversial Gay Parenting Study Is Severely Flawed, Journal's Audit Finds," *Chronicle of Higher Education*, July 26, 2012.

16. "Bristol Palin Loves Fake Sociology," Iranianredneck's Weblog, May 2, 2012, available at https://iranianredneck.wordpress.com/2012/05/02/bristol-palin-loves-fake-sociology/.

17. Bartlett, "Controversial Gay Parenting Study Is Severely Flawed, Journal's Audit Finds."

18. Darren E. Sherkat, "The Editorial Process and Politicized Scholarship: Monday Morning Editorial Quarterbacking and a Call for Scientific Vigilance," *Social Science Research*, 41(6), 2012: 1346–1349.

19. Sherkat, "The Editorial Process and Politicized Scholarship," 1346–1349.

20. Belinda Luscombe, "Do Children of Same-Sex Parents Really Fare Worse?" *Time*, July 11, 2012, available at http://healthland.time.com/2012/06/11/do-children-of-same-sex-parents-really-fare-worse/.

21. Douglas W. Allen, "The Regnerus Debate," *National Review Online*, June 14, 2012, available at http://www.nationalreview.com/article/302749/regnerus-debate-douglas-w-allen.

22. Christian Smith, "An Academic Auto-da-Fe," *The Chronicle Review*, July 23, 2012.

23. See the November 2012 issue of *Social Science Research*.

24. Simon Cheng and Brian Powell, "Measurement, Methods, and Divergent Patterns: Reassessing the Affects of Same-Sex Parents," *Social Science Research*, 52, 2015: 615–626.

25. Scott Rose, "Open Letter to the University of Texas regarding Professor Mark Regnerus' Alleged Unethical Anti-Gay Study," June 24, 2012, available at http://thenewcivilrightsmovement.com/open-letter-to-university-of-texas-regarding-professor-mark-regneruss-alleged-unethical-anti-gay-study/civil-rights/2012/06/24/41977.

26. Letter to Robert Robertson from Alan Price, August 24, 2012, available at http://www.utexas.edu/opa/wordpress/news/files/PRICE-Report.pdf.

27. Memo to Steven W. Leslie and others, "Regnerus Inquiry Report," from Robert Peterson, August 24, 2012.

28. Christine L. Williams, "Statement from the Chair regarding Professor Regnerus," April 12, 2014, accessed July 1, 2014, available at http://www.utexas.edu/cola/depts/sociology/news/7572.

29. Christian Smith, *The Sacred Project of American Sociology* (New York: Oxford University Press, 2013), 161–162.

CHAPTER 6

1. American Sociological Association, "Real Utopias: Emancipatory Projects, Institutional Designs, Possible Futures," Final Program of the 2012 Annual Meeting (Washington, DC: ASA, 2012), 1–19.

2. Jason Shafrin, "At the AEA," *Healthcare Economist*, January 7, 2012, available at http://healthcare-economist.com/2012/01/07/at-the-aea/.

3. Goffman noted this tendency in his work on stigma. "Presumably the more allied the individual is with normals," Goffman speculated, "the more he will see himself is non-stigmatic terms." Erving Goffman, *Stigma: Notes on the Management of Spoiled Identity* (New York: Simon and Schuster, 1963), 107.

4. Gintis reviewed *Basic Economics* on Amazon.com; see http://www.amazon.com/Basic-Economics-Common-Sense-Economy/product-reviews/0465002609?pageNumber=11.

5. Steven E. Rhoads, *The Economist's View of the World: Government, Markets, and Public Policy* (New York: Cambridge University Press, 1985), 75–81.

6. Everett Carl Ladd and Seymour Martin Lipset, *The Divided Academy: Professors and Politics* (New York: Norton, 1975), 107–124.

7. George Stigler, "The Politics of Political Economists," *Quarterly Journal of Economics*, 73(4), 1959: 522–532.

8. Rhoads, *The Economist's View of the World*, 86–87, 102–103.

9. Stigler, "The Politics of Political Economists," 522–532.

10. Jonathan Haidt, *The Righteous Mind: Why Good People Are Divided by Politics and Religion* (New York: Pantheon Books, 2012), 302–304.

11. Murray N. Rothbard, "The Politics of Political Economists: Comment," *Quarterly Journal of Economics*, 74(4), 1960: 659–665. In response, Stigler said Rothbard was guilty of "vast oversimplification" since private firms "collect much more information than government" and that data "cut in every direction." See George J. Stigler, "Reply," *Quarterly Journal of Economics*, 74(4), 1960: 670–671.

12. Donald W. Katzner, "On Quantifying the Nonquantifiable," *Journal of Post Keynesian Economics*, 1(2), 1978–1979: 113–128.

13. Examples cited in Daniel DiSalvo, "The Politics of Studying Politics: Political Science since the 1960s," *Society*, 50(2), 2013: 132–139.

14. Allan Bloom, *The Closing of the American Mind* (New York: Simon and Schuster, 1987), 365–366.

15. Ladd and Lipset, *The Divided Academy*, 120.

16. James W. Ceaser and Robert Maranto, "Why Political Science Is Left but Not Quite PC: Causes of Disunion and Diversity," in Robert Maranto, Richard E. Redding, and Frederick M. Hess, eds., *The Politically Correct University: Problems, Scope, and Reform* (Washington, DC: AEI Press, 2009), 219.

17. Ceaser and Maranto, "Why Political Science Is Left but Not Quite PC," 220. On similar influences in the field of international relations, see Patrick Thaddeus Jackson, "Rationalizing Realpolitik: US International Relations as a Liberal

Field," in Neil Gross and Solon Simmons, eds., *Professors and Their Politics* (Baltimore, MD: Johns Hopkins University Press, 2014), 267–290.

18. Peter L. Berger, *An Invitation to Sociology: A Humanistic Perspective* (New York: Doubleday, 1963), 13.

19. Peter Novick, *The Noble Dream: The 'Objectivity Question' and the American Historical Profession* (New York: Cambridge University Press, 1988), 464–465.

20. David Brooks, "Lonely Campus Voices," *New York Times*, September 27, 2003.

21. Nina J. Easton, *Gang of Five: Leaders at the Center of the Conservative Crusade* (New York: Simon and Schuster, 2000), 47.

22. Thomas Medvetz, "The Merits of Marginality: Think Tanks, Conservative Intellectuals, and the Liberal Academy," in Neil Gross and Solon Simmons, eds., *Professors and Their Politics* (Baltimore, MD: Johns Hopkins University Press, 2014), 291–308.

23. Thomas Sowell, *Intellectuals and Society* (New York: Basic Books, 2009), 6–8.

24. Christian Smith, *The Sacred Project of American Sociology* (New York: Oxford University Press, 2014), 140–142. Also see Jonathan Imber, "Other-Directed Rebels," *Contemporary Sociology*, 28(3), 1999: 255–259.

25. Alvin W. Gouldner, "Anti-Minotaur: The Myth of Value Free Sociology," *Social Problems*, 9(3), 1962: 199–213.

26. Goffman recognized this tendency in his work on stigma. "This stigmatized individual is likely to use his stigma," Goffman noted, "as an excuse for ill success that has come his way for other reasons." See Goffman, *Stigma*, 10–11.

CHAPTER 7

1. Luke Sheahan, "Missouri State Releases Report on Social Work Department, Foundation For Individual Rights in Education", *FIRE.org*, April 9, 2007, available at http://www.thefire.org/missouri-state-releases-report-on-social-work-department/.

2. David French, "Missouri State and Indoctrination's Final Frontier," *National Review Online*, November 2, 2006, available at http://www.nationalreview.com/phi-beta-cons/45471/missouri-state-and-indoctrinations-final-frontier.

3. Jim Sedanius et al., *The Diversity Challenge: Social Identity and Intergroup Relations on the College Campus* (New York: Russell Sage Foundation, 2010), 323.

4. Lisa Legault, Jennifer N. Gutshell, and Michael Inzlicht, "Ironic Effects of Antiprejudice Messages: How Motivational Interventions Can Reduce (but Also Increase) Prejudice," *Psychological Science*, 22(12), 2012: 1472–1477.

5. Stanley Rothman, April Kelly-Woessner, and Matthew Woessner, *The Still Divided Academy: How Competing Visions of Power, Politics, and Diversity Complicate the Mission of Higher Education* (Lanham, MD: Rowman and Littlefield, 2011), 74–78. Also see Robert Whaples, "Changes in Attitudes among College Economics Students about the Fairness of the Market," *Journal of Economic Education*, 26(4), 1995: 308–313.

6. Neil Gross, *Why Are Professors Liberal and Why Do Conservatives Care?* (Cambridge, MA: Harvard University Press, 2013), 78–86.

7. Kyle Dodson, "The Effects of College on the Social and Political Attitudes and Civic Participation," in Neil Gross and Solon Simmons, eds., *Professors and Their Politics* (Baltimore, MD: Johns Hopkins University Press, 2014), 135–157.

8. Jonathan Zimmerman, "The Context of Undergraduate Teaching and Learning," *Society*, 52(1), 2015: 42–46.

9. Jonathan Haidt, *The Righteous Mind: Why Good People Are Divided by Politics and Religion* (New York: Pantheon Books, 2012), 68–69, 309–312.

10. Bruce L. R. Smith, Jeremy D. Meyer, and A. Lee Fritschler, *Closed Minds? Politics and Ideology in American Universities* (Washington, DC: Brookings Institution Press, 2008), 141.

11. Paul Lazersfeld, Bernard Barelson, Hazel Gauder, *The People's Choice: How the Voter Makes Up His Mind in a Presidential Campaign* (New York: Columbia University Press, 1944); Thomas E. Patterson and Robert D. McGlure, *The Unseeing Eye: The Myth of Television Power in National Elections* (New York: Putnam's, 1976); Stephen Ansolabehere and Shanto Iyengar, *Going Negative: How Political Advertisements Shrink and Polarize the Electorate* (New York: Free Press, 1997).

12. Stephen R. Porter and Paul D. Umbach, "College Major Choice: An Analysis of Person-Environment Fit," *Research in Higher Education*, 47(4), 2006: 429–449.

13. Amy J. Binder and Kate Wood, *Becoming Right: How Campuses Shape Young Conservatives* (Princeton, NJ: Princeton University Press, 2013), 151–152.

14. Mack D. Mariani and Gordon J. Hewitt, "Indoctrination U? Faculty Ideology and Changes in Student Orientation," *PS: Political Science and Politics*, 41(4), 2008: 773–783.

15. Donald Lazere, "The Contradictions of Cultural Conservatism in the Assault on American Colleges," *Cultural Studies*, 19(4), 2005: 415–422.

16. Adam Kotsko, "Christians in Academe: A Reply," *Inside Higher Ed*, August 9, 2010, available at www.insidehighered.com/views/2010/08/09/kotsko#sthash.hEuFUaIg.dpbs.

17. Chris Gaither, "Berkeley Course on Mideast Raises Concerns," *New York Times*, May 16, 2002, available at http://www.nytimes.com/2002/05/16/us/berkeley-course-on-mideast-raises-concerns.html.

18. Dodson, "The Effects of College on Social and Political Attitudes and Civic Engagement," 155–157.

19. Whaples, "Changes in Attitudes among College Economics Students about the Fairness of the Market," 308–313.

20. Conservative students, meanwhile, might moderate slightly because they are persuaded by some of their professors' arguments.

21. Norval Glenn, *Closed Hearts, Closed Minds: The Textbook Story of Marriage* (New York: Institute for American Values, 1997), 1–21.

22. Haidt, *The Righteous Mind*, 287.

23. Stephen Hayward, "Conservatives & Higher Ed," *The New Criterion*, June 2014, available at http://www.newcriterion.com/articles.cfm/Conservatives—higher-ed-7920.

24. John Stuart Mill, *On Liberty* (Indianapolis, IN: Hackett Publishing Company, 1978), 35.

25. Hayward, "Conservatives & Higher Ed."

26. See Jon A. Shields, *The Democratic Virtues of the Christian Right* (Princeton, NJ: Princeton University Press, 2009), 156–159.

27. Haidt, *The Righteous Mind*, 81–91.

28. David Horowitz, *Reforming Our University: The Campaign for an Academic Bill of Rights* (Washington, DC: Regnery, 2010), ix–20.

29. Though a minority, conservatives seem to be stronger proponents of neutrality in the classroom. Gross and Simmons found that while 22% of conservative professors are strong proponents of neutrality, a mere 5% of liberals agreed. See Neil Gross and Solon Simmons, "The Social and Political Views of American Professors," Working Paper, September 24, 2007, 62–63.

30. Binder and Wood, *Becoming Right*, 9.

31. Commission on the Humanities and Social Sciences, *The Heart of the Matter: The Humanities and Social Sciences for a Vibrant, Competitive, and Secure Nation* (Cambridge, MA: American Academy of Arts and Sciences, 2013), 11, 22.

32. Albert O. Hirschman, *Exit, Voice, and Loyalty* (Cambridge, MA: Harvard University Press, 1970).

33. See Neil Gross and Solon Simmons, eds., *Professors and Their Politics* (Baltimore, MD: Johns Hopkins University Press, 2014).

34. Gross and Simmons, "The Social and Political Views of American Professors," 62–64.

35. Christian Smith, *The Sacred Project of American Sociology* (New York: Oxford University Press, 2014), 1–27, 189–197.

36. Deborah Prentice, "Liberal Norms and Their Discontents," *Perspectives on Psychological Science*, 7(5), 2012: 516–518.

37. Jose Duarte et al., "Political Diversity Will Improve Social Psychological Science," *Behavioral and Brain Sciences*, 38, 2015: e130. doi:10.1017/S0140525X14000430.

38. Harry Bruinius, *Better for All the World: The Secret History of America's Forced Sterilization and America's Quest for Racial Purity* (New York: Vintage, 2007), 18–19.

39. Sharon M. Leon, *An Image of God: The Catholic Struggle with Eugenics* (Chicago: University of Chicago Press, 2013).

40. Jon A. Shields, "Framing the Christian Right: How Progressives and Post-War Liberals Constructed the Christian Right," *Journal of Church and State*, 53(4), 2011: 635–655.

41. Edward J. Larson, *Summer for the Gods: The Scopes Trial and America's Continuing Debate over Science and Religion* (Cambridge, MA: Harvard University Press, 1997), 23–28.

42. John Earl Haynes and Harvey Klehr, *In Denial: Historians' Communism and Espionage* (San Francisco, CA: Encounter Books, 2003), 1–46.

43. For excellent work that challenges the radical orthodoxy, see Harvey Klehr, John Earl Haynes, and Fridrikh Igorevich Firsov, *The Secret World of American Communism* (New Haven, CT: Yale University Press, 1995); Harvey Klehr and John Earl Haynes, *The Soviet World of American Communism* (New Haven, CT: Yale University Press, 1998).

44. Haynes and Klehr estimate that the *Journal of American History* published twenty-two articles with a positive perspective on American communism over a thirty-year period, but not a single critical one.

45. Haynes and Klehr, *In Denial*, 59–87, 193–233.

46. David L. Chappell, *Stone of Hope: Prophetic Religion and the Death of Jim Crow* (Chapel Hill, NC: University of North Carolina Press, 2004), 1–8, 44–66, 87–104.

47. Chappell, *Stone of Hope*, 179–190.

48. Chappell, *Stone of Hope*, 3–4, 100–104.

49. Jeffrey K. Hadden, "Toward Desacralizing Secularization Theory," *Social Forces*, 65(3), 1987: 587–611.

50. Smith, *The Sacred Project of American Sociology*, 150–152.

51. Hadden, "Toward Desacralizing Secularization Theory," 587–611.

52. James T. Patterson, *Freedom Is Not Enough: The Moynihan Report and America's Struggle over Black Family Life from LBJ to Obama* (New York: Basic Books, 2010), 47–86, 129–165.

53. Sara McLanahan and Gary Sandefur, *Growing Up with a Single Parent, What Hurts, What Helps* (Cambridge, MA: Harvard University Press, 1997), 19–38.

54. For some examples of work in this tradition, see Judith Stacey, *Brave New Families: Stories of Domestic Upheaval in Late-Twentieth-Century America*, reprint ed. (Berkeley, CA: University of California Press, 1998); Stephanie Coontz, *The Way We Never Were: American Families and the Nostalgia Trap* (New York: Basic Books, 1993).

55. Smith, *The Sacred Project of American Sociology*, 189.

56. See Jerry Z. Muller, *Conservatism: An Anthology of Social and Political Thought from David Hume to the Present* (Princeton, NJ: Princeton University Press, 1997).

57. Richard H. Sander, "A Systematic Analysis of Affirmative Action in American Law Schools," *Stanford Law Review*, 57(2), 2004: 367–483. See also Richard H. Sandler and Stuart Taylor, Jr., *Mismatch: How Affirmative Action Hurts Students It's Intended to Help, and Why Universities Won't Admit It* (New York: Basic Books, 2012).

58. See, for example, Jesse Rothstein and Albert H. Yoon, "Affirmative Action in Law School Admissions: What Do Racial Preferences Do?" *NBER Working Paper*, No. 14276 (August 2008), 1–70.

59. Alex Rajczi, "What Is the Conservative Point of View about Distributive Justice?" *Public Affairs Quarterly*, 28(4), 2014: 341–373.

60. Rajczi, "What Is the Conservative Point of View about Distributive Justice?" 341–373.

61. Steven E. Rhoads, *Taking Sex Differences Seriously* (San Francisco, CA: Encounter Books, 2004).

62. Lloyd B. Lueptow, Lori Garovich-Szabo, and Margaret B. Lueptow, "Social Change and the Persistence of Sex Typing, 1974-1997," *Social Forces*, 80(1), 2001: 1–35.

63. Susan Moller Okin, *Justice, Gender, and the Family* (New York: Basic Books, 1989), 179.

64. Smith, *The Sacred Project of American Sociology*, 153–155.

65. Statement of Mary Ann Glendon, Learned Hand Professor of Law, Harvard University, Origins and Scope of Roe v. Wade, Hearing Before the Subcommittee on the Constitution of the Committee on the Judiciary, House of Representatives, 104th Congress, 2d Session, 22 April 1996.

66. Mary Ann Glendon, "Women and Roe," *First Things*, June 2003.

67. James Davison Hunter, *Before the Shooting Begins: Searching for Democracy in America's Culture War* (New York: Free Press, 1997), 87.

68. For some of the most influential examples, see Thedor W. Adorno et al., *The Authoritarian Personality* (New York: Harper and Brothers, 1950); Daniel Bell, ed., *The New American Right* (New York: Criterion Books, 1955); Richard Hofstadter, *Anti-Intellectualism in American Life* (New York: Vintage Books, 1962); Thomas Byrne Edsall and Mary D. Edsall, *Chain Reaction: The Impact of Race, Rights and Taxes on American Politics* (New York: Norton, 1991); Donald R. Kinder and Lynn M. Sanders, *Divided by Color: Racial Politics and Democratic Ideals* (Chicago: University of Chicago Press, 1996); Lisa McGirr, *Suburban Warriors: The Origins of the New American Right* (Princeton, NJ: Princeton University Press, 2002).

69. Gerard Alexander, "Why Are Liberals So Condescending?" *Washington Post*, February 7, 2010.

70. Perry Bacon, Jr. and Shailagh Murray, "Opponents Paint Obama as an Elitist," *Washington Post*, April 12, 2008; "'Bitter' Is Hard Pill for Obama to Swallow," *Washington Post*, April 13, 2008.

71. See, for example, Jacob S. Hacker and Paul Pierson, *Off Center: The Republican Revolution and the Erosion of Democracy* (New Haven, CT: Yale University Press, 2006); Barbara Sinclair, *Party Wars: Polarization and the Politics of National Policy Making* (Norman, OK: University of Oklahoma Press, 2006); Rick Perlstein, *Nixonland: The Rise of a President and the Fracturing of America* (New York: Scribner, 2008); Thomas E. Mann and Norman J. Ornstein, *It's Even Worse Than It Looks: How the American Constitutional System Collided with the New Politics of Extremism* (New York: Basic Books, 2013).

72. Report of the Committee on Political Parties, "Toward a More Responsible Two-Party System," supplement to the *American Political Science Review*, 44(3), 1950.

73. Hacker and Pierson, *Off Center*, 187.

74. For a more developed discussion of these developments, see Jon A. Shields, "In Praise of the Values Voter," *Wilson Quarterly*, 31(4), 2007: 32–38.

75. Matt McFarland, "Why Clay Christensen Is Abandoning the Traditional Approach to Academic Research," *The Washington Post*, June 12, 2014, available at http://www.washingtonpost.com/blogs/innovations/wp/2014/06/12/why-clay-christensen-is-abandoning-the-traditional-approach-to-academic-research/.

76. Vincent Larivière et al. "The Decline in the Concentration of Citations, 1900–2007," *Journal of the American Society for Information Science and Technology*, 60(4), 2009: 858–862.

77. Kieran Healy, "Lewis and the Women," KieranHealy.org, June 2013, available at http://kieranhealy.org/blog/archives/2013/06/19/lewis-and-the-women/.

78. Cyril C. Means, Jr., "The Law of New York concerning Abortion and the Status of the Foetus, 1664–1658: A Case of Cessation of Constitutionality," *New York Law Forum*, 14(3), 1968: 411–515.

79. Cyril C. Means, Jr., "The Phoenix of Abortional Freedom: Is a Penumbral Right or Ninth Amendment Right about to Rise from the Nineteenth-Century Legislative Ashes of a Fourteenth-Century Common-Law Liberty", *New York Law Forum*, 17(2), 1971: 336.

80. Justin Buckley Dyer, *Slavery, Abortion, and the Politics of Constitutional Meaning* (New York: Cambridge University Press, 2013), 59–61.

81. Dyer, *Slavery, Abortion, and the Politics of Constitutional Meaning*, 110–118.

82. Hunter, *Before the Shooting Begins*, 176–177.

83. Dyer, *Slavery, Abortion, and the Politics of Constitutional Meaning*, 110–118.

84. "Brief for 281 Historians as Amici Curiae in Support of Appellees," *Webster v. Reproductive Health Services*, 492 U.S. 490 (1989): 44, 48.

85. Sylvia Law, "Conversations between Historians and the Constitution," *Public Historian*, 12(3), 1990: 11–17.

86. Quotations from Dyer, *Slavery, Abortion, and the Politics of Constitutional Meaning*, 129–131.

87. "Brief of 250 American Historians as Amici Curiae in Support of Planned Parenthood of Southeastern Pennsylvania," *Planned Parenthood v. Casey*, 505 U.S. 833 (1992).

88. Quoted in Hunter, *Before the Shooting Begins*, 179.

89. Ronald Dworkin, *Life's Dominion: An Argument about Abortion, Euthanasia, and Individual Freedom* (New York: Knopf, 1993), 112.

90. Leslie Reagan, *When Abortion Was a Crime: Women, Medicine, and the Law in the United States, 1867–1973* (Berkeley, CA: University of California Press, 1997), 14.

91. Dyer, *Slavery, Abortion, and the Politics of Constitutional Meaning*, 124.

92. Douglas W. Allen, "High School Graduation Rates among Children of Same-Sex Households," *Review of Economics of the Household*, 11(4), 2013: 635–658.

93. 358 F.3d 804 (11th Cir.).

94. Sonya D. Winner et al., "Brief of American Anthropological Association and others as *Amicus Curiae* Supporting Appellees," filed in *Perry v. Schwarzenegger*, October 25, 2010, 1–28, available at http://cdn.ca9.uscourts.gov/datastore/general/2010/10/27/amicus39.pdf.

95. Kass and Mansfield quotation from Andrew Ferguson, "The 'Science' of Same-Sex Marriage," *Weekly Standard*, April 1, 2013, available at http://www.weeklystandard.com/articles/science-same-sex-marriage_708842.html.

96. See Joshua M. Dunn, *Complex Justice: The Case of Missouri v. Jenkins* (Chapel Hill, NC: University of North Carolina Press, 2008); Joshua M. Dunn and Martin West, "Calculated Justice: Education Research and the Courts," in Frederick M. Hess, ed., *When Research Matters: How Scholarship Influences Education Policy* (Boston, MA: Harvard Education Press, 2008), 155–176.

97. Hunter, *Before the Shooting Begins*, 180.

98. Scott Jaschick, "Florida GOP vs. Social Science," *Inside Higher Ed*, October 12, 2011, available at www.insidehighered.com/news/2011/10/12/florida_governor_challenges_idea_of_non_stem_degrees#sthash.Kzp6BnIW.dpbs.

99. Mark Binker and Julia Sims, "McCrory: Fund Higher Education Based on Results," WRAL.com, January 29, 2013, available at http://www.wral.com/mccrory-fund-higher-education-based-on-results/12037347/.

100. Jedediah Purdy, "Ayn Rand Comes to UNC," *The New Yorker*, March 19, 2015, available at http://www.newyorker.com/news/news-desk/new-politics-at-the-university-of-north-carolina?mbid=social_facebook.

101. Paul Basken, "Senate Moves to Limit NSF Spending on Political Science," *Chronicle of Higher Education*, March 21, 2013, available at http://chronicle.com/article/Senate-Moves-to-Limit-NSF/138027/?cid=at.

102. Stephen Carter, *God's Name in Vain: The Wrongs and Rights of Religion in Politics* (New York: Basic Books, 2000), 67–82; Anna Greenburg, "The Church and Revitalization of Politics and Community," *Political Science Quarterly*, 115(3), 2000: 377–394.

103. Binker and Sims, "McCrory: Fund Higher Education Based on Results."

EPILOGUE

1. Jonathan Zimmerman, "US Colleges Need Affirmative Action for Conservative Professors," *Christian Science Monitor*, December 13, 2012, available at http://www.csmonitor.com/Commentary/Opinion/2012/1213/US-colleges-need-affirmative-action-for-conservative-professors.

2. Jose Duarte et al., "Political Diversity Will Improve Social Psychological Science," *Behavioral and Brain Sciences*, 38, 2015: e130. doi:10.1017/S0140525X14000430.

3. Valerie Richardson, "CU Donors Give $1 Million to Hire Conservative Prof," *The Colorado Observer*, March 17, 2012, available at http://thecoloradoobserver.com/2012/03/cu-donors-give-1-million-to-hire-conservative-prof/.

4. Neil Gross, *Why Are Professors Liberal and Why Do Conservatives Care?* (Cambridge, MA: Harvard University Press, 2013), 8–9, 62.

5. James W. Ceaser and Robert Maranto, "Why Political Science Is Left but Not Quite PC: Causes of Disunion and Diversity," in Robert Maranto, Richard E. Redding, and Frederick M. Hess, eds., *The Politically Correct University: Problems, Scope, and Reform* (Washington, DC: AEI Press, 2009), 210.

6. Everett Carl Ladd and Seymour Martin Lipset, *The Divided Academy: Professors and Politics* (New York: Norton, 1975), 93–124.

7. Bruce L. R. Smith, Jeremy D. Mayer, and A. Lee Fritchler, *Closed Minds? Politics and Ideology in American Universities* (Washington, DC: Brookings Institution Press, 2008), 92–137.

8. Smith, Mayer, and Fritchler, *Closed Minds?* 92–137.

9. Lyndon B. Johnson, "To Fulfill These Rights," Commencement address at Howard University, June 4, 1965, available at http://www.lbjlib.utexas.edu/johnson/archives.hom/speeches.hom/650604.asp.

10. 438 U.S. 265.

11. Benjamin Ginsberg, *The Fall of the Faculty: The Rise of the All-Administrative University and Why It Matters* (New York: Oxford University Press, 2011), 110–116.

12. In our own sample, 89% of professors are men and 95% are white.

13. Neil Gross, "Liberals and Conservatives in Academia: A Reply to My Critics," *Society*, 52(1) 2015: 47–53.

14. Part of the political appeal of the *Bakke* rationale is that it provided colleges and universities a justification for extending affirmative action to nonblacks. As Richard Kahlenberg pointed out years ago, the "compensatory argument did not work well for women" in particular. "[W]hite women," noted Kahlenberg, "are much less economically disadvantaged than blacks and can readily compete in a number of educational and employment arenas without preference." Richard D. Khalenberg, *The Remedy: Class, Race, and Affirmative Action* (New York: Basic Books, 1997), 38–41.

15. See Hanna Rosin, *The End of Men: And the Rise of Women* (New York: Riverhead Books, 2012).

16. Kahlenberg, *The Remedy*, 38–41.

17. Jonathan Haidt, *The Righteous Mind: Why Good People Are Divided by Politics and Religion* (New York: Pantheon Books, 2012).

Index

Tables are indicated by "t" following the page numbers.